Reading Strategies
for Fiction

Author

Jessica Hathaway

SHELL EDUCATION

Publishing Credits

Robin Erickson, *Production Director;* Lee Aucoin, *Creative Director;*
Timothy J. Bradley, *Illustration Manager;* Sara Johnson, M.S.Ed., *Editorial Director;*
Grace Alba Le, *Designer;* Sandra Canchola, *Editorial Assistant;*
Corinne Burton, M.A.Ed., *Publisher*

Image Credits

Cover, p. 1 The Bridgeman Art Library; All other images Shutterstock

Standards

© 2010 National Governors Association Center for Best Practices and Council of Chief State School Officers (CCSS)
© 2004 Mid-continent Research for Education and Learning (McREL)
© 2007 Teachers of English to Speakers of Other Languages, Inc. (TESOL)
© 2007 Board of Regents of the University of Wisconsin System. World-Class Instructional Design and Assessment (WIDA). For more information on using the WIDA ELP Standards, please visit the WIDA website at www.wida.us.

Shell Education

5301 Oceanus Drive
Huntington Beach, CA 92649-1030
http://www.shelleducation.com
ISBN 978-1-4258-1005-4
© 2014 Shell Education Publishing, Inc.

Table of Contents

Table of Contents *(cont.)*

What Is Reading?

Reading is a complex act to learn. As Emerald Dechant (1991) outlines, it is a visual process that begins with one's ability to use one's vision to interpret graphic symbols. Reading requires great visual acuity. To read, one must be able to visually distinguish each letter, to identify each letter, have a visual memory for each letter, and recode those letters so that one can re-create the letters, pronounce the letters, or associate sound with the letters. But can one understand what the words mean? Comprehension is the essence of reading; to comprehend what is read, readers must be able to cognitively process the words by drawing meaning from their own experience and knowledge to understand the author's message. In essence, reading is a dialogue between the reader and the author, and during this dialogue, the reader should generate questions to help anticipate meaning, search for information, respond intellectually and emotionally, and infer ideas from and explain further the content of the text.

The Importance of Reading

The ability to read and comprehend written text is one of the key fundamental skills students learn in school. Research shows that the amount that children read directly affects their verbal skills, academic success, and overall knowledge about the world (Shefelbine 2002). Additionally, correlational research studies indicate that a greater volume of reading is linked to better achievement in reading fluency, vocabulary, and comprehension (National Reading Panel 2000). In other words, the poorest readers read the least and the best readers read the most. The ability to read well affects many aspects of students' lives, and without the requisite reading skills, a student's ability to navigate the complexities of today's print-dependent society, both in and out of the classroom, are severely limited. For these reasons, a large portion of school curriculum focuses on teaching the decoding and comprehension skills necessary to read all types of literature.

Why Teach Fiction?

Within the field of education, various types of literature serve different educational goals. While nonfiction effectively conveys facts and information about a variety of topics, fictional literature plays a critical role in teaching students about social situations, morals, personal dilemmas, and the experiences of different people in diverse situations. By reading fiction, students also learn about the technical aspects of literature such as story structure and vocabulary. Fictional literature provides a gateway for students to explore worlds of fantasy, science fiction, mystery, historical fiction, humor, drama, and adventure. Furthermore, and perhaps most importantly, fiction introduces students to the pleasure of reading and the beauty of written language.

What Is Reading? *(cont.)*

Many of the strategies that students use to comprehend fictional literature are different from those that they use for nonfiction. Such elements as plot sequence, theme, and character development often play a critical role in fiction, but these features may not be present at all in nonfiction text. Students must learn strategies for comprehending fiction, including identifying and analyzing these elements, in order to become successful readers. Given the importance of reading comprehension, it is imperative that teachers strive to enhance their students' ability to understand reading material, and this can be accomplished by working directly with reading comprehension strategies.

Literacy Demands

The literacy needs for the 21st century are tremendous. Literacy was defined a century ago as one's ability to write one's name. A literate person could write his or her name; an illiterate person could not. In 1940, more than "half of the U.S. population had completed no more than an eighth grade education," which is an evolving statistic as education continues to change and develop into the 21st century (National Center for Education Statistics 2013).

Education, as an institution, is evolving to meet the demands of what it means to be considered literate in the 21st century. With the advent of the Common Core State Standards (National Governors Association Center for Best Practices, Council of Chief State School Officers 2010), students are considered literate individuals when:

1. They demonstrate independence.

2. They build strong content knowledge.

3. They respond to the varying demands of audience, task, purpose, and discipline.

4. They comprehend as well as critique.

5. They value evidence.

6. They use technology and digital media strategically and capably.

7. They come to understand other perspectives and cultures.

This means a person should be able to effectively read, for example, a given paragraph from a work of fictional literature. In doing so, this person demonstrates both reading independence and comprehension, both of which hinge on the reader's ability to understand the content and purposefully respond to that particular reading experience (i.e., by evaluating the passage to determine if he or she understands the scene being described, which inherently requires the reader to not only comprehend the text on the page but also to use sound reasoning and prior knowledge to connect any personal experiences to the fictional text to aid in comprehension). The box on the next page is an excerpt from *Alice's Adventures in Wonderland*, a text which a literate individual would have little to no difficulty comprehending.

What Is Reading? *(cont.)*

Alice in Wonderland by Lewis Carroll

"[Alice] was considering, in her own mind (as well as she could, for the hot day made her feel very sleepy and stupid), whether the pleasure of making a daisy-chain would be worth the trouble of getting up and picking the daisies, when suddenly a White Rabbit with pink eyes ran close by her.

"There was nothing so very remarkable in that; nor did Alice think it so very much out of the way to hear the Rabbit say to itself, 'Oh dear! Oh dear! I shall be too late!' (when she thought it over afterward, it occurred to her that she ought to have wondered at this, but at the time it all seemed quite natural); but, when the Rabbit actually *took a watch out of its waistcoat-pocket*, and looked at it, and then hurried on, Alice started to her feet, for it flashed across her mind that she had never before seen a rabbit with either a waistcoat-pocket, or a watch to take out of it, and, burning with curiosity, she ran across the field after it."

In order to understand the passage, the reader must first comprehend all of the words, such as *waistcoat*, *remarkable*, and *started*. Moreover, the reader needs to understand the implications of multiple types of punctuation. For example, the author uses several exclamation marks to denote the rabbit's state of excitement and uses parentheses to separate comments about Alice's state of mind. The reader must understand that quotation marks signify that someone is speaking and that a semi-colon separates two connected thoughts. The reader must also infer that "burning with curiosity" does not signify that Alice was actually on fire. A strong reader with keen comprehension skills would think of a number of questions when reading this passage: *Why did a talking white rabbit have a waistcoat with a pocket watch? Was Alice imagining the rabbit? What type of girl is Alice? Was it safe for Alice to follow the rabbit?* A good reader would also make predictions about the rest of the story and begin to make assumptions about the characters based on this introductory passage. Only a strong basis in reading and comprehension skills would allow the reader to grasp the full meaning of the passage and enable the reader to use this knowledge to enhance his or her understanding of the rest of the story. This is why teachers must incorporate the strategic teaching of reading comprehension strategies into their daily instruction.

But the demands of literacy extend beyond the definition of 21st-century literacy. Given the complex world in which we live, the need for literacy in today's workforce is unprecedented. The aforementioned qualities of a literate individual in the 21st century also represent the qualities of students who are, according to the Common Core State Standards, "college and career ready."

What Is Reading? *(cont.)*

Furthermore, students who meet the standards outlined in the Common Core State Standards by the time they leave high school are "prepared to enter college and workforce training programs" with success (National Governors Association Center for Best Practices, Council of Chief State School Officers 2010). There is a clear movement toward fostering the skills necessary for students to succeed in real-world contexts in order to succeed and thrive as productive citizens and workers. This need to develop productive members of the workforce is in line with alarming findings related to dropout rates and the U.S. economy (Wolk 2011, 75):

> *An analysis by the Alliance for Excellent Education (2010) shows that the U.S. economy would grow significantly if the number of high school dropouts were cut in half. If just half of these students had graduated, research shows, they would have generated more than $4.1 billion in additional earning every year, and states and localities would have received additional taxes of more than $535 million. If the nation continues to lose students at the present rate, about 13 million students will drop out in the next 10 years at a financial loss of $3 trillion (Alliance for Excellent Education, 2009).*

The cost of high school dropouts to the economy is clear and an unfortunate statistic that cannot be ignored in the midst of today's economic state. But what can classroom teachers do to remedy these findings? Why are students dropping out of high school at such an alarming rate? Does the desire to drop out begin in high school or long before? Research suggests that the reasons behind student dropout rates take root long before students make the active choice to drop out. In fact, experts in the field claim that to make a lasting difference in high school dropout rates, "we must understand and focus on why students choose to leave school. Dropping out is not an impulsive decision. The process begins long before high school, often by the 4th or 5th grade. More often than not *it is rooted in the failure of students to learn to read*—not just decode the English language, but to read and understand what they read" (Wolk 2011, 77; italics added).

Teachers need to develop in students the *desire* to read, to actively read, to habitually read, and to read with comprehension and purpose. Students are experiencing failure in reading at an early age, which significantly impacts their motivation to read and develop the skills necessary to be considered college and career ready. We must examine how to effectively motivate students to read and instill the lifelong love for reading that goes hand-in-hand with reading independence, comprehension, and deep learning. But to understand how to instill this thirst for reading, teachers must first understand *who* their students are and how 21st-century learners have very different learning needs from previous generations during a time when technology and digital learning played a small role in students' lives both in and out of the classroom.

What Is Reading? *(cont.)*

Technology and 21st-Century Learning

It is no secret that technology is changing education like never before and, consequently, the lives of young people growing up in the "Net Generation." As such, what it means to be literate in the context of advanced technology is not the same definition even from a decade ago. In "Comprehending and Learning From Internet Sources: Processing Patterns of Better and Poorer Learners," Susan Goldman et al. (2012) note that technology is "changing the face of literacy," stating that people of all ages look to the Internet to resolve a variety of problems that "arise in academic, personal, interpersonal, and occupational contexts" (356–357). Students are looking to the Web for their schoolwork, which makes the development of 21st-century skills crucial to students' ability to strategically navigate and "critically evaluate information sources for their relevance, reliability, and consistency" since nearly anyone can post information—regardless of its validity—to the Internet.

Having said that, it is no wonder that the strategic use and navigation of technology and digital media is included in the Common Core State Standard definition of literacy in the 21st century. Students must learn to integrate and evaluate the information that they encounter on a daily basis from diverse media, including both print and digital resources, whether in school or at home. We have entered a new era in education, and this era is deeply tied to the technological advances that now permeate our modern lives. Today, children can use a cell phone to take a picture before they can speak. A typical three-year-old can turn on a computer and begin a game program without assistance from an adult. Students in school can use the Internet and online libraries to access information from remote locations. They can interview experts in faraway locations through email. According to Susan Metros, Professor of Clinical Education at the University of Southern California, college students today are "media-stimulated, but not necessarily media-literate" (quoted in Wagner 2008, 183–184). But today's college students are not the same learners who are presently immersed in today's elementary and secondary education system. Bearing this in mind, the Common Core State Standards emphasize the development of those skills in preparation for college and careers beyond the classroom. The hope is that students become media-literate as they meet the standards outlined by the Common Core and are able to navigate the complexities of the digital realm. Now, more than ever, it is each teacher's responsibility and duty to prepare students for the reading demands of our technological age. In order to become effective and efficient readers, students need to use comprehension strategies automatically and independently. Students need teacher guidance to help them become independent readers and learners so that they not only understand what they read but can also question it and create beyond it.

Differentiation

As teachers, we know that students come into our classrooms at varying reading and readiness levels to access the content at hand. As such, this resource provides suggestions for differentiating the reading strategies for different groups of students so that they can benefit from the reading strategy being implemented, whether those groups are English language learners or below- or above-level students.

What Is Reading? *(cont.)*

English Language Learners

The ability to access content and demonstrate mastery of particular skills and knowledge hinges on each student's ability to dissect and interact with texts, unquestionably marking the act of reading as a crucial skill in any classroom. Additionally, the demographics of students in our classrooms today is becoming increasingly more diverse, prompting teachers to differentiate their instruction to allow for students of all backgrounds and languages to develop the skills necessary to succeed. And with this growing diversity, it is important to note that English language learners often struggle with more than just accessing content but also with developing reading skills in the context of unfamiliar cultural references, tales, and legends that native English speakers are naturally more familiar with. Because the Common Core State Standards emphasize the shared responsibility of teachers across content areas to help students learn to read critically, providing English language learners with access to texts that will help develop their overall reading ability is essential in any classroom. English language learners "will benefit from actively seeking exposure to language and social interaction with others who can provide meaningful input in the second language. Furthermore, they—and you, the teacher—can enhance students' English language skills by placing language learning in meaningful and interesting contexts" (Dunlap and Weisman 2006, 11).

As teachers, our goal is to help students demonstrate mastery of content knowledge as they climb the " 'staircase' of increasing complexity" in their reading skills as outlined in the Common Core State Standards (National Governors Association Center for Best Practices, Council of Chief State School Officers 2010). As part of this goal, it is our responsibility to provide students with meaningful and interesting contexts to learn language and build their reading skills. When implementing the reading strategies in this book, discuss with students, and English language learners in particular, the importance of using a variety of reading strategies to understand the new information that they glean from their reading of fictional literature so that the importance of reading and developing fine-tuned reading skills is effectively communicated and made known. The explicit instruction of the reading strategies provides students with *meaningful* contexts for learning language, so this discussion is of the utmost importance in establishing a reason for reading, not only for your English language learners, but for all of your students. In doing so, teachers simultaneously aid in the development of students' collaborative, communicative, and group-based skills emphasized in the Common Core State Standards' Speaking & Listening Skills, subsequently helping all students to strategically communicate and interact with those around them within the context of the English language.

Motivating Students to Read

Without the proper guidance from teachers, students will continue to experience failure in reading at an early age, which will contribute to the detrimental high school dropout statistic that currently plagues the nation. But to what extent can teachers be held responsible for preparing students to navigate today's world? To what degree are students themselves held responsible? What can be done to reverse students' negative reading experiences? Research suggests that the answer is rooted in the ways teachers instill motivation to read in their students. After all, today's students are radically different learners from those of us who Marc Prensky rightfully terms "digital immigrants" in today's digital age (quoted in Wolk 2011, 166).

Intrinsic and Extrinsic Motivation

To provide students with a motive to read is to provide them with relevant and real reasons to read, instilling within them a desire or a need for reading. In order to motivate today's 21st-century learners who are, according to John Seely, "growing up digital," teachers must explore new motivational strategies to adapt to the changing needs of today's students (quoted in Wagner 2008, 170).

There is no doubt that today's world is drastically different from the world 100 years ago. So why is it often the case that educators implement motivational strategies that are similarly outdated and no longer relevant to the students they seek to motivate? In Bob Sullo's *Activating the Desire to Learn*, he makes the argument that teachers' instruction should evolve to meet the motivational needs of their students instead of rigidly adhering to ineffective strategies of the past (2007, 5):

> *Given that we've spent a century or so believing that external stimuli explain human behavior, teacher training programs typically require educators to learn how to systematically reward and punish students. Many educators thus see themselves as responsible for shaping the behavior of students by extrinsically rewarding them for compliance. Yet ironically, our system of rewarding students for academic achievement devalues the very thing we say we want: learning. 'If it weren't for the reward we are offering, what we are teaching you would not be worth learning.' In short, a system of education based on rewards and punishment is fundamentally anti-educational.*

In this sense, *extrinsic* motivation is a form of motivation external to students, a form in which rewards and punishments are tangible and concrete. But as Sullo (2007) argues, extrinsic motivation does not seek to instill the lasting desire or need to read. *Intrinsic* motivation is the alternative to extrinsic motivation, and a form of motivation that has long-term, lasting results.

Motivating Students to Read (cont.)

Interests

Many motivational strategies exist to help generate student interest in particular reading tasks, but one strategy in particular focuses on fostering the lifelong love for reading that extends beyond the day-to-day reading tasks of classroom life. As aforementioned, *intrinsic motivation* has long-term results, which makes intrinsically motivating students the preferred method of motivation. To do this, teachers should become familiar with students' interests as early in the school year as possible with the goal of providing students with reading materials throughout the year that are tailored to their interests. Once these high-interest texts are made available, students are more likely to be self-motivated to read because they *want* to discover more about the topics that interest them. Although students are not necessarily delving into fictional literature at this point, this self-motivated act of reading develops students' desire to read that is so important in accessing content from a wide range of texts and text types beyond their interests. Reading texts of interest allows students to fine-tune their reading skills in the context of reading experiences that are interesting, familiar, and comfortable for them, in turn providing them with the confidence and practice needed to effectively navigate texts that are more advanced, unfamiliar, or unexciting.

Unfortunately, many students do very little reading, and some do not read at all outside of school. It is for this reason that teachers, especially language arts teachers, must encourage and provide many opportunities for students to read engaging materials. Some students dislike reading the informational texts in science or social studies instruction, and they, in turn, seem to dislike reading, in general. That very same child may love reading fables, poetry, chapter books, and other types of fictional texts, so it is important to remember that reading skills can and should be developed when teaching any subject.

Assessing students' interests is easy to do and is an effective means of gathering important data about your students. According to Rosalie Fink, "reading interest inventories are easy to administer and modify to fit each student's age or developmental stage" (2006, 18). Distributing surveys is a quick and confidential way to ask questions of your students that are geared toward discovering interests that may otherwise be overlooked. As we all know, interests can take many shapes, so ask questions that are purposeful in determining your students' interests and helpful in locating texts about these interests, such as categorical topics related to favorite authors, genres, time periods, books, poems, screen adaptations of famous literary works, or any other fiction-related subject that would elicit purposeful responses from your students. There are a variety of student-interest surveys available online you can use to inspire your own survey, or you can create a survey of entirely your own making.

Outside Reading

In addition to discovering students' interests and providing texts based on your findings, one of the easiest and most effective ways to improve comprehension in language arts is to promote extensive reading outside of class. Students who frequently read a wide variety of materials have better vocabularies and better reading comprehension skills. As Randall Ryder and Michael Graves (2003) point out, wide reading fosters automaticity in students because it exposes them to more words in different contexts, provides them with knowledge on a variety of topics, and promotes lifelong reading habits.

Motivating Students to Read (cont.)

A teacher's attitude toward reading, especially pleasure reading outside of school, has a tremendous effect on the students in the classroom. Teachers who talk enthusiastically about books they have read and who model reading as an enjoyable and fulfilling experience foster a love for reading in their students. Teachers who can recommend books that are particularly engaging and interesting can increase student motivation tremendously. Language arts teachers should have an intimate knowledge of fictional reading materials for a wide range of reading abilities so they can recommend books to any student to read outside of class.

The Classroom Library

The first step is to set up a classroom library. Why is it important to have a classroom library? According to Lesley Mandel Morrow (2003), president of the International Reading Association (2003–04), research indicates that children in classrooms with book collections read 50 percent more books than children in classrooms without such collections.

High-Interest Texts

Teachers should work with the school librarian or media specialist and parent organizations to build a sizeable collection of texts for their classrooms, which can be a mixture of informational and fictional books from which students can choose to read based on their interests. Bear in mind that this library may serve to generate the interest to read a variety of texts on many different subjects, so providing students with a wide range of texts from which to choose will be beneficial in fostering students' desire and motivation to read. In addition to simply providing students with informational and fictional texts, be sure to provide texts that are at your students' readiness levels and also texts that may present more of a challenge. Especially with interest-based texts, students can build their prior knowledge about a given topic at a less challenging reading level, in turn preparing them to apply a variety of reading strategies to navigate more advanced texts on the same topic. "Michael Pressley and his colleagues (2003)... found high-motivational and high-performing classrooms were, above all, filled with books at different levels of text difficulty. Conversely, on their list of the characteristics of classroom practices that undermine motivation and achievement is: 'The teacher does not give students opportunities to have power over their own learning. Students do not have choice in their work'" (Calkins, Ehrenworth, and Lehman 2012, 50), which is counterproductive to what we as teachers aim to achieve in the context of the Common Core: fostering the reading skills students need to be "college and career ready." This notion is in line with Rosalie Fink's (2006, 81) findings regarding the language acquisition of English language learners, which is applicable to all students' language acquisition: "to encourage striving readers... to read about their interests, teachers should create their own content area libraries full of enticing materials at all readability levels."

Motivating Students to Read (cont.)

Often students are unaware they have interest in a particular topic until they encounter it for the first time, so providing a variety of interest-based texts can only serve to offer students a wide variety of texts from which to read. Additionally, research suggests that the most influential factor in motivating students to read is "ensuring the students [have] easy access to high-interest texts," so making these high-interest texts available to your students is an important factor to consider when developing your classroom library (Calkins, Ehrenworth, and Lehman 2012, 50).

To support learning in language arts, it is important to provide a variety of types of literary works. To find these types of texts, go to used book stores, library sales, and garage sales to gather inexpensive, quality materials. Locate scholarly articles online, print them, and place them in thin folders to preserve their quality. Invite students to locate and donate materials they find on relevant language arts topics or literature. Students should have access to a wide variety of materials about:

- **Science Fiction** (e.g., *The Magic School Bus* books by Joanna Cole and *The Hunger Games* by Suzanne Collins)
- **Historical Fiction** (e.g., *Little House on the Prairie* by Laura Ingalls Wilder and *The Midwife's Apprentice* by Karen Cushman)
- **Mystery** (e.g., *Chasing Vermeer* series by Blue Balliet and *The Westing Game* by Ellen Raskin)
- **Fantasy** (e.g., the *Harry Potter* series by J.K. Rowling and *Ella Enchanted* by Gail Carson Levine)
- **Adventure** (e.g., *Heroes of Olympus* series by Rick Riordan and *Hatchet* by Gary Paulsen)

The reading materials should be housed in bookcases that provide easy access for students to use, as needed. Use tubs to hold magazines and articles on related language arts topics and themes. Most importantly, provide reading materials for a wide range of reading skills. Some students read at a much lower level than others, so include many picture books in addition to articles about literature from newspapers and journals. Students will be better able to incorporate their new learning through independent reading into their existing prior knowledge if the materials are purposefully organized: science fiction, historical fiction, mystery, fantasy, adventure, and other types of fictional literature. Once the materials are in place, create opportunities to incorporate them into your instruction. Assign projects that require students to use the classroom library materials to independently learn more about different topics and themes. Also encourage wide reading by making free voluntary reading a regular classroom activity. If students are not doing any reading outside of the school, school should provide some time for students to read in class. It may be nearly impossible to imagine blocking out any time for silent reading in today's demanding classrooms, but as Stephen Krashen (2009) makes clear in his "81 Generalizations about Free Voluntary Reading," more reading leads to better reading, faster reading, better writing, more writing, and better language acquisition for English language learners. Additionally, Lucy Calkins, Mary Ehrenworth, and Christopher Lehman support these findings in *Pathways to the Common Core: Accelerating Achievement* where they identify that "the engine that motors readers' development is the time spent engaged reading and in talking and writing about that reading. It will be important, therefore, for you to organize the school day so that students have long blocks of time for reading" (2012, 50).

Motivating Students to Read *(cont.)*

Tablets and Interactive Devices

If the technology is available to you, use iPads®, tablets, or other interactive devices for your classroom library to further engage the "Net Generation" so that the reading experience is more interactive and relevant to students' lives. In Lisa Perez's "Re-Imagine Your Library with iPads®," she makes a point that the use of iPads® in her classroom library "was a powerful way to engage students in a variety of reading, writing, speaking, and listening skills" that help students meet many of the Common Core State Standards in ways that are fun and motivational for students (2013, 24). iPads®, tablets, and other interactive devices also engage learners in a variety of purposeful activities that paperbound books cannot offer, such as recording videos, recording voices while reading aloud, and creating digital sketches or other representations to demonstrate their understanding. The reading experience becomes more engaging as students collaborate and share their learning, in turn helping them to meet the Speaking & Listening skills targeted in the Common Core State Standards while also taking ownership of their reading experience by actively engaging with the text in a digital format. The emphasis here is on students' engagement with *active* learning experiences, which serves to further motivate and engage students: "The overwhelming majority of students today want learning to be active, not passive," so providing students with tablets or other interactive devices where this type of work is possible is a great way to motivate students while also supplying them with engaging, high-interest texts (Wagner 2008, 200).

The Reading Process

Teachers can easily optimize the use of reading materials with students by utilizing the three-part framework of the reading process to plan for and facilitate learning. To do this, break reading assignments into three comprehension-building components: before, during, and after reading. It is important to note that what teachers and students do during each of these stages during the reading process is crucial to student learning.

Before Reading

As the teacher prepares for a student reading experience, he or she should carefully read the text ahead of time to determine how to best prepare students for the reading task, being mindful to not overly scaffold or "frontload" the text for students prior to the actual reading task. Leaving a "just right" degree of challenge allows students to grapple with the text and draw their own conclusions, which is an important skill highlighted in the Common Core State Standards. Use before-reading time to purposefully set students up for the selected reading in order to allow them to take ownership of their reading experience and be ready to create meaning as they read. Prior to beginning a reading assignment, the teacher may engage students through a variety of activities so that they can successfully enter the reading task. Constructing before-reading activities that match the students' strengths and needs, address the demands of the text, and consider the instructional context requires careful teacher preparation and includes choices such as generating student interest in the topic, activating prior knowledge/experience or building background knowledge, and setting the purpose for reading.

Teachers who motivate students and create interest prior to assigning the reading can actually improve their students' overall comprehension. Students who are motivated to read a particular text are more engaged and actively involved in the process of learning than those who are unenthusiastic about reading. Motivated readers are also more likely to have better long-term recall of what they read.

Teachers can motivate students by addressing their prior knowledge and stimulating their curiosity about the topic. Knowing students' current knowledge on a topic makes it easier to activate that knowledge and then build on it during reading. The mind holds information in the form of frameworks called schemata, and as we learn new information, we store it in frameworks that link new learning to what we already know. Teachers who build on and activate students' prior knowledge and experience before reading prepare students to more efficiently process, sort, and comprehend the new information that they read. For students who do not have the critical background knowledge necessary to enter into a text with meaning, the teacher may use the before-reading time to briefly share significant information that is not provided by the text and is essential to set the context or concept for the reader.

Prior to reading, teachers can prepare students to be strategic readers by helping them set a purpose for their reading. There are a number of different purposes that readers have for a reading assignment such as to understand a new literary concept, to identify literary devices in a text, to learn new vocabulary, to summarize the information, and so on. Students need to have a purpose in mind as they read. Students utilize all their strategies during reading to create meaning, but a purpose for reading helps students attend to particular aspects of how they are reading and comprehending that text. Once a purpose is established, students read and respond to the text with that focus in mind.

The Reading Process *(cont.)*

Sometimes before reading, teachers find that they must present a concept or directly teach several academic or content-specific vocabulary words that are not supported contextually. Therefore, language arts teachers may also use the before-reading time to introduce that key concept or critical, selected vocabulary prior to reading. This information is often shared in a brief introduction before the students dive into the text. Teachers only scaffold what is absolutely necessary so that students can successfully negotiate the text reading. In doing so, teachers facilitate students' comprehension and fluency as they read.

Finally, as students prepare to read, teachers may coach students into a metacognitive awareness of their reading strategies. Teachers prompt students to note what they are thinking and doing as they are reading. Developing metacognitive awareness allows students to better understand the strategies they use during effective reading and meaning construction. It also enables students to take control of their own learning thereby developing more independent readers and learners, a goal emphasized by the Common Core State Standards' College and Career Readiness Anchor Standards for Reading. Within these Anchor Standards for Reading, students "read and comprehend literary and informational texts independently and proficiently." Creating opportunities for students to demonstrate independence as they engage in before-reading activities is crucial to students' academic success (National Governors Association Center for Best Practices, Council of Chief State School Officers 2010).

At this point, it is important to note that before-reading activities are limited when the teacher engages students in a close reading of a text. Close reading is done with a short, grade-level challenging text where the text itself becomes the "teacher." Therefore, the "frontloading" or pre-teaching of the text during close reading is minimal, and, instead, the teacher leads the students into digging out the layers of meaning on their own through several repeated readings of the text and well-selected, thought-provoking questions that probe for students' understanding. Therefore, most of the following before-reading activities listed below would not be a part of a close reading experience. However, even in close reading sessions, the teacher may recognize that before a close reading of a particular text, students might need essential background information to understand the context or meaning of the selected text.

The activities and/or questions selected to use before reading differ depending on the text selected, the students' strengths/needs and prior knowledge, and the identified purpose/focus for reading. Most often, teachers employ these activities before a shared, interactive read-aloud text or as a part of a small, instructional reading group time. During independent reading with self-selected texts, students set themselves up for reading based on the many strategies they have learned.

Before-Reading Activities
Examples of before-reading activities are as follows:

- Have students scan any text features that accompany the text (e.g., illustrations, images, or captions). *Look at the illustration on page 6. What do you think this passage will be about?*
- Have students preview for chapter titles. *Are the chapters numbered or are they named? Will this change how you read the passage?*

The Reading Process *(cont.)*

- Encourage students to skim the text to activate prior knowledge. *What do you already know about Greek mythology?*
- Preview only essential unknown vocabulary that is not morphologically or contextually supported within the text. *Let's discuss the meaning of* earnest. *Do you think the double meaning of this word will be important in this book?*
- Activate and build on students' prior knowledge/experience about the text's topic or build critical background knowledge about the topic. *What do you know about dystopian societies? What other texts have we read with an unreliable narrator?*
- Work with students to generate a few guiding questions to consider while reading. *From what point of view is this story told? How will this character change from the beginning to the end of this story based on _____?*
- Briefly allow the students to predict some of the possible plot developments. *Look at the description of the story from the cover. What are some things that you expect to happen? What do you think will happen to the main character? Do you think the title gives away the ending? Why or why not?*
- Converse with students to develop a purpose or focus for their reading. *As you read, note especially how the main character develops over the story. Which events or individuals impact this character?*

During Reading

During this stage of the reading, students read text, ask and answer questions (either self-generated or teacher-generated), monitor their comprehension of the text, consider their purpose for reading, visualize the information, and integrate new learning into their existing knowledge from various texts, concepts, and contexts. Most often, students are engaged in answering questions while they read. Proficient readers self-question as they read to make sure they understand the reading material. In addition, students search for the answers to questions they may have generated prior to reading. As students process the text, they begin to infer what the author intended and begin to summarize and analyze the specific details in the information provided. They also look for textual evidence for the questions they must answer.

Students are involved in monitoring and regulating their reading strategies while they are actively reading. If a section of the text is confusing, students problem solve by rereading the section, use fix-up strategies to clear up any confusions, or adjust the speed of reading to suit their purposes or to match the difficulty of the text. Thus, students modify or self-correct as needed to successfully access the content being presented. As a significant component of monitoring, students also determine or clarify the meaning of unknown words as they actively read. If they do not know what a word means, they may attempt to employ word-meaning strategies as they attend to context clues or word parts to decode the meaning of the word. As students address vocabulary needs, they also observe the text structure and features as they read, which helps them organize the new information and identify main ideas.

During reading, teachers can refocus students' attention on the objectives of the reading task established during the before-reading activities. Students may adjust their processing and thinking based on the information they are reading and on their prior knowledge.

Explicit Instruction of Reading Comprehension Strategies

Good teachers use many strategies to enhance students' reading comprehension, and it is helpful to identify which strategies they use in order to explain why the technique successfully improves their students' skills. Even more important is the explicit instruction of the individual strategies, including modeling, guided practice, and independent practice. These steps ensure that students learn to independently and consistently use a wide variety of reading comprehension strategies for a broad range of reading experiences.

Teaching students the strategies to improve their comprehension is nothing new to educators. Research has demonstrated that students greatly benefit from the direct instruction of reading comprehension strategies when reading a text (Block 1999; Dole, Brown, and Trathen 1996; Durkin 1978–1979; Pressley and Afflerbach 1995, as cited by Kragler, Walker, and Martin 2005) (Duke and Pearson 2002). Simply put, strategy instruction is an effective means of assisting students in comprehension and improving understanding.

The *Report of the National Reading Panel* (2000), commissioned by the U.S. Congress to evaluate research in the area of reading, identified a number of effective comprehension strategies. Michael Pressley (2000) echoes these findings. These strategies include vocabulary development, prediction skills (including inference), the building of prior knowledge, think-alouds, visual representations, summarization, and questioning. This book provides a detailed explanation of each strategy and describes a number of activities that language arts teachers can incorporate into their lessons.

Students also need to develop their metacognitive skills when reading and learning in language arts. Scholars agree that metacognition plays a significant role in reading comprehension (e.g., Baker and Brown 1984; Garner 1987; Gourgey 1998; Hacker et al. 1998; Mastropieri and Scruggs 1997; Mayer 1998; Paris, Wasik, and Turner 1991; Schraw 1998, as cited by Baker 2002). Research shows that teachers should foster metacognition and comprehension monitoring during comprehension instruction because in doing so, students will be able to monitor and self-regulate their ability to read. "Developing engaged readers involves helping students to become both strategic and aware of the strategies they use to read" (McCarthy, Hoffman, and Galda 1999, as cited by Baker 2002).

It is important to note that educators should never take a "one-size-fits-all" approach when teaching reading comprehension. Some strategies work for some students and other strategies work for other students, just as some strategies work best with certain types of reading material and other strategies work best with other types of reading material. The most important thing to remember when trying to improve reading comprehension in students is that the skill level, group dynamic, and make-up of students should determine the approach to take.

Explicit Instruction of Reading Comprehension Strategies *(cont.)*

The Steps Involved in Explicit Instruction of Reading Comprehension Strategies

According to Nell Duke and P. David Pearson (2002), research supports that a balanced approach to teaching reading comprehension is more than teaching students specific reading strategies and providing opportunities to read. Teachers should begin with direct explanation and instruction of how to use the strategy so that after a series of steps, students will be able to use the strategy independently, which is emphasized in the Common Core State Standards' Anchor Standards for Reading. Following are the five steps for explicit instruction of comprehension strategies:

1. **Provide an exact description of the strategy and explain when and how it should be used.** Teachers need to explain what the strategy is called, why students should use it, what it helps them understand, and how often students should use it.

2. **Provide modeling of the strategy.** Teachers should model how to use the strategy when students are in the process of reading. Students can also model the strategy, while the teacher reinforces an explanation of how the strategy is being used.

3. **Provide opportunities for collaborative use of the strategy in action.** Teachers and students should work together and share their use of the strategy while they are reading.

4. **Lead guided-practice sessions using the strategy, and allow for a gradual release of responsibility from teacher to student.** At this stage, teachers can remind students of how to use the strategy and of the steps involved, but teachers should allow students to work on the technique independently.

5. **Encourage students' independent use of the strategy.** In the final stage, teachers might gently remind students of the name of the strategy, but students should be using the technique automatically and independently.

Duke and Pearson (2002) emphasize the importance of remembering that students need to be able to use more than one comprehension strategy to understand a reading selection. Throughout the five phases, other strategies should be referenced and modeled for students. When working with reading materials in language arts, teachers should use the very same techniques to introduce a new learning strategy to students as they would during language arts time or in an English class. Students master the use of reading comprehension strategies when instruction follows the five steps listed above. When covering language arts topics, teachers must take the time to allow students to master the strategy so that they can become independent readers.

What Great Teachers Do

Many language arts teachers use a variety of strategies that go beyond simply answering the questions at the end of the chapter. Research shows, however, that there is a big difference between teaching reading comprehension strategies well and teaching them in a dynamic, ingenious way that motivates and excites students about reading and learning. Through research, observations, and conversations with teachers who have been successful with the direct instruction of reading comprehension strategies, Ellin Oliver Keene (2002) has identified five traits specific to outstanding and consistently effective teachers. What makes these teachers effective?

1. **They take the time to understand each strategy in their own reading.** Reading about the techniques and activities is not enough. Great teachers of reading comprehension strategies take the time to figure out how to use and understand every strategy with the texts they are reading. In doing so, they increase their own metacognitive skills and can better articulate their own thinking during reading.

2. **They incorporate reading comprehension strategy instruction into predictable daily, weekly, and monthly activities.** Effective teachers of reading comprehension strategies set goals for strategy learning and create a predictable schedule to ensure that those goals are met. These teachers also set aside time to work more intensively with small groups, as needed. They also set aside time for students to reflect on their progress toward the goals they set.

3. **They ask students to apply each comprehension strategy to a wide variety of texts and text levels in different contexts.** Great teachers use beautifully written texts or excerpts from larger works with challenging and profound themes that can be read in their entirety in a mini-lesson. For example, they ask students to summarize the text, to preview the passage, and to use background knowledge to understand a reading selection. In order to comprehend actively and assertively, students must read from texts with appropriately challenging words and concepts.

4. **They vary the size of groupings for strategy instruction.** Changing the group size and configuration helps teachers focus on different goals during comprehension strategy instruction.

Large groups are best for:

- introducing a new strategy
- modeling think-alouds to show students how good readers use the strategy
- practicing think-alouds with new genres and allowing students to share their experiences using the strategy

What Great Teachers Do (cont.)

Small groups are best for:

- providing more intensive instruction for students who need it
- introducing above-level students to the strategy so that they can apply it independently to more challenging texts and to new genres
- introducing new activities that enable students to share their thinking (new maps, charts, thinking notebooks, sketches, logs, etc.)
- allowing students to discuss books and comprehension strategies without teacher involvement

Conferences are best for:

- checking students' understanding of how to apply the strategy they are studying to their own books
- providing intensive strategy instruction to a text that may be particularly challenging to students
- coaching students in how they might reveal their thinking to others
- encouraging students to use a strategy to think more deeply than they might have imagined possible

5. **They gradually release the responsibility for the application of a comprehension strategy to students.** Great teachers follow the steps involved in the explicit instruction of reading comprehension strategies (Duke and Pearson 2002): over several weeks, teachers provide thorough explanations of the strategy, model how to use it, allow for group work with the strategy, transition to more independent use, and then release the responsibility to students.

What Do Good Readers Do When They Read?

Duke and Pearson (2002) have established that good readers:

- **read** actively
- **set goals** for their reading tasks and constantly **evaluate** whether the text and their reading of it is meeting their goals
- **preview** the text prior to reading, noting the **text organization and structure** to locate the sections most relevant to their reading goals
- **make predictions** about what is to come in the text
- **read selectively**, continually making decisions about their reading process: what to read carefully, what to read quickly, what to skim, what not to read, and what to reread
- **construct, revise, and question the meanings they develop** as they read
- **determine the meanings of unfamiliar or unknown words and concepts** in the text
- **draw from, compare, and integrate their prior knowledge** with the material in the text
- **consider the author(s) of the text**, style, beliefs, intentions, historical perspective, and so on
- **monitor their understanding of the text**, making adjustments in their reading as necessary and dealing with inconsistencies or gaps, as needed
- **evaluate the text's quality and value**, and interact with the text in multiple ways, both intellectually and emotionally
- **read different kinds of texts differently**
- **construct and revise summaries** of what they have read when reading fictional texts
- **think about the text before, during, and after reading**
- **feel satisfied and productive** when reading, even though comprehension is a consuming, continuous, and complex activity

Teachers will find the job of teaching fictional literature much easier if every student has the skills of a good reader.

How to Use This Book

This book includes a variety of strategies that can be used within language arts lessons to improve students' reading comprehension skills: promoting word consciousness, analyzing word parts, activating knowledge through vocabulary development, using and building prior knowledge, predicting and inferring, think-alouds and monitoring comprehension, questioning, summarizing, using visual representations and mental imagery, using text structure and text features, and using multiple reading comprehension strategies instruction.

Each section opens with an overview of research in that area to emphasize the importance of that particular reading comprehension skill. There is also a clear and detailed definition of the skill, suggestions for instruction, and best practices. This information provides teachers with the solid foundation of knowledge to provide deeper, more meaningful instruction to their students.

Following each skill overview is a variety of instructional strategies to improve students' comprehension in that area. Each strategy in the book includes a description and purpose of the strategy, the research basis for the strategy, and the reasons why the strategy is effective in improving comprehension. The grade level spans for which the strategy is most appropriate (1–2, 3–5, 6–8, or 9–12) and the language arts standards that are addressed are listed. A detailed description of the strategy includes any special preparation that might be needed and extension ideas where appropriate. Finally, suggestions for differentiating instruction are provided for English language learners, below- and above-level students. Following the strategy descriptions are grade-level examples of how the strategy is applied to language arts. A blank template of the activity sheet is included as a reproducible, where applicable, as well as on the accompanying Digital Resource CD. Reproducibles are available on the Digital Resource CD in PDF form and often as Word documents to allow for customization of content and text for students of diverse abilities and needs.

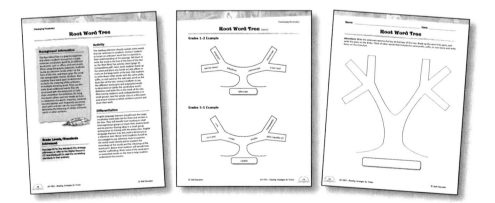

Correlation to Standards

Shell Education is committed to producing educational materials that are research and standards based. In this effort, we have correlated all of our products to the academic standards of all 50 United States, the District of Columbia, the Department of Defense Dependent Schools, and all Canadian provinces.

How to Find Standards Correlations

To print a customized correlation report of this product for your state, visit our website at **http://www.shelleducation.com** and follow the on-screen directions. If you require assistance in printing correlation reports, please contact Customer Service at **1-877-777-3450**.

Purpose and Intent of Standards

Legislation mandates that all states adopt academic standards that identify the skills students will learn in kindergarten through grade twelve. Many states also have standards for Pre-K. This same legislation sets requirements to ensure the standards are detailed and comprehensive.

Standards are designed to focus instruction and guide adoption of curricula. Standards are statements that describe the criteria necessary for students to meet specific academic goals. They define the knowledge, skills, and content students should acquire at each level. Standards are also used to develop standardized tests to evaluate students' academic progress. Teachers are required to demonstrate how their lessons meet state standards. State standards are used in the development of all of our products, so educators can be assured that they meet the academic requirements of each state.

Common Core State Standards

Many of the lessons in this book are aligned to the Common Core State Standards (CCSS). The standards support the objectives presented throughout the lessons and are provided on the Digital Resource CD (standards.pdf).

McREL Compendium

We use the Mid-continent Research for Education and Learning (McREL) Compendium to create standards correlations. Each year, McREL analyzes state standards and revises the compendium. By following this procedure, McREL is able to produce a general compilation of national standards. Each lesson in this product is based on one or more McREL standards, which are provided on the Digital Resource CD (standards.pdf).

TESOL and WIDA Standards

The lessons in this book promote English language development for English language learners. The standards correlations can be found on the Digital Resource CD (standards.pdf).

Correlation to Standards (cont.)

The main focus of the strategies presented in this book is to promote the implementation of explicit reading instruction in the language arts classroom. The correlating standards for the strategies in this resource are provided on the Digital Resource CD (standards.pdf).

Common Core State Standards

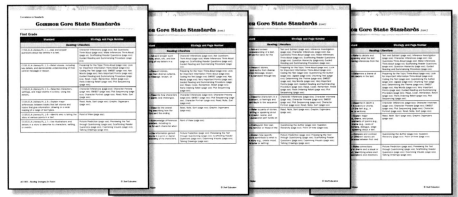

McREL Standards

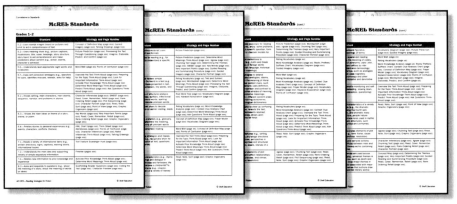

TESOL and WIDA Standards

Developing Vocabulary Overview

What Is Vocabulary?

What comes to mind when you hear the word *vocabulary*? For most, the word suggests a list of words ready for use in one's speech and writing. Educators and researchers in the field of reading have long recognized that vocabulary knowledge plays an integral role in a student's ability to comprehend reading material. Students with wider vocabularies find it easier to comprehend more of what they are reading than do students with limited vocabularies. Moreover, students who have strong vocabularies have less difficulty learning unfamiliar words because those words are more likely to be related to words that students already know (Rupley, Logan, and Nichols 1999).

As William Nagy and Judith Scott (2000) point out, for many, the word *vocabulary* suggests a reductionist attitude toward word learning. The term *vocabulary* begs the reader to look just at words and their meanings rather than at how the words are part of the overall reading process. It also suggests that students learn words by memorizing short definitions or sentences. This limited perception about vocabulary, combined with the traditional and unsound methods of introducing words and asking students to look them up in the dictionary, goes against all that is known about the reading process. The process of using word knowledge to comprehend reading is rather complex and merits much discussion, particularly because many fictional texts introduce more unknown vocabulary words to the reader than are taught in most foreign language classes.

Levels of Word Knowledge

Researchers have established that there are different levels of word knowledge: *unknown*, *acquainted*, and *established* (Lapp, Flood, and Farnan 1996; Ryder and Graves 2003). *Unknown* words are words that students neither recognize nor understand. Few kindergartners are able to define *symbol*. *Acquainted* words are those that students may recognize but must consciously think about to determine their meanings. Fourth graders are acquainted with the phrase *metaphor*, but they may not be able to define it in detail. *Established* words are those words that students recognize and can define easily and automatically. The word *simile* should be well established in the vocabularies of every eighth grader.

The goal is to move new vocabulary into the established level for students so that they can use the words in their own speech and writing. It is not enough for students to be acquainted with artifacts—the goal is for students to use the term easily when speaking and writing. To achieve this, teachers must expose students to the word a number of times and in a variety of contexts.

Knowing a word completely involves a number of skills: recognizing the word automatically; knowing the denotations, connotations, synonyms, antonyms, metaphors, and analogies for the word; associating the word with different experiences; and being able to explain one's understanding of the nuances of the word. Obviously, students cannot learn all of these skills with only a single exposure to the word (Lapp, Flood, and Farnan 1996). Word learning is an incremental process—a series of encounters that leads to mastery of the word. Sometimes brief instruction just before or after reading is all that students need to develop a thorough understanding of an unknown word.

Developing Vocabulary Overview *(cont.)*

Word-Learning Tasks

In addition to different levels of word knowledge, there are different word-learning tasks that students engage in. Lapp, Flood, and Farnan (1996) categorize word learning into six distinct tasks:

- **Learning to Read Known Words**—Students may have words already in their oral vocabularies, but they may not recognize them in print. There is no need to teach the meanings of these words because students already know and understand them when they hear them; they just cannot read them. For example, students may have heard the word *dystopian*, but they may not recognize it in print.

- **Learning New Meanings for Known Words**—If the new meanings of known words do not represent new and difficult concepts, teachers should acknowledge the known meaning, give the new meaning, and note the similarities between the meanings. Students usually recognize the word *practices*, and may associate it with sports teams, but they may not know it has a definition related to religion.

- **Learning New Words Representing Known Concepts**—Sometimes the words are not in students' oral or reading vocabularies, but they do have prior knowledge of the concept. For example, students may not know the word *motivation*, but they know *motivate* and the suffix *-tion*, so the concept of motivation is present. Most words that students learn in middle school are this type.

- **Learning New Words for New Concepts**—When students do not know the words or the concepts associated with the word, they have the demanding task of learning both. For these words, it is best to activate as much prior knowledge as possible with students. For example, students probably have never heard of the word *primitive* and will need to develop the background knowledge to understand it.

- **Clarifying and Enriching the Meanings of Known Words**—As students become more sophisticated with their vocabularies, they begin to learn the nuances involved in words with varying shades of meaning. In language arts, students will learn to distinguish *bear* from *bare*.

- **Moving Words into Students' Expressive Vocabularies**—It is one thing to know a word, to recognize it, to know what it means, and to understand its shades of meaning. It is another task to use the word in speech or in writing.

Developing Vocabulary Overview (cont.)

Effective Vocabulary Instruction

Typically, teachers focus on teaching specific words and their definitions in vocabulary instruction, but this is not the most effective method due to complexity of word knowledge. Instead, students should be invited to build on their previous understandings of words to learn new meanings and nuances, to connect words to greater concepts, to associate words with other related words, to categorize words in unique and useful ways, and to enjoy using language creatively to express themselves and their ideas.

Blachowicz and Fisher (2000) feel that reading research suggests four main principles to guide vocabulary instruction. Students should:

1. Be active in developing their understanding of words and ways to learn them
2. Personalize word learning
3. Be immersed in words
4. Build on a variety of resources to learn words through multiple exposures

Increasing students' awareness of words and how they can learn them is the first step involved in vocabulary instruction. Obviously, language arts teachers have an enormous task before them: they must teach a large number of complex and wholly unfamiliar concepts that involve lots of unfamiliar vocabulary. The first step in improving reading comprehension skills in students is to develop their vocabularies.

Selecting Vocabulary to Teach

It is not enough to know that word knowledge is complex; teachers must also know how and when to select the vocabulary for explicit instruction in the classroom.

Students themselves are the best resources for determining the words that they know and do not know. Teachers can make up a list of vocabulary words about a particular topic or for a selected reading assignment and ask students to indicate their level of understanding for each word. For example, if the book is *Number the Stars* by Lois Lowry the list might include *Nazi, kroner, rabbi, synagogue,* and *halte*. If students indicate that they do not recognize any of the terms, the teacher can better plan the unit to address this issue. This task can make assessing student knowledge of specific words efficient and effective.

Ryder and Graves (2003) also suggest that students skim the reading material in advance and create their own list of words that are difficult, are particularly essential, or may need more clarification in class for successful comprehension of the reading material. This is a task that can be completed in cooperative groups.

Developing Vocabulary Overview (cont.)

The following guidelines from Ryder and Graves (2003) will help teachers select vocabulary words to teach in class:

1. The words are important to the understanding of the reading selection.

2. Students can use context or their structural knowledge to determine the general meaning. If students can glean the meaning of the word because they recognize the root or compound parts, it is not always necessary to teach the word.

3. The words are useful outside of the assigned reading selection. If students are likely to encounter the word in another reading task outside of class, it is a valuable word to teach.

When selecting vocabulary for instruction, be sure to account for the incidental words that come up in class discussions and question-answer sessions. For example, when the word *boycott* comes up in a class discussion, take the time to explain it as it is a word that will be used across disciplines. Addressing vocabulary questions as they arise promotes word consciousness. Also, it is important to note that most teachers assign too many vocabulary words at one time.

Teach no more than ten new words to middle and high school students, no more than five to upper-grade students, and only one or two to primary-grade students for each reading selection (chapter, article, or short story).

Promoting Word Consciousness

Students who are word conscious know the power of words, and they know a lot about words and how to use them. Word-conscious students enjoy using words cleverly in precise and effective ways. They are interested in words, in general, like to play with language, and pay close attention to the ways in which others use words. Word consciousness is directly connected to vocabulary development, which, in turn, helps students comprehend reading materials more efficiently and effectively. Developing word consciousness in language arts helps students become more critical thinkers and strategic readers.

Promoting curiosity and interest in words takes effort on the part of the language arts teacher. Ryder and Graves (2003) suggest the following ways to promote word consciousness:

- Include precise, novel, and perhaps colorful words when talking with students.
- Point out particularly adept word choices in the material students are reading.
- Compliment students when they make adroit word choices in their speech or writing.
- Discuss connotations and other subtleties of words, particularly value-laden ones.
- Engage students in empirical inquiries about words.

In this section, you will find the following strategies for promoting word consciousness:

- Word Wall
- Rating Vocabulary
- Word Knowledge Analysis

Developing Vocabulary Overview *(cont.)*

Analyzing Word Parts

Breaking down and examining word parts—prefixes, suffixes, base words, blends, digraphs, and Greek and Latin roots—is another approach to teaching vocabulary that can help students learn the thousands of words they need to know. There is increasing evidence that it helps to teach students the major word chunks in English (Ryder and Graves 2003; Pressley 2000). *Morphology* is the ability to use word structures to make meaning of new vocabulary. Explicit instruction that teaches students to use their prior knowledge to make sense of root words, suffixes, prefixes, and other word parts builds confidence in understanding words and ultimately increases reading comprehension skills. Simply put, when students recognize Greek and Latin roots and other word parts in unfamiliar words, they are better able to make accurate guesses at the definitions, and therefore better understand what they are reading.

Prefix	Words with Prefixes	Prefix Definition
mis-	misbehave	wrongly
pre-	prehistoric	before
re-	rewind	again
anti-	antisocial	against
dis-	dishonest	not, opposite
under-	underweight	below, less than
tri-	tripod	three

Suffix	Words with Suffixes	Suffix Definition
-en	earthen	made of
-ful	sorrowful	full of
-ment	movement	action of
-ible	combustible	can be, is
-some	meddlesome	inclined to
-ize	popularize	to make
-ism	socialism	doctrine of, principle of

Before teachers do direct instruction on word parts in language arts, it is best to assess students' understanding of what they already know about word parts. Ryder and Graves (2003) suggest a few activities to determine what students know about prefixes and suffixes. Give students a list of words that have various prefixes. Have students remove the prefixes from the words and then define the prefixes. Then, give students a list of words that have a variety of suffixes. Have them remove the suffixes from the words and define the suffixes.

Ask any adult who studied Greek or Latin in school and that adult will extol the virtues of teaching Greek and Latin to all students. This is because most modern English words originated from these languages. This is particularly important in language arts where students encounter a large number of Greek- and Latin-based words. Teachers can do a similar activity with common Greek and Latin root words. Make a list of words that contain Greek or Latin roots, and ask students to identify and define the root. Teachers can also group words with common roots and ask students to determine what the root means.

Developing Vocabulary Overview (cont.)

Prefix	Words with Root	Meaning
aud-	audience, audiology, audiologist, audible	hear
cred-	credible, credit, incredible, discreditable, creed	believe
fin-	finite, infinite, final, definite, define	end
hydr-	hydrate, hydrant, hydrogen, hydrangea, hydrology	water
micro-	microscope, microbiology, microgram, microbe	very small

Ryder and Graves (2003) also suggest that teachers use direct instruction to teach common Greek and Latin roots as well as prefixes and suffixes. Teachers can teach the word parts that are most useful in language arts, that appear most frequently in the reading material, and that will appear in contexts outside language arts class. It is important to provide students with a resource to locate the definitions of word parts as they read independently. Language arts teachers should create bulletin boards of common roots, prefixes, and suffixes with examples of words that include the word parts and provide students with comprehensive lists to keep in their notebooks for easy reference. See Appendix A: Additional Resources (page 272–273; greeklatinroots.pdf) for a list of Greek and Latin roots.

In this section, you will find the following strategies for analyzing word parts:

- Root Word Tree
- Roots/Prefixes/Suffixes Chart
- Context Clue Analysis Chart

Developing Vocabulary Overview (cont.)

Activating Knowledge through Vocabulary Development

Building Vocabulary Connections

Effective vocabulary instruction in language arts involves helping students relate new vocabulary words to what they already know. By helping students make strong connections between their prior knowledge on a topic and new words and concepts in class, teachers can greatly increase the long-term retention of vocabulary. Furthermore, relating new words to previous experiences leads to improved reading comprehension (Lenski, Wham, and Johns 1999).

Associating an experience or a concept with a word is fundamental to the reading process, and word knowledge is absolutely necessary when learning how to comprehend texts efficiently. Students come to school and to each classroom with a variety of experiences and knowledge. They arrive with finite vocabularies to describe the world around them and their own experiences. It is through new experiences and interactions with reading materials, classmates, and teachers that they articulate their experiences and new understandings and expand the meaning of the words they use.

Personalizing Word Learning

The most important aspect of activating knowledge through vocabulary instruction is to personalize what is learned for students. Making this personal connection greatly enhances students' ability to retain the meaning of new vocabulary words so that they can recognize them in print and use them in their own speech and writing. Research in vocabulary instruction supports the active engagement of students in making connections between and among words (Blachowicz and Fisher 2000). Students should be encouraged to articulate their personal understanding of words as they encounter them, to select what words they will study and learn, and to determine which strategies to use when they become more independent at comprehending reading material.

In this section, you will find the following strategies for activating knowledge through vocabulary development:

- Concept of Definition Map
- Frayer Model
- Vocabulary Diagram
- Keyword Association

Developing Vocabulary Overview (cont.)

Standards Addressed

The following chart shows the correlating standards for each strategy in this section. Refer to the Digital Resource CD (standards.pdf) to read the correlating standards in their entirety.

Strategy	McREL Standards	Common Core State Standards
Word Wall	Grades 1–2 (5.6) Grades 3–5 (5.7) Grades 6–8 (5.3) Grades 9–12 (5.2)	Grade 1 (L.1.6) Grade 2 (L.2.6) Grade 3 (L.3.6) Grade 4 (L.4.6) Grade 5 (L.5.6) Grade 6 (L.6.6) Grade 7 (L.7.6) Grade 8 (L.8.6) Grades 9–10 (L.9-10.6) Grades 11–12 (L.11-12.6)
Rating Vocabulary	Grades 3–5 (5.3, 5.5) Grades 6–8 (5.2–5.4) Grades 9–12 (5.2)	Grade 3 (L.3.4) Grade 4 (L.4.4) Grade 5 (L.5.4) Grade 6 (L.6.4) Grade 7 (L.7.4) Grade 8 (L.8.4) Grades 9–10 (L.9-10.4) Grades 11–12 (L.11-12.4)
Word Knowledge Analysis	Grades 3–5 (5.3, 5.5) Grades 6–8 (5.2–5.4) Grades 9–12 (5.2)	Grade 3 (L.3.4, L.3.6) Grade 4 (L.4.4, L.4.6) Grade 5 (L.5.4, L.5.6) Grade 6 (L.6.4, L.6.6) Grade 7 (L.7.4, L.7.6) Grade 8 (L.8.4, L.8.6) Grades 9–10 (L.9-10.4, L.9-10.6) Grades 11–12 (L.11-12.4, L.11-12.6)
Root Word Tree	Grades 1–2 (5.4) Grades 3–5 (5.4)	Grade 1 (L.1.4, L.1.6) Grade 2 (L.2.4, L.2.6) Grade 3 (L.3.4, L.3.6) Grade 4 (L.4.4, L.4.6) Grade 5 (L.5.4, L.5.6)
Roots/Prefixes/Suffixes Chart	Grades 3–5 (5.4) Grades 6–8 (5.2) Grades 9–12 (5.2)	Grade 3 (L.3.4, L.3.6) Grade 4 (L.4.4, L.4.6) Grade 5 (L.5.4, L.5.6) Grade 6 (L.6.4, L.6.6) Grade 7 (L.7.4, L.7.6) Grade 8 (L.8.4, L.8.6) Grades 9–10 (L.9-10.4, L.9-10.6) Grades 11–12 (L.11-12.4, L.11-12.6)

Developing Vocabulary Overview (cont.)

Strategy	McREL Standards	Common Core State Standards
Context Clue Analysis Chart	Grades 3–5 (5.5) Grades 6–8 (5.3, 5.4) Grades 9–12 (5.2)	Grade 3 (L.3.4, L.3.5, L.3.6) Grade 4 (L.4.4, L.4.5, L.4.6) Grade 5 (L.5.4, L.5.5, L.5.6) Grade 6 (L.6.4, L.6.5, L.6.6) Grade 7 (L.7.4, L.7.5, L.7.6) Grade 8 (L.8.4, L.8.5, L.8.6) Grades 9–10 (L.9-10.4, L.9-10.5, L.9-10.6) Grades 11–12 (L.11-12.4, L.11-12.5, L.11-12.6)
Concept of Definition Map	Grades 1–2 (5.1) Grades 3–5 (5.6–5.7) Grades 6–8 (5.3) Grades 9–12 (5.2)	Grades 1–2 (L.1-2.4) Grade 3 (L.3.5) Grade 4 (L.4.5) Grade 5 (L.5.5) Grade 6 (L.6.5) Grade 7 (L.7.5) Grade 8 (L.8.5) Grades 9–10 (L.9-10.5) Grades 11–12 (L.11-12.5)
Frayer Model	Grades 3–5 (5.6) Grades 6–8 (5.3) Grades 9–12 (5.2)	Grade 3 (L.3.5, L.3.6) Grade 4 (L.4.5, L.4.6) Grade 5 (L.5.5, L.5.6) Grade 6 (L.6.5, L.6.6) Grade 7 (L.7.5, L.7.6) Grade 8 (L.8.5, L.8.6) Grades 9–10 (L.9-10.5, L.9-10.6) Grades 11–12 (L.11-12.5, L.11-12.6)
Vocabulary Diagram	Grades 3–5 (5.4, 5.6) Grades 6–8 (5.2, 5.3) Grades 9–12 (5.1, 5.2)	Grade 3 (L.3.4, L.3.5, L.3.6) Grade 4 (L.4.4, L.4.5, L.4.6) Grade 5 (L.5.4, L.5.5, L.5.6) Grade 6 (L.6.4, L.6.5, L.6.6) Grade 7 (L.7.4, L.7.5, L.7.6) Grade 8 (L.8.4, L.8.5, L.8.6) Grades 9–10 (L.9-10.4, L.9-10.5, L.9-10.6) Grades 11–12 (L.11-12.4, L.11-12.5, L.11-12.6)
Keyword Association	Grades 1–2 (5.2) Grades 3–5 (5.4) Grades 6–8 (5.3) Grades 9–12 (5.2)	Grades 1–2 (L.1-2.4) Grade 3 (L.3.5, L.3.6) Grade 4 (L.4.5, L.4.6) Grade 5 (L.5.5, L.5.6) Grade 6 (L.6.5, L.6.6) Grade 7 (L.7.5, L.7.6) Grade 8 (L.8.5, L.8.6) Grades 9–10 (L.9-10.5, L.9-10.6) Grades 11–12 (L.11-12.5, L.11-12.6)

Word Wall

Background Information

A Word Wall is a bulletin board display of key vocabulary, concept words, and other domain-specific vocabulary. Word Walls are a common component of elementary classrooms because they are a great way to expose students to new academic words and phrases. However, Word Walls can be just as effective in middle and high school. Teachers who work with multiple student groups throughout the day may use a flip chart as a Word Wall so that words can be added and removed for each individual class. It is a great idea to involve students in the creation of Word Walls, so they feel a sense of ownership and pride in the wall as they acquire and learn to use new vocabulary. Exposing students repeatedly to the words on a larger scale helps imprint the words in their long-term memories so they can accurately and appropriately use the newly acquired terms.

Grade Levels/Standards Addressed

See page 36 for the standards this strategy addresses, or refer to the Digital Resource CD (standards.pdf) to read the correlating standards in their entirety.

Preparation

Using strips of tagboard or brightly colored construction paper, have students neatly print the words by hand. The strips should be large enough

for the print to be easily read from a distance. Illustrations may be included. Always place the words on a specific wall area so that students will know to refer to this site for the current vocabulary. When "new" academic terms are introduced, move the "old" words to a different location where they are still accessible. Have students periodically "read the wall" for review. Encourage students to use the Word Wall as a reference for correct spelling. Advocate the accurate application of new and old vocabulary in class discussions and assignments.

Activity

Prior to reading about a specific topic or genre, have students create a bulletin board display that includes domain-specific words about the topic. For example, if students are studying mystery novels, have them print words such as *sleuth, forensics, suspense, detective, inference,* and *deduction.* Have students draw pictures or search through texts to find examples of the words and place the examples near the words. Students can also group into categories the words on the bulletin board.

Differentiation

This strategy is particularly helpful for English language learners because it exposes them to the target academic terms, and they can easily refer to the words any time. Include photos and/or illustrations for words whenever possible and provide students with take-home versions of the words on the board so that they can refer to them outside the classroom. Encourage above-level students to use more challenging words such as *inscrutable* and *arcane.* Give below-level students copies of the words from the Word Wall for their notebooks and repeatedly prompt them to refer to the Word Wall or their lists. It may help to provide additional words on the list to help stimulate their thinking.

Word Wall (cont.)

Grades 1–2 Example

Blueberries for Sal by Robert McCloskey

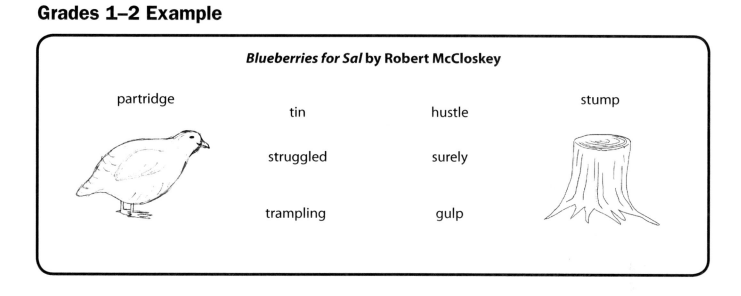

partridge

tin   hustle   stump

struggled   surely

trampling   gulp

Grades 3–5 Example

Stuart Little by E. B. White

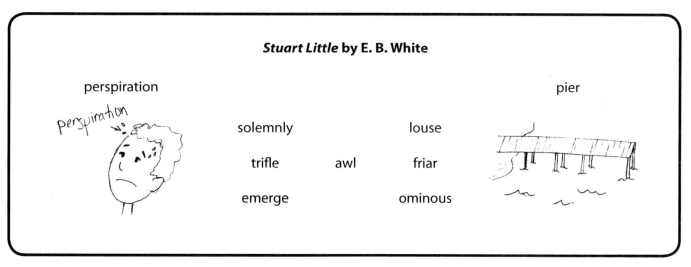

perspiration   pier

solemnly   louse

trifle   awl   friar

emerge   ominous

Word Wall (cont.)

Grades 6–8 Example

A Separate Peace by John Knowles

inane

tacit   erratic

fey

irate   vindicated

enmity

Grades 9–12 Example

All Quiet on the Western Front by Erich Maria Remarque

aberration	convalescent	palatial
barrage	gnaw	pallid
congeal	impinge	voracity

Rating Vocabulary

Background Information

Rating Vocabulary is an activity that allows students to rate their knowledge of target vocabulary words at specific points during the reading process. In order to clarify the definition of unknown words, or words with multiple meanings, students must first be able to identify words that are unfamiliar to them. In this activity, the teacher generates a list of key words for the lesson and asks students to evaluate their understanding of each before reading, after reading, and after discussing the words. The activity encourages students to think metacognitively about their understanding of each word and the related concepts. It also promotes the independent acquisition of new vocabulary.

Grade Levels/Standards Addressed

See page 36 for the standards this strategy addresses, or refer to the Digital Resource CD (standards.pdf) to read the correlating standards in their entirety.

Activity

Prior to assigning a reading selection, choose the most essential words in the lesson or unit, making sure to include words that may be unknown to students. Create a *Rating Vocabulary* activity sheet (page 43, ratingvocabulary.pdf) with the selected words. Give students the *Rating Vocabulary* activity sheet and explain that they will be thinking about

their understanding of particular words at three different points: before reading, after reading, and after discussing the words with the class. Explain the rating values: (+) indicates students know the word; (–) indicates students do not know the word; and (?) indicates students have heard of the word but are not sure of the meaning.

Ask students to read the words silently and rate the words in the Before Reading column on their activity sheets. After students have read the selected text, ask them to rate the words again in the After Reading column. Place students in small cooperative groups, or hold a class discussion in which students share which words they knew before reading, which words they were able to figure out during reading, and what they think the words mean. Clarify any words they still do not know. Have students complete the After Discussion column of the activity sheet. As a class, discuss which strategies students used to determine or clarify the meaning of unknown words.

Differentiation

Recite the words on the list or have students recite them to make sure English language learners understand the target words. Include known forms of the target words—like *magnet* for *magnetism*—because they will be better able to build on their prior knowledge. Select more challenging words for the same concepts for above-level students and encourage their independent exploration of their meanings. Below-level students may get discouraged during the before-reading stage if they do not recognize any of the words, so select two or three words that they are sure to know in order to build their confidence and motivation.

Rating Vocabulary (cont.)

Grades 3–5 Example

Word	Before Reading	After Reading	After Discussion
1. annual	–	?	+
2. ascend	–	–	+
3. coax	?	?	+
4. disclose	–	+	+
5. limb	+	+	+
6. queasy	+	+	+
7. sole	–	–	+
8. valiant	–	?	+
9. vast	–	+	+
10. weary	+	+	+

Grades 6–8 Example

Word	Before Reading	After Reading	After Discussion
1. avid	+	+	+
2. benign	–	?	+
3. deface	?	+	+
4. dire	–	?	+
5. epoch	+	+	+
6. fastidious	–	–	+
7. formidable	–	?	+
8. pithy	?	+	+
9. porous	–	?	+
10. pungent	?	?	+

Grades 9–12 Example

Word	Before Reading	After Reading	After Discussion
1. abject	+	+	+
2. agnostic	–	+	+
3. effigy	–	?	+
4. indictment	–	+	+
5. moot	?	+	+
6. prestigious	+	+	+
7. surveillance	+	+	+
8. travesty	–	+	+
9. valor	?	+	+
10. venerate	–	–	+

Name: _____ Date: _____

Rating Vocabulary

Directions: Fill out each column at three different stages of reading a section of the text: before reading, after reading, and after discussion. Use the following key to indicate your understanding of the word: (+) I know the word; (–) I do not know the word; and (?) I have heard of the word but am not sure of the meaning.

Word	Before Reading	After Reading	After Discussion
1.			
2.			
3.			
4.			
5.			
6.			
7.			
8.			
9.			
10.			

Word Knowledge Analysis

Background Information

Word Knowledge Analysis is a strategy that allows students to consciously examine their existing understanding of a word by analyzing the type and depth of their knowledge about it. Students often have knowledge about words even if they cannot explicitly define them (Graves 1984, as cited by Maria 1990). This strategy asks students to rank domain-specific words according to three levels of knowledge: established, acquainted, and unknown (Beck and McKeown 1991, as cited by Lapp, Flood, and Farnan 1996 and Ryder and Graves 2003). At the highest level, established, students understand and can produce the definition of the word. The next level, acquainted, refers to the ability to associate the new word with other words or concepts but not supply a clear definition of the word. The lowest level of knowledge, unknown, indicates that the student has no awareness or understanding of the word. Once students have a better awareness of their own preexisting knowledge about the words, they can use this information to focus their learning on the acquisition of new academic vocabulary words both during and after reading the selection.

Grade Levels/Standards Addressed

See page 36 for the standards this strategy addresses, or refer to the Digital Resource CD (standards.pdf) to read the correlating standards in their entirety.

Activity

Scan the reading selection and select six new or challenging words from the text that are important for students to comprehend. Make sure these words are grade-appropriate, significant to the main concepts of the text, and relevant to future learning and comprehension. Create a *Word Knowledge Analysis* activity sheet (page 47, wordanalysis.pdf) with the chosen words. Distribute the *Word Knowledge Analysis* to students and explain that they will be analyzing their familiarity with six words. Discuss the various levels of word knowledge and model how to complete the activity sheet. Instruct students to complete their own *Word Knowledge Analysis* activity sheets independently.

After students are finished, have the class read the text, asking students to pay particular attention to the selected vocabulary words. Once they have completed the reading, have students revisit the *Word Knowledge Analysis* activity sheet and add any additional knowledge they gained from reading the text. Then, review the words as a class, clarifying any words students still do not know.

Differentiation

Read through the list of words independently with English language learners to ensure they can identify the target vocabulary words. After they have independently rated their own levels of word knowledge, encourage English language learners to work together to develop definitions and associations for the words. Select more challenging words for above-level students and encourage them to write detailed definitions for the words. For below-level students, take the time to ensure that they understand the target vocabulary words and explain that the point of this strategy is to truthfully gauge one's knowledge about these new words, not to write accurate definitions for each one before reading the text.

Word Knowledge Analysis (cont.)

Grades 3–5 Example

1. curious __X__ established _____ acquainted _____ unknown *wanting to know more about something*	**4.** alarm __X__ established _____ acquainted _____ unknown *a signal of danger*
2. tremble _____ established _____ acquainted __X__ unknown	**5.** prove _____ established __X__ acquainted _____ unknown *rue, false, lies, truth, show*
3. soar _____ established __X__ acquainted _____ unknown *birds, flying, kites*	**6.** eager _____ established _____ acquainted __X__ unknown

Grades 6–8 Example

1. barren __X__ established _____ acquainted _____ unknown *deserted, clear of anything*	**4.** impede __X__ established _____ acquainted _____ unknown *progress, story, prohibit, make difficult*
2. dormant _____ established __X__ acquainted _____ unknown *sleeping, still, volcano*	**5.** abhor __X__ established _____ acquainted _____ unknown *to hate*
3. edict _____ established _____ acquainted __X__ unknown	**6.** induct _____ established __X__ acquainted _____ unknown *hall of fame, club membership, ceremony*

Word Knowledge Analysis (cont.)

Grades 9–12 Example

1. ambiguous __X__ established _____ acquainted _____ unknown *unclear, not precise*	**4.** kindred _____ established __X__ acquainted _____ unknown *friendship, family, relationships*
2. congenial _____ established _____ acquainted __X__ unknown	**5.** lenient __X__ established _____ acquainted _____ unknown *permissive, tolerant*
3. dilapidated _____ established __X__ acquainted _____ unknown *building, disrepair, dangerous, poverty*	**6.** perpetrate _____ established __X__ acquainted _____ unknown *crime, commit, bad, evil, wrongdoing*

Word Knowledge Analysis

Directions: For each word, mark your level of knowledge. Mark *established* if you know the definition of the word and then write the definition is the space below. Mark *acquainted* if you do not know the exact definition but can think of words or concepts associated with the word. Write the associated words in the space below. Mark *unknown* if you have no knowledge or understanding of the word.

1.

_____ established
_____ acquainted
_____ unknown

4.

_____ established
_____ acquainted
_____ unknown

2.

_____ established
_____ acquainted
_____ unknown

5.

_____ established
_____ acquainted
_____ unknown

3.

_____ established
_____ acquainted
_____ unknown

6.

_____ established
_____ acquainted
_____ unknown

Root Word Tree

Background Information

The Root Word Tree is a graphic organizer that allows students to examine a single, unknown vocabulary word for its different word parts, such as affixes and root words. When using the graphic organizer, students locate an unknown word, write it at the base of the tree, and break apart the word into recognizable chunks. Students then examine these word parts to determine or clarify the meaning of the unknown or multiple-meaning word. They can also write down additional words that are associated with the word parts to help them remember the definition. By using the word's affixes and root words as clues to determine the word's meaning, students become familiar with frequently occurring word parts and can use this knowledge to determine the meaning of similar unknown words in other contexts.

Grade Levels/Standards Addressed

See page 36 for the standards this strategy addresses, or refer to the Digital Resource CD (standards.pdf) to read the correlating standards in their entirety.

Activity

The reading selection should contain some words that are unknown to students. Instruct students to locate an unknown word that is essential to their understanding of the passage. Tell them to write the word in the box at the base of the tree on the *Root Word Tree* activity sheet (page 50, rootwordtree.pdf). Next, have students break up the word and place any Greek or Latin affixes or roots on the large limbs of the tree. Ask students to write down other words with the same prefix, suffix, or root word as the unknown word on the branches of the tree. Instruct students to use the different word parts and associated words to determine or clarify the vocabulary word's definition and write this in the trunk of the tree. After having students work independently or in small groups, lead the whole class in a discussion and review session in which students present and share their work.

Differentiation

English language learners should have the target vocabulary word selected for them and written in the box. They will benefit from working in small heterogeneous groups to lower their anxiety levels and to practice sharing ideas in a small-group setting prior to sharing with the entire class. English language learners may also need a dictionary as a reference tool. Above-level students should be encouraged to use reference tools to examine the words more closely and to research the etymology of the words and the meanings of the word parts. Below-level students will benefit from teacher scaffolding. Write some of the word parts or associated words on the tree to help students understand the process.

Root Word Tree *(cont.)*

Grades 1–2 Example

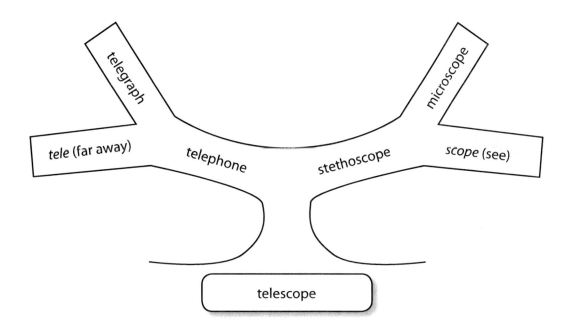

- telegraph
- *tele* (far away)
- telephone
- stethoscope
- microscope
- *scope* (see)
- telescope

Grades 3–5 Example

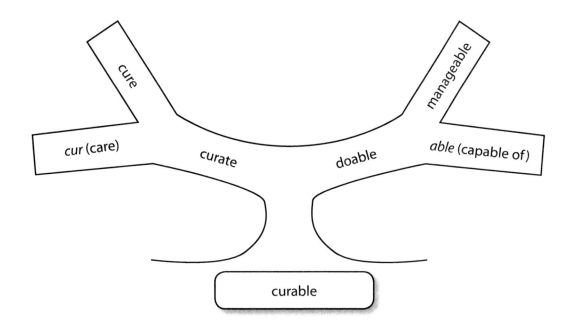

- cure
- *cur* (care)
- curate
- doable
- manageable
- *able* (capable of)
- curable

Root Word Tree

Directions: Write the unknown word in the box at the base of the tree. Break up the word into parts, and write the parts on the limbs. Think of other words that include the same prefix, suffix, or root word, and write those on the branches.

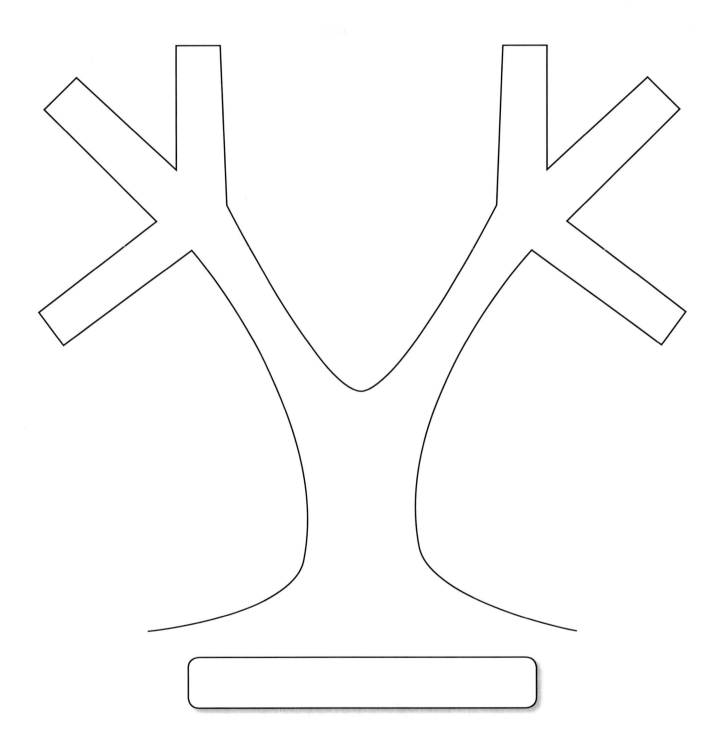

Roots/Prefixes/Suffixes Chart

Background Information

The Roots/Prefixes/Suffixes Chart helps students determine or clarify the meaning of the unknown words they encounter while reading independently. The chart specifically asks students to write down unknown words, record any Greek or Latin roots, prefixes, and suffixes that may be a part of the word. Students then guess the word's definition. When students examine unknown words in this way, they can use the information from affixes and root words as clues to comprehend unknown words as they read. Furthermore, allowing students to guess at the definition enables them to personalize their learning (Nagy and Scott 2000). Word part analysis can be introduced informally, beginning in kindergarten when students learn the orthographic patterns of many words. For example, kindergartners, although they may not be able to explain it, can easily understand that number words that end in -th are ordinal numbers (fifth, sixth, twelfth). As students progress through the upper grades, they will encounter hundreds of general and domain-specific words that have roots, prefixes, and suffixes within them in many different subject areas. In grades 1–2, students should analyze one or two words per reading selection. In grades 3–5, students should examine no more than three words per reading selection. In grades 6–12, students should examine no more than five words per reading selection.

Grade Levels/Standards Addressed

See page 36 for the standards this strategy addresses, or refer to the Digital Resource CD (standards.pdf) to read the correlating standards in their entirety.

Activity

Distribute the *Roots/Prefixes/Suffixes Chart* activity sheet (page 53, rootschart.pdf) to students prior to beginning a reading selection from a book or passage. Ask students to pay attention to words they do not know as they read. Have students work independently or in pairs to record the unknown words. Ask them to look up the Greek or Latin roots, prefixes, and suffixes and record these as well. Encourage students to guess the meaning of the unknown word based on the clues provided by the word parts. When students have completed the activity sheet, meet as a class to discuss the unknown words and what students think they mean. Encourage students to discuss how they arrived at their preliminary definitions. Verify or refute their guesses by reviewing the true definitions as a class and comparing and contrasting them to their guesses.

Differentiation

English language learners will benefit from working with a partner during this activity. Cooperative learning lowers the anxiety levels of English language learners and promotes collaboration. Encourage above-level students to locate additional words that include the same roots, prefixes, and suffixes on the back of their charts that they can later share with the whole group. Below-level students may need the teacher to scaffold some of the graphic organizer as it will lower anxiety by making the task seem less overwhelming.

Roots/Prefixes/Suffixes Chart (cont.)

The following books are great resources for teaching roots, prefixes, and suffixes:

All Grades
Greek & Latin Roots: Keys to Building Vocabulary (Rasinski et al. 2008)

Grades 2–4
Starting with Prefixes and Suffixes (Rasinski et al. 2013)

Grades 5–8
Practice with Prefixes (Rasinski et al. 2012)

Grades 3–5 Example

Unknown Word	Roots	Prefixes	Suffixes	Guess Definition
autobiography	*bio* (life) *graph* (write)	*auto* (self)		to write about one's life
incredible	*cred* (believe)	*in-* (not)	*-ible* (capable of)	not able to believe
revival	*viv* (to live)	*re-* (again)	*-al* (process of)	the process of making someone come back to life

Grades 6–8 Example

Unknown Word	Roots	Prefixes	Suffixes	Guess Definition
repopulate	*popular* (people)	*re* (again)	*-ate* (state or quality of)	to fill with people again
inscribable	*scrib* (write)	*in* (inside, into)	*-able* (capable of)	able to write in
immigrate	*migrate* (to move)	*im* (into, upon)	*-ate* (state of)	state of moving somewhere
psychology	*psych* (of the mind)		*-ology* (study)	study of the mind

Grades 9–12 Example

Unknown Word	Roots	Prefixes	Suffixes	Guess Definition
antebellum	*bellum* (war)	*ante* (before)		before the war
rectify	*rect* (straight)		*-ify* (to make)	to make straight
misanthrope	*anthro* (man)	*mis* (hate)		hater of mankind
polygamist	*gamos* (marriage)	*poly* (many)	*-ist* (a person who is involved in)	someone who has multiple marriages

Roots/Prefixes/Suffixes Chart

Directions: Identify the unknown words. Look up the Greek or Latin affixes and root words. Use this information to determine or clarify the word's definition.

Unknown Word	Roots	Prefixes	Suffixes	Guess Definition

Context Clue Analysis Chart

Background Information

In addition to inferring meaning from the etymology of words, students should also use context clues as a strategy to surmise the meaning of unknown or multiple-meaning words. Context can provide clues about word meaning through word relationships, such as synonyms, antonyms, and analogies. Edwards and her colleagues (2012) recommend teaching students five different types of context clues: *definition, synonym, antonym, example,* and *general.* The first context clue, definition, refers to when the author explicitly states the meaning of a word within the context of the sentence or selection. A synonym context clue provides meaning for a vocabulary word by using a word similar in meaning within the same sentence or passage. An antonym context clue suggests the definition of the vocabulary word by contrasting it with a word of opposite meaning. Authors may also choose to explain words by giving example context clues. Finally, words can be understood through general context clues, or several words or statements that give meaning to the target word. The goal of this strategy is to teach students to identify and use these five types of context clues to infer meaning about unknown vocabulary words.

Grade Levels/Standards Addressed

See page 37 for the standards this strategy addresses, or refer to the Digital Resource CD (standards.pdf) to read the correlating standards in their entirety.

Activity

Explain that writers often embed clues about word definitions within the text, and as a result, students can use these context clues to determine or clarify the meaning of unknown words. Explain that context clues can be words, phrases, or sentences within the same sentence or paragraph as the unknown word. Before beginning the lesson, select five new vocabulary words from the story that warrant further study. These words may be general academic or domain-specific words, but should be grade-appropriate and add significant value to the comprehension of the text. Display the *5 Types of Context Clues Reference Sheet* (page 274, contextclues.pdf) and discuss the clues and their examples. Provide several example sentences with unknown words and work together as a class to determine the type of context clue used to infer the meaning of the words in each sentence. Distribute the *Context Clue Analysis Chart* activity sheet (page 57, contextcluechart.pdf) to students with the five selected words filled in under the "unfamiliar word" column. Have students complete the activity sheet.

Differentiation

Provide English language learners with assistance in reading the vocabulary words. Because they may not be familiar with the words used in context (in addition to the chosen vocabulary words), it is beneficial to allow these students to work with a language-proficient partner to complete the activity sheet. Challenge above-level students by providing them with advanced vocabulary words and ask them to develop alternative sentences using different types of context clues for their vocabulary words. Below-level students will benefit from scaffolding in this activity. Provide these students with their own set of vocabulary words and attempt to give them words that are novel but not too challenging. The ideal type of words for these students are words that they have seen and heard before but still do not fully comprehend.

Context Clue Analysis Chart (cont.)

Grades 3–5 Example

Unfamiliar Word	Context	Type of Context Clue	Possible Definition
feeble	The feeble old man was frail and sickly.	synonym	weak or without physical strength
solitary	Instead of going to parties, Allison liked solitary activities like reading a book.	antonym	alone or by oneself
obsolete	An obsolete comic book is one that is no longer printed or produced.	definition	no longer created or used
compensate	To compensate for her poor eyesight, Sally used a guide dog to help navigate her surroundings. The guide dog's skills made up for her lack of vision.	general	to counterbalance or make the same
amphibian	We saw many different types of amphibians, such as toads, salamanders, and frogs, on our hike around the pond.	example	group of animals with wet skin and four legs

Grades 6–8 Example

Unfamiliar Word	Context	Type of Context Clue	Possible Definition
formidable	I had the formidable task of getting my little brother out of bed in the morning. I dreaded this job more than just about anything else.	general	causing fear or apprehension
agile	The agile dancer glided across the stage. Her quick and graceful movements made her appear as if she was floating.	synonym	quick or nimble
rebuke	He thought his father would applaud his performance. The sharp rebuke he received stunned him instead.	antonym	reprimand or scold
aboriginal	Aboriginal forests are the earliest known forests in a region.	definition	indigenous or native
prehistoric	Prehistoric dinosaurs, such as the tyrannosaurus rex, triceratops, and stegosaurus, roamed the earth during this time.	example	preceding the modern world

Context Clue Analysis Chart *(cont.)*

Grades 9–12 Example

Unfamiliar Word	Context	Type of Context Clue	Possible Definition
bucolic	The bucolic setting was quite a contrast to noisy, chaotic city life.	antonym	quiet or peaceful
nuance	She explained the nuances, or subtle differences, between the two chosen words.	definition	subtle variation
elucidate	I tried to clarify the situation, but my explanation failed to clearly elucidate the issue.	synonym	to explain clearly
etymology	The etymology of a word can help you understand the word's meaning. For example, studying a word's prefix, suffix, and root word can provide clues about its definition.	example	the parts of a word
irreverent	His irreverent tone took the teacher by surprise. Normally his students were respectful when discussing the serious nature of the disease.	antonym	flippant or disrespectful

Context Clue Analysis Chart

Directions: In the chart below, locate the unfamiliar words from the reading passage. Write the phrase, sentence, or passage that provides context clues about the meaning of the word. Using your knowledge of context clues, decide which type of context clue the author uses to help you understand the new word: *definition*, *synonym*, *antonym*, *example*, or *general*. Then, write a possible definition for the word in the space provided.

Unfamiliar Word	Context	Type of Context Clue	Possible Definition

Concept of Definition Map

Background Information

The Concept of Definition Map (Schwartz and Raphael 1985) is a graphic organizer used to teach the definitions of the most essential vocabulary terms. These terms should represent important concepts in the reading material. The Concept of Definition Map encourages students to learn more than just the dictionary definition of key terms. It helps them learn the subtleties and nuances of particular words, which are reinforced by the visual organization of the information in a graphic organizer. Included in the Concept of Definition Map are the categories or classes for the term (*What is it?*), the properties or characteristics of the term (*What are some things you know about it?*), comparison terms (*What is it like?*), and illustrations or examples (*What is it an example of?*). Through the creation of a Concept of Definition Map, students learn to sort words into categories, define them by key attributes, identify real-life connections between the words and their uses, and distinguish shades of meaning between words. The analogies that students create promote long-term memory by personalizing the association of the concept.

Grade Levels/Standards Addressed

See page 37 for the standards this strategy addresses, or refer to the Digital Resource CD (standards.pdf) to read the correlating standards in their entirety.

Activity

Prior to assigning a reading selection, choose a concept word that is important to comprehending the text. Write the term on the board and at the center of the *Concept of Definition Map* (page 61, conceptdefinition.pdf). Guide students in adding to the map by asking them the following questions:

- *What is it?*
- *What are some things you know about it?*
- *What is it like?*
- *What is an example of it?*

Encourage students to then read the text and add information as they read. Ask students in grades 6–12 to think of an original analogy to explain what the concept is like. After completing the activity, ask students to use their maps as guidelines to write a definition of the concept. Meet as a class to discuss student answers, and write examples of good definitions on the board to model for students.

Differentiation

English language learners will benefit from working with a partner during this activity. Cooperative learning lowers the anxiety levels of English language learners and promotes collaboration. Encourage above-level students to complete further research by using other resources to find definitions and examples, instead of the textbook, and combining them into a definition that is a synthesis of what they have learned. Below-level students will benefit from the teacher filling out a section of the graphic organizer prior to distributing them to students. This will help students orient themselves with concepts and ideas and lower their anxiety.

Concept of Definition Map (cont.)

Grades 1–2 Example

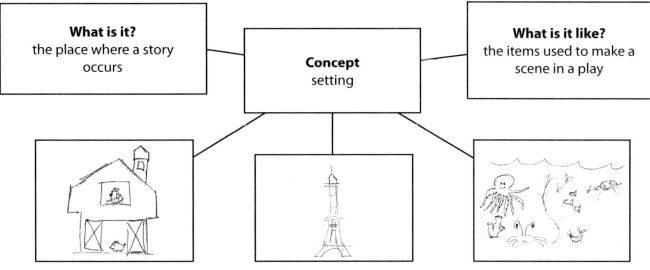

What is it?
the place where a story occurs

Concept
setting

What is it like?
the items used to make a scene in a play

Examples and Illustrations

Grades 3–5 Example

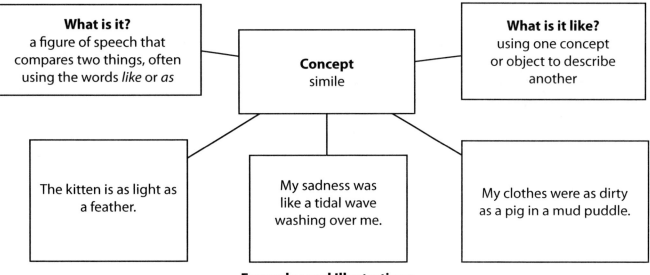

What is it?
a figure of speech that compares two things, often using the words *like* or *as*

Concept
simile

What is it like?
using one concept or object to describe another

The kitten is as light as a feather.

My sadness was like a tidal wave washing over me.

My clothes were as dirty as a pig in a mud puddle.

Examples and Illustrations

Concept of Definition Map (cont.)

Grades 6–8 Example

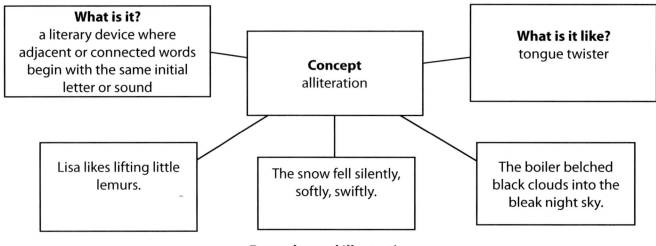

What is it?
a literary device where adjacent or connected words begin with the same initial letter or sound

Concept
alliteration

What is it like?
tongue twister

Lisa likes lifting little lemurs.

The snow fell silently, softly, swiftly.

The boiler belched black clouds into the bleak night sky.

Examples and Illustrations

Grades 9–12 Example

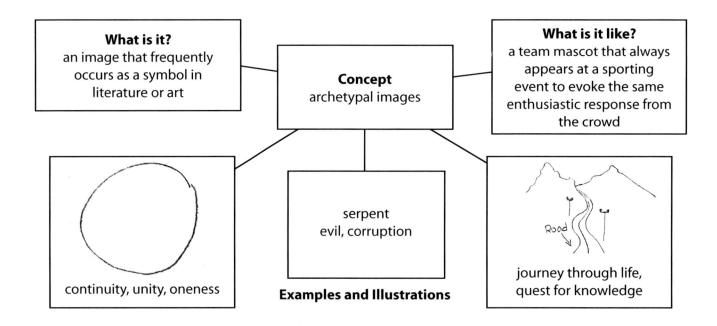

What is it?
an image that frequently occurs as a symbol in literature or art

Concept
archetypal images

What is it like?
a team mascot that always appears at a sporting event to evoke the same enthusiastic response from the crowd

continuity, unity, oneness

serpent
evil, corruption

Road

journey through life, quest for knowledge

Examples and Illustrations

Concept of Definition Map

Directions: Fill out the different categories for the selected word. Use a dictionary or another reference source, if necessary.

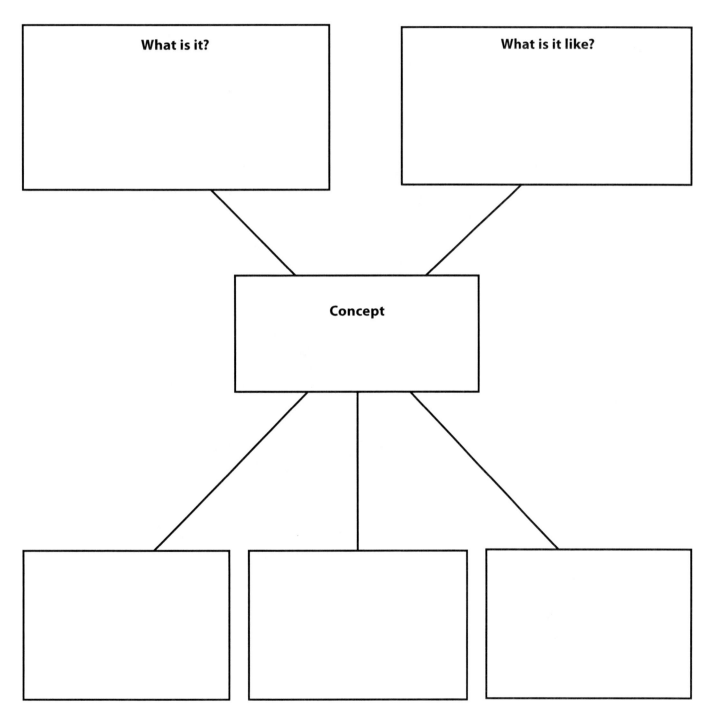

Examples and Illustrations

Frayer Model

Background Information

The Frayer Model (Frayer, Frederick, and Klausmeier 1969) is a strategy in which students use the graphic organizer as a means to better understand a concept and to distinguish that concept from others they may know or may be learning. The framework of the Frayer Model includes the concept word, the definition, the characteristics of the concept word, examples of the concept word, and nonexamples of the concept word. It is important to include both examples and nonexamples so that students are able to clarify what the concept word is and what it is not. The Frayer Model is especially useful for teaching grade-appropriate vocabulary that describes complex concepts or domain-specific words that describe concepts students may already know but cannot yet clearly define. This strategy takes a substantial amount of the teacher's and students' time and effort, but it provides students with a rich understanding of important concepts.

Grade Levels/Standards Addressed

See page 37 for the standards this strategy addresses, or refer to the Digital Resource CD (standards.pdf) to read the correlating standards in their entirety.

Activity

Instruct students to write the word for a concept they are learning on a *Frayer Model* activity sheet (page 65, frayermodel.pdf). Define the concept, as a class and list its attributes. Students may refer to their textbooks, using information in the margins or the glossary or apposition in the text itself, consult other resources to find the definition, or use the definition provided by the teacher.

Next, distinguish between the concept and similar academic concepts with which it might be easily confused. When doing this, help students to understand the concept in some depth. This can be accomplished through question-and-answer during a short discussion. Also, provide students with examples of the concept and explain why they are examples. Next, provide students with nonexamples of the concept and explain why they are nonexamples. Discuss the examples and nonexamples, including the nuances between the concept and other related, but different, concepts. Encourage students to generate their own examples and non-examples, and allow them to discuss their findings with the class. Once students are skilled at using the strategy, the entire class can work in pairs to complete a *Frayer Model* activity sheet for different essential concepts and then present their findings to the class.

Differentiation

Coach above-level students to model how to complete the organizer for the class. By placing a small group of two to three on- and above-level students in the center of the room and allowing the class to observe their discussion and how they complete the organizer, English language learners will learn from the discussion the small group holds. Encourage students who are modeling the technique to think aloud as they work through their ideas. Provide one-on-one instruction during the small group work for below-level students and select a reasonable concept word.

Frayer Model (cont.)

Grades 3–5 Example

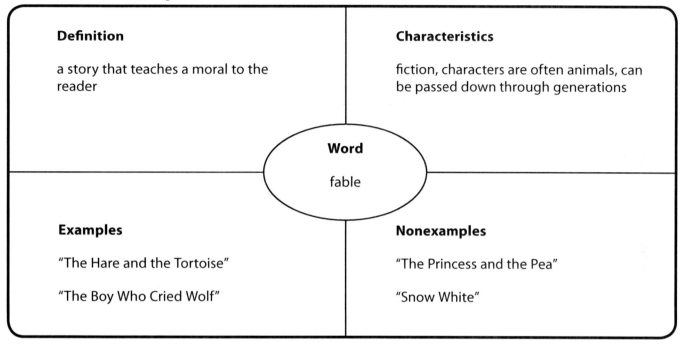

Definition

a story that teaches a moral to the reader

Characteristics

fiction, characters are often animals, can be passed down through generations

Word

fable

Examples

"The Hare and the Tortoise"

"The Boy Who Cried Wolf"

Nonexamples

"The Princess and the Pea"

"Snow White"

Grades 6–8 Example

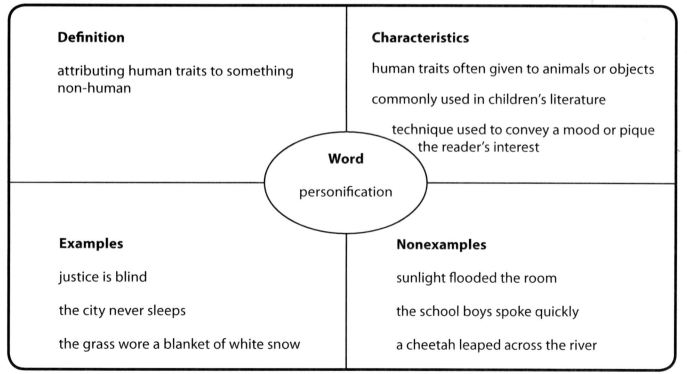

Definition

attributing human traits to something non-human

Characteristics

human traits often given to animals or objects

commonly used in children's literature

technique used to convey a mood or pique the reader's interest

Word

personification

Examples

justice is blind

the city never sleeps

the grass wore a blanket of white snow

Nonexamples

sunlight flooded the room

the school boys spoke quickly

a cheetah leaped across the river

Frayer Model (cont.)

Grades 9–12 Example

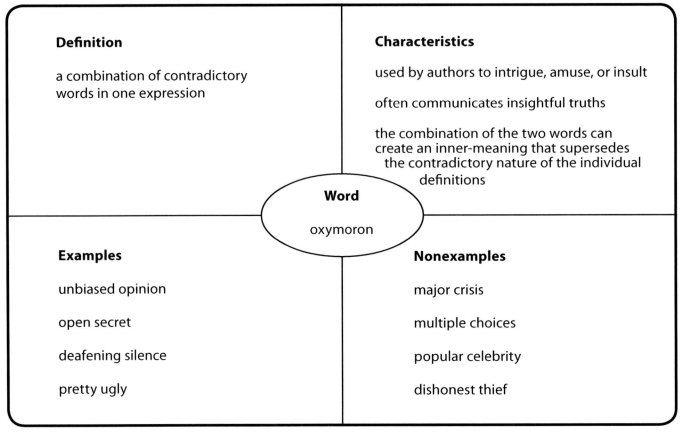

Definition

a combination of contradictory words in one expression

Characteristics

used by authors to intrigue, amuse, or insult

often communicates insightful truths

the combination of the two words can create an inner-meaning that supersedes the contradictory nature of the individual definitions

Word

oxymoron

Examples

unbiased opinion

open secret

deafening silence

pretty ugly

Nonexamples

major crisis

multiple choices

popular celebrity

dishonest thief

Name: _____ **Date:** _____

Frayer Model

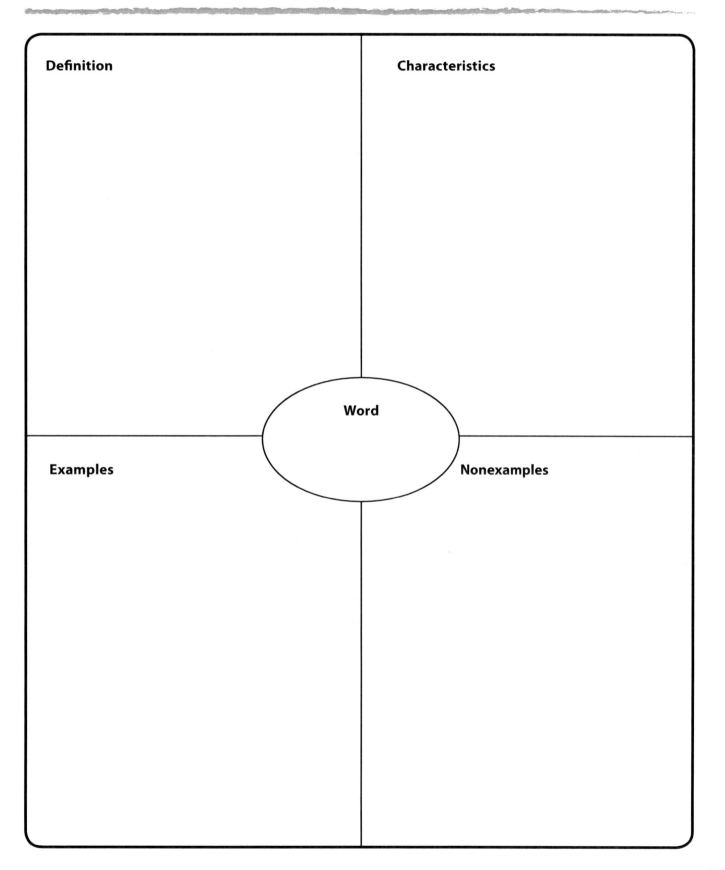

Definition

Characteristics

Word

Examples

Nonexamples

Vocabulary Diagram

Background Information

The Vocabulary Diagram enables students to break down individual words and examine them in different categories. Students look at a unknown word in terms of its part of speech, its Greek or Latin roots, affixes, its synonyms and antonyms, its cognates (related words), the people or things that illustrate the word, a drawing, a sentence from their reading, and original sentences. By examining words in this dynamic manner, students gain a clearer understanding of the multidimensional nature of the words they study (Nagy and Scott 2000). Analyzing a single word through examples, word relationships, and etymology makes it possible for students to recognize and decode a greater number of unknown words during reading and promotes better long-term retention of vocabulary words. The language arts teacher should select the target word for this graphic organizer carefully, making sure that students will be able to complete each category. Students should only complete one Vocabulary Diagram per lesson or unit, otherwise the word study becomes overwhelming and tedious.

Grade Levels/Standards Addressed

See page 37 for the standards this strategy addresses, or refer to the Digital Resource CD (standards.pdf) to read the correlating standards in their entirety.

Activity

As students are reading a selection from a textbook, trade book, or article, locate a dynamic word that is essential to understanding the text. Distribute the *Vocabulary Diagram* activity sheet (page 70, vocabularydiagram.pdf) to students and instruct them to place the selected word in the diamond at the center of the graphic organizer and identify its part of speech. Have students write the sentence from the text that contains the word in the rectangle at the bottom left. Have them identify any synonyms and antonyms for the word and place those in the oval on the left. Discuss the connections between these words and how these word relationships can help determine or clarify the meaning of the unknown word. Next, have students break down the word to identify the Greek or Latin roots and any affixes, if present, and place these in the oval to the right. Instruct students to include words that have the same Greek or Latin root as the selected word in the trapezoid. Ask them to draw a picture illustrating the meaning of the word in the square. Instruct them to think of a person or thing that exemplifies the word and add this to the circle. Require students to write one or two sentences that clearly demonstrate the word's definition in the rectangle at the bottom right. As a class, share ideas with a document camera and discuss each word as needed.

Differentiation

Complete some portions of the *Vocabulary Diagram* activity sheet for English language learners to allow them to concentrate on other areas (e.g., synonyms, antonyms, part of speech, affixes, and roots). They will also benefit from whole classroom instruction and completion of the diagram. Above-level students should be encouraged to select a word that they find challenging and complete the form independently. Below-level students can work with the teacher instead of small groups to complete the activity page.

Vocabulary Diagram (cont.)

Grades 3–5 Example

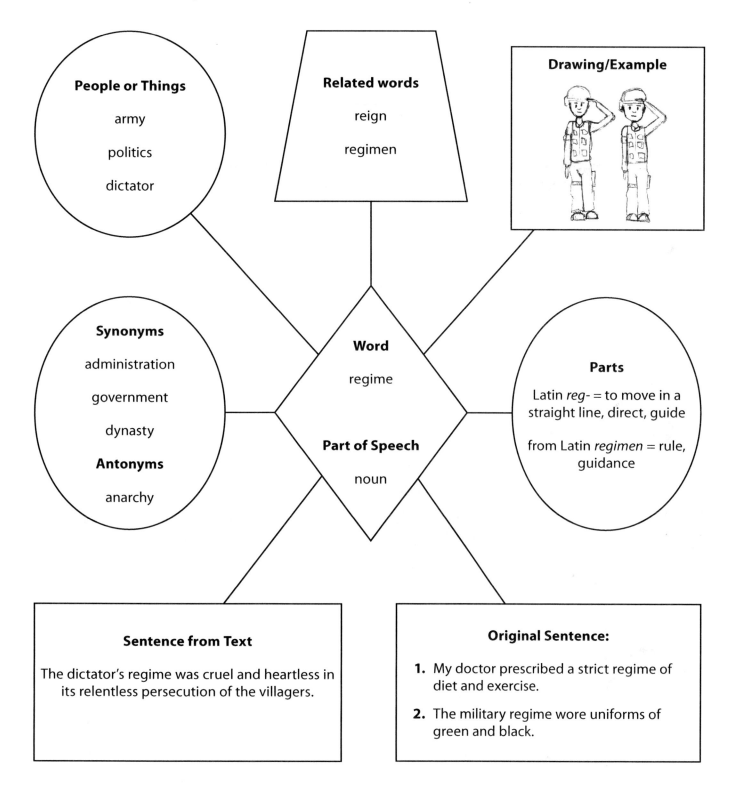

People or Things

army

politics

dictator

Related words

reign

regimen

Drawing/Example

Synonyms

administration

government

dynasty

Antonyms

anarchy

Word

regime

Part of Speech

noun

Parts

Latin *reg-* = to move in a straight line, direct, guide

from Latin *regimen* = rule, guidance

Sentence from Text

The dictator's regime was cruel and heartless in its relentless persecution of the villagers.

Original Sentence:

1. My doctor prescribed a strict regime of diet and exercise.

2. The military regime wore uniforms of green and black.

Vocabulary Diagram *(cont.)*

Grades 6–8 Example

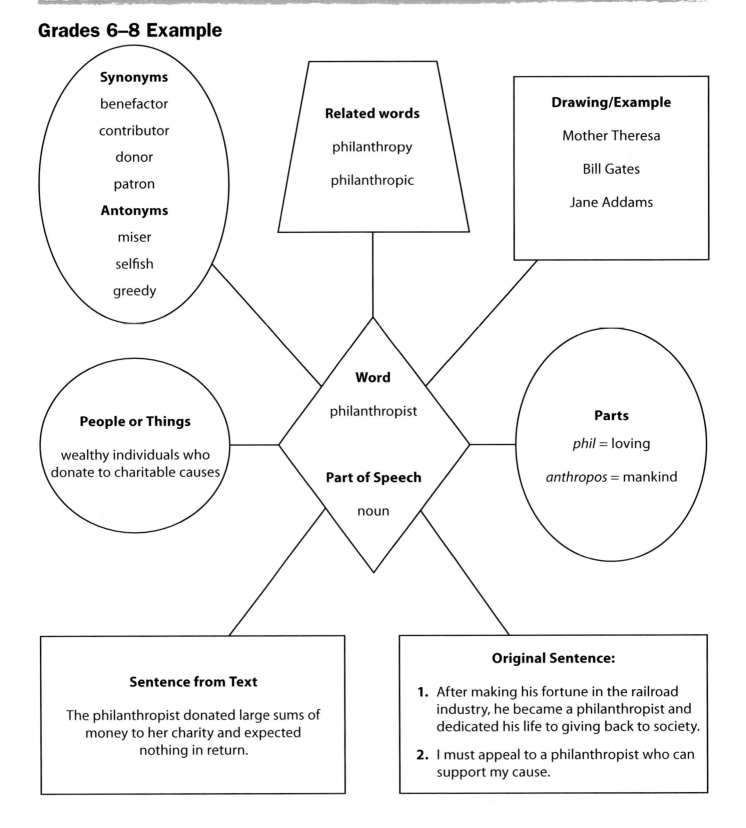

Synonyms

benefactor

contributor

donor

patron

Antonyms

miser

selfish

greedy

Related words

philanthropy

philanthropic

Drawing/Example

Mother Theresa

Bill Gates

Jane Addams

Word

philanthropist

Part of Speech

noun

People or Things

wealthy individuals who donate to charitable causes

Parts

phil = loving

anthropos = mankind

Sentence from Text

The philanthropist donated large sums of money to her charity and expected nothing in return.

Original Sentence:

1. After making his fortune in the railroad industry, he became a philanthropist and dedicated his life to giving back to society.

2. I must appeal to a philanthropist who can support my cause.

Vocabulary Diagram *(cont.)*

Grades 9–12 Example

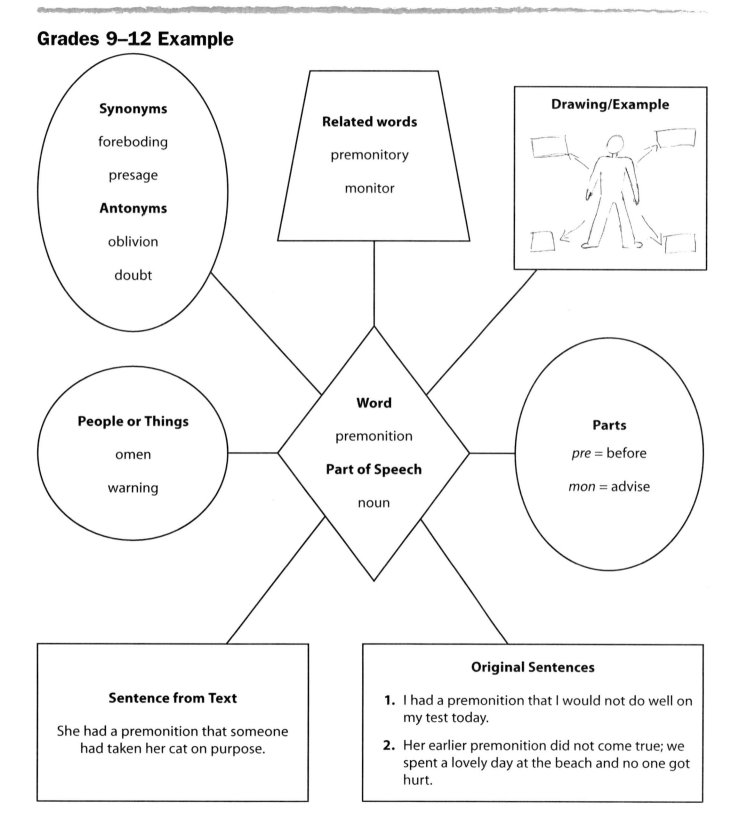

Synonyms

foreboding

presage

Antonyms

oblivion

doubt

Related words

premonitory

monitor

Drawing/Example

People or Things

omen

warning

Word

premonition

Part of Speech

noun

Parts

pre = before

mon = advise

Sentence from Text

She had a premonition that someone had taken her cat on purpose.

Original Sentences

1. I had a premonition that I would not do well on my test today.

2. Her earlier premonition did not come true; we spent a lovely day at the beach and no one got hurt.

Name: _____ **Date:** _____

Vocabulary Diagram

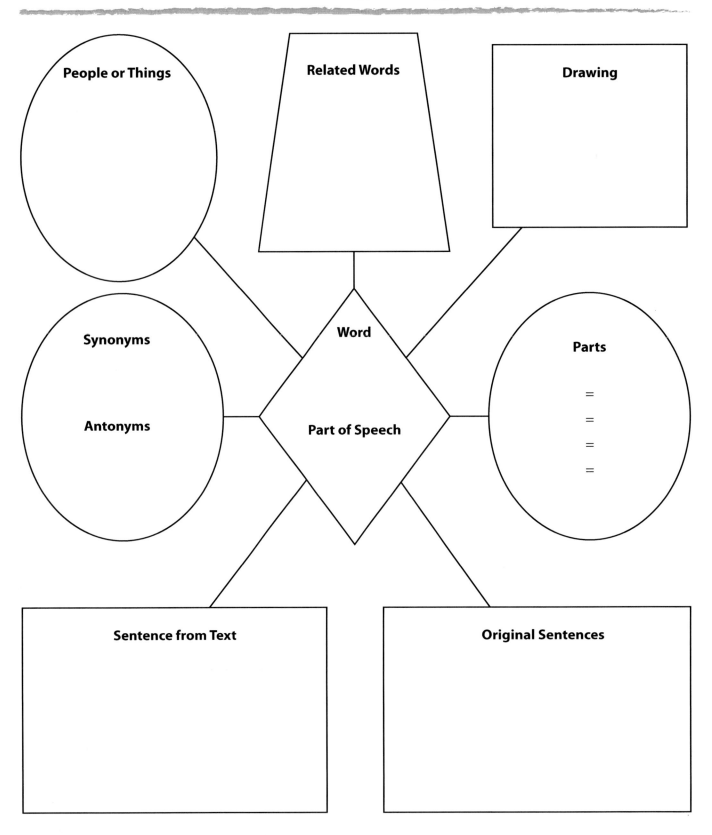

People or Things

Related Words

Drawing

Synonyms

Antonyms

Word

Part of Speech

Parts

=
=
=
=

Sentence from Text

Original Sentences

Keyword Association

Background Information

According to Katherine Maria (1990), successful direct vocabulary instruction teaches students strategies that enable them to "determine the meanings of words independently and make connections between new knowledge and their already existing knowledge." To this end, the Keyword Association strategy facilitates vocabulary recognition, recall, and comprehension by enabling students to make mental connections between new, unfamiliar words and existing, familiar words. In order to strengthen the relationship between the two words, students create mental images or sentences combining them. At first, students practice making these connections and mental images consciously so that eventually they will be able to internalize this strategy and learn to develop these types of associations and images automatically when learning new words. By utilizing this strategy to improve retention and recall of new words, students increase their ability to acquire and use a greater variety of grade-appropriate vocabulary words.

Grade Levels/Standards Addressed

See page 37 for the standards this strategy addresses, or refer to the Digital Resource CD (standards.pdf) to read the correlating standards in their entirety.

Activity

After carefully reading the literature selection, have each student identify an unknown word from the passage that he or she wishes to study. Encourage students to select words that play an important role in the selection and whose meaning will facilitate their overall comprehension rather than arbitrary or insignificant words. Distribute the *Keyword Association* activity sheet (page 73, keywordassociation.pdf) to students. Each student writes his or her unknown word in the first box. Next, students find the definition of their word. You may choose to define words through a collaborative class discussion or by having students use a dictionary. Then, ask each student to think of a keyword that he or she associates with the new words. Make sure to model this process aloud by using your own word so students can understand your decision process. This associated word may be related to the new word in any number of ways (e.g., definition, spelling patterns, or sound). For example, for the word *enshroud* (noun), one student might choose *cover* (definition), one might choose *shroud* (spelling patterns), and one might choose *cloud* (sound). Students then write their related word in the appropriate box and create a drawing or sentence linking the two words.

Differentiation

It is important that English language learners obtain the correct definition for their new word so that the new associations they make are accurate. If necessary, these students may select a word from their native language as their related word to facilitate comprehension and retention. Challenge above-level students to choose more complex words to study and encourage them to create extra keyword associations if the new word has multiple meanings or uses. Provide assistance for below-level students by choosing the new words for them. After finishing, have them share their drawings or sentences with a partner so that they can practice explaining their keyword association aloud.

Keyword Association (cont.)

Grades 1–2 Example

New Word	Related Keyword	Drawing/Sentence

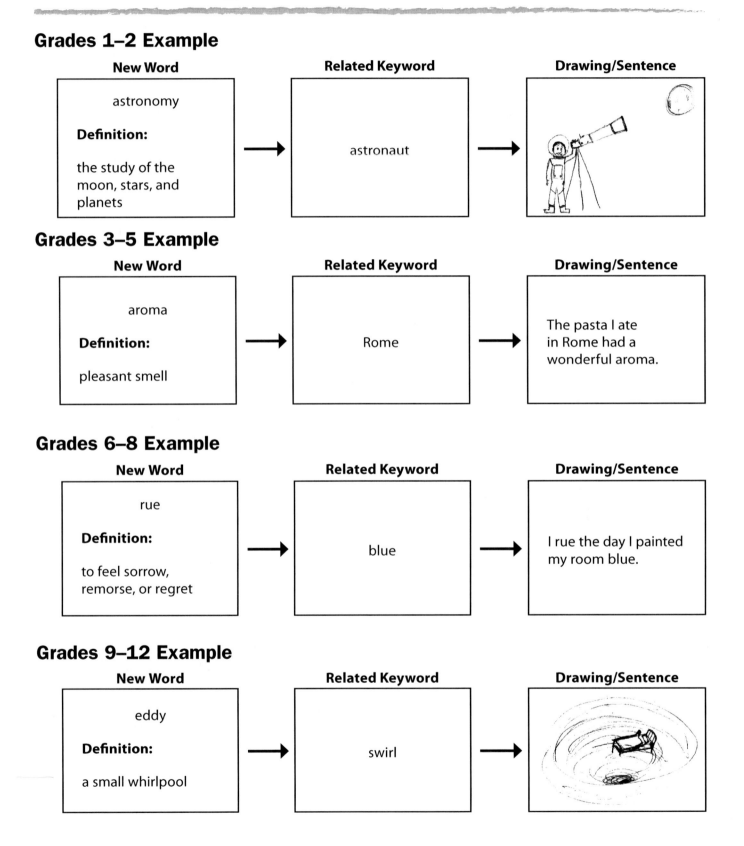

astronomy

Definition:

the study of the moon, stars, and planets

→

astronaut

→

Grades 3–5 Example

New Word	Related Keyword	Drawing/Sentence

aroma

Definition:

pleasant smell

→

Rome

→

The pasta I ate in Rome had a wonderful aroma.

Grades 6–8 Example

New Word	Related Keyword	Drawing/Sentence

rue

Definition:

to feel sorrow, remorse, or regret

→

blue

→

I rue the day I painted my room blue.

Grades 9–12 Example

New Word	Related Keyword	Drawing/Sentence

eddy

Definition:

a small whirlpool

→

swirl

→

Keyword Association

Directions: Write the new vocabulary word and its definition in the first box. Write a familiar word that you associate with the new word in the second box. Create a drawing or sentence combining the new word and the related keyword in the third box.

New Word	Related Keyword	Drawing/Sentence

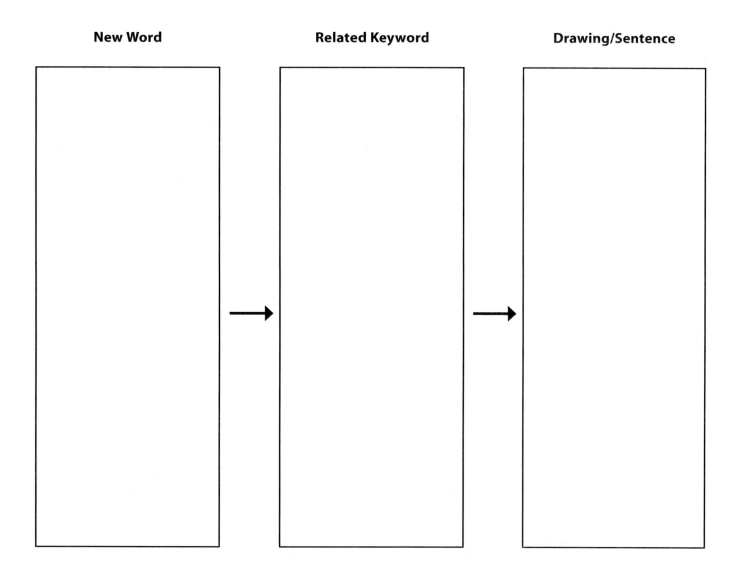

Using and Building Prior Knowledge Overview

What Is Prior Knowledge?

Students learn more effectively when they already know a little something about a topic and when the concepts involved in the topic mean something to them. Research on enriching background knowledge has demonstrated that activating such knowledge increases comprehension (Christen and Murphy 1991). Linking new information to the students' prior, or background, knowledge activates students' interest and curiosity and gives instruction a sense of purpose. Furthermore, building on students' familiarity with a topic enables the students to connect the curriculum content to their personal lives and experiences. Using and building prior knowledge during reading tasks is essential to improving reading comprehension skills, and there are a number of strategies teachers can utilize to make this happen.

But what is prior knowledge? Experts often use the words *schema*, *schemata*, and *schema theory* when discussing prior knowledge, but many teachers do not know exactly what these terms mean. It is important to understand that when one reads, one associates any new information with information one already knows. Researchers have established that readers build a *schema*, or a mental representation, of what they learn in order to organize their prior knowledge on a topic. A schema is essentially a large database in the brain that holds all of an individual's experiences and knowledge. This means the new information that one acquires from reading must be associated with and connected to the prior knowledge that one already has. This is known as the spiral of knowledge (Dechant 1991). Because of this, the newly constructed meaning that the reader forms is a product of the transformation that occurs between the new experience and all other previous experiences (Dechant 1991). *Schema theory* provides an explanation for how information is stored in the mind. *Schemata* is the plural for schema, so imagine that individuals hold a number of databases in their brains. When one learns something new, one finds a database and looks through the database to find the right column and row to store the new information. Once the new information is placed in the desired location, one sees the information in the column and row in a whole new way. One may even look at the entire database in a whole new way.

Dechant (1991) explains that researchers generally use the term *assimilation* to describe the ways individuals fit the new information in with the old information. Every new experience one has is related to and becomes a part of one's previous experience, which in turn becomes the basis for new understandings and meanings. When readers come across new information, they may just incorporate it into their existing schema by merely attaching it to the existing organizational structures. Researchers since Piaget have called this assimilation, but recent scholarship refers to it as *accretion*. Sometimes, however, it is necessary to alter the schema slightly to accommodate the new information by fine-tuning the structure. This is known as *accommodation*, but recent cognitive psychologists refer to this as *tuning*. At other times, in contrast, it is necessary to restructure the schemata entirely when readers cannot make sense of what they are reading with their existing schemata. *Restructuring* is the term most commonly used for this process.

Using and Building Prior Knowledge Overview (cont.)

Assimilation of Knowledge

To make this clear, look at this example. When a baby first learns about her family, she may merely recognize the different faces and names for the different family members. This establishes her schema about family. Later the child may learn more details about each person, like their favorite foods, and she will assimilate the information into her existing schema about family. In her brain, the connection is made. As the child learns more about her family, the child may learn that mealtime has always been an important part of their traditions. At this time, the child may not distinguish her own family traditions from those of another family, so if she spends time away from home, she may be confused about the differences in the routine and matter of mealtime. Therefore, the child must alter her schema about mealtime to accommodate this new information. At some point, the child will learn more about traditions and culture and will begin to distinguish the practices in her own family from other families in the community. Later, she will learn that traditions are different all over the world. Later still, the child may learn about the cooking traditions and methods for making meals all over the world.

What Good Teachers Do

Researchers (Readence, Bean, and Baldwin 2000) have developed guidelines for teachers to help students actively link new knowledge to existing knowledge. Following these guidelines also increases student motivation.

To help students actively link new knowledge to existing knowledge:

- Provide a supportive, well-structured classroom environment.

- Assign projects that are meaningful and challenging but not frustrating.

- Break up complex, lengthy tasks into manageable increments.

- Teach students to set realistic goals.

- Provide explicit, immediate feedback.

- Reward success through enjoyable activities, points, or praise.

- Provide opportunities for active student responses to text.

Using and Building Prior Knowledge Overview (cont.)

What Is Prior Knowledge?

Reading comprehension is not just affected by prior knowledge or experience with the topic being learned. Prior knowledge is a combination of the students' established *attitudes*, *experiences*, and *knowledge* (Kujawa and Huske 1995) as explained below:

Attitudes

- beliefs about themselves as learners/readers
- awareness of their individual interests and strengths
- motivation and their desire to read

Experiences

- everyday activities that relate to reading
- events in their lives that provide background understanding
- family and community experiences that they bring to school with them

Knowledge

- of the reading process itself
- of content (e.g., literature, science, and math)
- of topics (e.g., fables, photosynthesis, fractions)
- of concepts (e.g., main idea, theory, numeration)
- of different types of style and form (e.g., fiction and nonfiction)
- of text structure (e.g., narrative or expository)
- of academic and personal goals (e.g., career and college)

It is generally accepted that the more elaborate the schemata, the richer the learning experience for students. The breadth and depth of the prior knowledge that students bring to the classroom is strongly connected to their achievement in reading. But what happens when students do not have adequate prior knowledge on the topics that teachers present? It is the teacher's responsibility to activate and build on the prior knowledge of students in order to help them comprehend the new information. Teachers must set up the schemata, so students can place the new information in the columns and rows of their databases, as needed.

Generally, teachers begin each term or year by formally and informally assessing the students' attitudes toward learning, reading, and themselves, as well as their experiences and knowledge about a wide variety of topics. Having this basic information about each student helps teachers differentiate instruction and helps increase motivation. The more teachers know about their students, the better they can prepare to teach them.

Using and Building Prior Knowledge Overview (cont.)

Shared Learning Experiences

The best way to build on prior knowledge is to create shared learning experiences for students. Let's say the new unit for first graders is about friendship. The teacher can hold a class discussion in which the students answer questions. The teacher might record shared ideas on the board as a brainstorming activity to activate the students' knowledge about what makes a good friend. Regardless of the prior knowledge of the students, creating shared learning experiences in which background information is activated provides all students with enough information to effectively read about new concepts. Following are ways to create shared learning experiences:

- demonstrations (e.g., Show videos of stories having to do with friends.)

- role playing or theatrical performances (e.g., Show how friends treat one another in different kinds of situations.)

- hands-on activities (e.g., Make books about friendships.)

- independent research (e.g., Conduct research about what makes a good friend.)

- debates (e.g., Debate what makes the best friend.)

- visuals (e.g., Analyze pictures, film, or multimedia presentations having to do with the book, *Frog and Toad are Friends* by Arnold Lobel.)

- read alouds (e.g., Read various stories having to do with the same theme.)

- free writing (e.g., Create imaginary diaries from the characters' perspectives.)

The best way to build on prior knowledge is through shared learning experiences.

Using and Building Prior Knowledge Overview (cont.)

Standards Addressed

The following chart shows the correlating standards for each strategy in this section. Refer to the Digital Resource CD (standards.pdf) to read the correlating standards in their entirety.

Strategy	McREL Standards	Common Core State Standards
KWL Chart	Grades 1–2 (Standards 6.4) Grades 3–5 (Standards 6.8) Grades 6–8 (Standard 6.10) Grades 9–12 (Standard 6.9)	Grade 1 (RL.1.10) Grade 2 (RL.2.10) Grade 3 (RL.3.10) Grade 4 (RL.4.10) Grade 5 (RL.5.10) Grade 6 (RL.6.10) Grade 7 (RL.7.10) Grade 8 (RL.8.8) Grades 9–10 (RL.9-10.10) Grades 11–12 (RL.11-12.10)
Concept Map	Grades 3–5 (6.6, 6.8) Grades 6–8 (6.9, 6.10) Grades 9–12 (6.6, 6.9)	Grade 3 (RL.3.10) Grade 4 (RL.4.10) Grade 5 (RL.5.10) Grade 6 (RL.6.10) Grade 7 (RL.7.10) Grade 8 (RL.8.8) Grades 9–10 (RL.9-10.10) Grades 11–12 (RL.11-12.10)
Think Sheet	Grades 1–2 (6.4) Grades 3–5 (6.8) Grades 6–8 (6.10) Grades 9–12 (6.9)	Grade 1 (RL.1.10) Grade 2 (RL.2.10) Grade 3 (RL.3.10) Grade 4 (RL.4.10) Grade 5 (RL.5.10) Grade 6 (RL.6.10) Grade 7 (RL.7.10) Grade 8 (RL.8.8) Grades 9–10 (RL.9-10.10) Grades 11–12 (RL.11-12.10)

Using and Building Prior Knowledge Overview *(cont.)*

Strategy	McREL Standards	Common Core State Standards
Alphaboxes	Grades 1–2 (6.4) Grades 3–5 (6.8) Grades 6–8 (6.10) Grades 9–12 (6.9)	Grade 1 (RL.1.10, L.1.6) Grade 2 (RL.2.10, L.2.6) Grade 3 (RL.3.10, L.3.6) Grade 4 (RL.4.10, L.4.6) Grade 5 (RL.5.10, L.5.6) Grade 6 (RL.6.10, L.6.6) Grade 7 (RL.7.10, L.7.6) Grade 8 (RL.8.8, L.8.6) Grades 9–10 (RL.9-10.10, L.9-10.6) Grades 11–12 (RL.11-12.10, L.11-12.6)
Points of Confusion	Grades 1–2 (5.6, 6.4) Grades 3–5 (5.7, 6.8) Grades 6–8 (5.3, 6.10) Grades 9–12 (5.2, 6.9)	Grade 1 (RL.1.10, L.1.4) Grade 2 (RL.2.10, L.2.4) Grade 3 (RL.3.10, L.3.4) Grade 4 (RL.4.10, L.4.4) Grade 5 (RL.5.10, L.5.4) Grade 6 (RL.6.10, L.6.4) Grade 7 (RL.7.10, L.7.4) Grade 8 (RL.8.8, L.8.4) Grades 9–10 (RL.9-10.10, L.9-10.4) Grades 11–12 (RL.11-12.10, L.11-12.4)

KWL Chart

Background Information

The KWL Chart is a three-part strategy to encourage active reading that was first described by Donna Ogle (1986). A KWL Chart is divided into three columns: *K* (What I Know), *W* (What I Want to Know), and *L* (What I Learned). The strategy involves recording ideas during each of the three stages of the reading process: pre-reading, during reading, and post-reading. During the pre-reading stage (*K*), students are asked to explain what they know about the topic they will be reading about. This stage is used to activate prior knowledge. As students share their ideas, it is typical for some disagreements to occur, and they begin to question what they know. From these disagreements, teachers can help students formulate questions to clarify any uncertainty they may have. In the during-reading stage (*W*), students again are asked what they wonder or want to find out in further reading. During the post-reading stage (*L*), students explain what they have learned from the reading and other activities, and the class discusses what has been learned, which questions have been answered, and what new questions have emerged. This phase of the activity provides students with the opportunity to practice answering questions by referring back to details and examples in the text. This strategy makes it possible for teachers to model an interactive study approach for students. Depending on the types of questions developed through the activity, the KWL chart can help students clarify challenging vocabulary terms, analyze story elements, and determine the theme or central idea of the text, in addition to activating prior knowledge.

Students in the primary grades can complete a KWL Chart as a class. Older students can complete one independently, but at the end of completing each column, the teacher should gather together students' ideas, questions, and answers so that all students can review the information together. Questions can be recorded using a variety of methods. Teachers can use a document camera to display a KWL Chart and record student responses for the class to review. Teachers can also record questions on butcher paper.

For young learners, teachers also can record the questions on sentence strips and insert each question into a pocket chart. An advantage in using a pocket chart is that questions can be added, rearranged, grouped, and used for other purposes during subsequent stages of an investigation. Using graphic organizer software and a document camera can be a highly effective strategy for gathering, sorting, and sharing information during the span of an investigation for students at all levels.

Grade Levels/Standards Addressed

See page 78 for the standards this strategy addresses, or refer to the Digital Resource CD (standards.pdf) to read the correlating standards in their entirety.

KWL Chart (cont.)

Activity

Re-create the *KWL Chart* activity sheet (page 84, kwlchart.pdf) on a large sheet of butcher paper and display for the class to view. Before beginning a language arts unit, ask students to brainstorm everything they know about the topic of study. While recording their ideas in the *K* column, ask students probing questions to activate any prior knowledge they may have about the topic of study. Distribute the *KWL Chart* activity sheet to students to record their own ideas as you complete the chart as a class. Encourage students to make connections between the information and their prior experiences. Students may present conflicting information and may begin to question what they know, but do not correct any false information provided by students at this stage. Help students to develop questions to clear up any uncertainty that they may have. Write these questions in the *W* column.

Next, present students with a reading selection on the topic of study. As students read, encourage them to articulate anything they may wonder about or want to find out more about through additional research and reading. Record their ideas in the *W* column below the questions they have already generated. After students complete the reading, present the partially completed KWL Chart again, and this time, ask them to review the information in the *K* and *W* columns. Have students discuss what they learned from the reading, answer the questions they generated prior to reading, and generate additional questions that they feel should be addressed in further study. Record items of note from the discussion in the *L* column. Be sure to post the KWL Chart in the classroom throughout the unit to guide students in their studies.

Variation

The KWL Chart can be extended to include other categories or columns to the chart:

H—How to Find Out

One extension involves adding an *H* for a How-to-Find-Out column to create a KWHL Chart. Asking students to articulate how they will search for answers to their questions encourages them to develop strong research skills.

S—Still want to Learn

Another extension involves adding an *S* category to enable students to explore what they Still-Want-to-Learn. Adding this category encourages students to explore language arts topics in more depth and independently.

Differentiation

Give English language learners time to discuss their prior knowledge and what they wonder about with a partner or in a small group before they share in a large group discussion. This will allow them more time to practice and will reduce any anxiety they may feel. Above-level students may inadvertently dominate the class discussion when adding to the *K* column if they have a great deal of prior knowledge, so ask them to write an essay or generate their own list of knowledge independent of the class. Invite these students to independently explore the topics of further study generated by the class during the *W* stage and report their findings later. Prior to introducing a new unit of study, inform below-level students of the next topic of study. Provide them with additional time to build any prior knowledge on the topic, which may assist them in the reading task.

KWL Chart *(cont.)*

Grades 1–2 Example

Topic: *Rooster's Off to See the World* by Eric Carle

K	W	L
The world is very large.	Will Rooster really be able to see the whole world?	Rooster explored some of the area near his home. He did not explore the whole world.
Roosters can walk, run, and fly.	How does Rooster plan to see the world?	Rooster planned a walking journey to see the world. But it only lasted one day.

Grades 3–5 Example

Topic: *Ramona the Pest* by Beverly Cleary

K	W	L	S
Ramona has a sister named Beezus.	Do Ramona and Beezus get along well?	Ramona often annoys Beezus.	Will they get along better when they are older?
Ramona is about to start kindergarten.	Will Ramona like going to school?	Yes, Ramona likes school, but she still gets into trouble.	Will Ramona get into trouble in first grade too?
Ramona likes to get into mischief at home.	Will Ramona get into trouble at school?	Yes, Ramona gets in trouble for pulling Susan's curly hair.	Do Ramona and Susan ever become friends?

KWL Chart *(cont.)*

Grades 6–8 Example

Topic: *A Wrinkle in Time* by Madeleine L'Engle

K	W	L
Meg Murray is in high school.	What is she like? Is she adventuresome?	Meg is an awkward, but loving, girl who overcomes her lack of self-confidence to save her family.
Meg's father is missing.	Where is he? Is he alive?	He is being held by evil forces on another planet.
Meg wants to find her father.	Will she be capable of finding and saving her father?	Yes, Meg was able to find and save her father by traveling through time.
The word *wrinkle* has several meanings including, a line on one's skin, a change in customary procedure, or something new or different.	What is a wrinkle in time?	In the story, Meg and the other characters travel through tesseracts, or gaps in time and space, to search the fifth dimension for Mr. Murray.

Grades 9–12 Example

Text: *The Scarlet Letter* by Nathaniel Hawthorne

K	W	L
The main character, Hester Prynne, lives in a Puritan society.	Was Hester religious?	Yes, she considered herself a Puritan and went to church.
Puritans were extremely religious and governed their society through religious laws.	How did these laws affect Hester?	Hester was an outcast in society because she had a child out of wedlock.
The letter A is an important symbol in the story.	What does it represent?	The scarlet letter A represents adultery and is supposed to represent a shameful sign of Hester's sinful actions.
Unmarried or single women did not have many rights in this time period.	How does Hester's lack of a husband affect her life?	Hester is considered an outcast in society and people often gossip about her.

KWL Chart

Topic: _____

K	W	L

Concept Map

Background Information

A Concept Map is a graphic representation of the information related to a concept or concepts discussed in fictional texts (West, Farmer, and Wolff 1991). Most often, teachers construct a Concept Map about the new reading material and present it to the class prior to reading. In doing so, teachers better prepare students to read and comprehend the literature selection. As students read from the text, they can incorporate the relationships or links among the new concepts learned in the Concept Map.

There are many variations to the Concept Map, and some may suggest that it is merely a visual representation of traditional outlining, but Concept Maps allow students to learn more than just facts. The Concept Map allows students to develop organizational skills because they can view the concepts and details in terms of how they are related to one another in a visual, hierarchical format. Using a Concept Map helps students develop strong organizational skills in their writing, as well. Generally, the information presented in a Concept Map is hierarchical, so it moves from general categories to specific details. The appearance is similar to a flow chart in that the links between the concepts are demonstrated through lines and arrows. This structure can help students plan the organization of paragraphs rather easily. Please note that students should use the same shapes (e.g., circles, rectangles, ovals) in their Concept Maps to represent the same categories of information.

Grade Levels/Standards Addressed

See page 78 for the standards this strategy addresses, or refer to the Digital Resource CD (standards.pdf) to read the correlating standards in their entirety.

Preparation

Begin the process by conducting a thorough reading of the material students will be expected to read. Identify the most important themes, central ideas, or literary elements that are directly related to the reading, and note the concepts, words, and phrases that are related to these important terms. Then, organize the concepts and identify the relationships and connections among those concepts. Organize the concepts and details into different categories. It may help to place the title and the terms on separate strips of paper so that they can be manipulated in various ways to demonstrate the links and relationships. The last stage in the process is to refine the information presented in the Concept Map to enhance students' learning. It is important to keep the amount of information presented simple to minimize confusion. Use different shapes for different categories of information to demonstrate the hierarchical relationships among the concepts, information, and details. Make sure to leave adequate room for students to add their prior knowledge to the map.

Concept Map (cont.)

Activity

Present the prepared Concept Map to the class to introduce students to the new concept. Also, provide students with a blank map so that they can write down the information presented. Plan to share a version of the map using a document camera and either fill it out using notes as you present the information, or display the concepts one at a time by covering up the Concept Map with a sheet of paper that you can move around as you discuss each concept. This will reduce the amount of information presented to students at any given time and will enable them to focus more intently on the concepts you discuss.

Start with a clear explanation of the purpose of a Concept Map and explain how it can be effectively used as a learning tool. Read the title and ask students to predict what concepts may be presented in relation to the main topic of inquiry.

As you present the information on the map, encourage students to become more actively involved by asking them to share their prior knowledge and ideas related to the information. Incorporate their information into the map. Use the presentation time to clarify any misinformation and to determine the level of prior knowledge students have developed on the topic.

While students read the selection, they can use the Concept Map as a study guide. They can add information to their maps by taking notes or highlighting pertinent information.

Variation

List all of the terms and categories that belong in a concept map prior to presenting it to students. Distribute blank sheets of paper to students, and ask them to create a concept map using the list.

Differentiation

When students complete Concept Maps independently, it is important to scaffold the map for English language learners and below-level students. Provide some of the concepts for them in the blank map to help guide them as they fill out the map independently. It may also help both groups to place students in pairs so that they can work cooperatively to complete the map. It is important in both cases that the teacher review the maps completed independently as a class to discuss the variations in the connections and organizational structure students create. Above-level students may need very little instruction to complete Concept Maps independently. They should be encouraged to add another dimension to their organization (e.g., color).

Concept Map (cont.)

Grades 3–5 Example (after presentation)

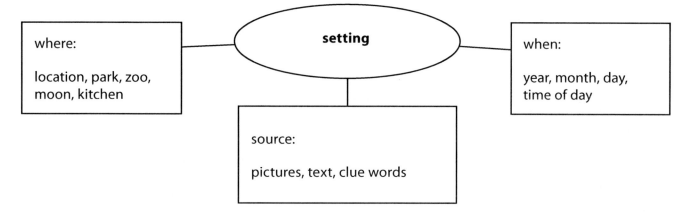

Grades 6–8 Example (homework assignment)

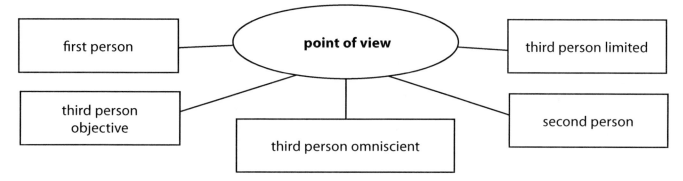

Grades 9–12 Example (after reading)

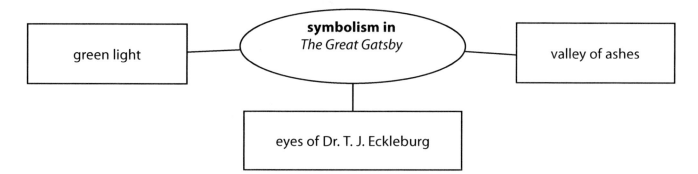

Think Sheet

Background Information

The Think Sheet strategy enables students to compare and contrast their pre-reading ideas with their post-reading understandings. Teachers encourage students to examine their own background knowledge and questions on literary issues to be studied so that they will be better prepared to read. After engaging in a close reading of the text and when students compare and contrast their ideas and questions with the new information in the reading materials, they are better able to make connections between their prior knowledge and their new conceptual knowledge. This technique helps new information remain in long-term memory because students have made the connections among their schemata. This strategy also gives students practice with citing evidence in the text to support or refute their ideas, facilitating greater comprehension as a result.

This strategy works best when there is an issue that involves some debate or controversy. The teacher models the process using a document camera so that students better understand the procedure.

Grade Levels/Standards Addressed

See page 78 for the standards this strategy addresses, or refer to the Digital Resource CD (standards.pdf) to read the correlating standards in their entirety.

Activity

Determine the main topic of the selected passage. Distribute the *Think Sheet* activity sheet (page 91, thinksheet.pdf) to students and display it for the class. Present the main issue, and ask students to generate questions that they have about the topic. Ask them to explain what they hope to learn from reading. Write their questions down in the first column, My Questions. Next, ask students to explain what they already know about the main issue, and encourage them to share even if they are not sure if their information is correct. Write their information in the second column, My Thoughts. Explain to students that they should read the text carefully to locate the answers to their questions and determine if their thoughts were supported or countered by the information in the text. As students read, they record the important ideas from the text in the last column (Text Support/Evidence) on the activity sheet. After reading, students share what they have learned and make connections between their questions, their thoughts, and the information presented in the text.

The reading can be completed as a read aloud for the younger students, paired reading, or as a homework assignment for the older students. Discuss what students learned from the reading, and show them how their questions, their thoughts, and the information in the text are all related and connected. Ask questions such as *What did the text say about your question? Did you have any questions that were not answered by the text? Were any of your thoughts inaccurate? Which ones?*

Differentiation

Model how to formulate questions for English language learners. Above-level students should be encouraged to conduct further reading to find the answers to any questions left unanswered by the text and share their findings in small groups or with the teacher. Allow below-level students to do a paired reading or hear the reading selection aloud as a scaffold.

Think Sheet *(cont.)*

Grades 1–2 Example

Main Issue: plot

My Questions	My Thoughts	Text Support/Evidence
What is a plot in a story?	I think the plot is what happens in the story.	The plot is the order of events that happen in the story. This book follows this pattern.
How does the author present the plot in the story?	The author describes the events.	The author starts each piece of the plot in a certain order. Page 1 starts with the beginning.
Is it always the same?	The plot for each story is different.	Sometimes stories have plots that are almost the same, but usually they are different. I read a book in a different order.

Grades 3–5 Example

Main Issue: flashback

My Questions	My Thoughts	Text Support/Evidence
What is the purpose of a flashback in a story?	A flashback indicates that a character is mentally unstable.	A flashback interrupts the action to go back in time to show something that happened earlier. Page 10 starts a flashback.
Do flashbacks only happen in stories?	No, I think that people can have real flashbacks where they remember something and feel like they are experiencing it again.	Not in the text.
Is it always the main character that has the flashback in the story?	Yes, I think the main character has the flashbacks.	Any character can have a flashback. Usually it is the main character, but not always. The main character ends the flashback on page 11.

Think Sheet (cont.)

Grades 6–8 Example

Main Issue: imagery

My Questions	My Thoughts	Text Support/Evidence
How is imagery used in fiction?	The author describes things in the story so the reader can make a mental image to accompany the text.	The author uses imagery on page 53 to describe the building.
How does imagery work?	The descriptive words help the reader imagine the text in mental images.	The words engage the reader's senses and provide details and comparisons to make the text come alive. Page 53 uses very descriptive words.
Is imagery only used in fiction?	Yes, I think it is.	No, imagery can be used in any type of text, but it is frequently used in fiction.

Grades 9-12 Example

Main Issue: allusion

My Questions	My Thoughts	Text Support/Evidence
What is allusion?	I think allusion is a literary device used to purposely confuse or mislead the reader.	Allusion is a reference in one literary work to a person, place, or passage from another literary work. The author makes a Biblical allusion on page 74.
What is the purpose of using allusion in fiction?	Allusion can be used to make the text more interesting.	Authors use allusion to associate the tone or theme of one literary work with another. Usually the reader must infer the connection between the two pieces of literature. The allusion on page 74 helps develop the main character.
Do allusions always reference famous or well-known works?	Yes, I think they do.	Allusions usually reference well-known pieces of literature because the meaning of the allusion is lost if the reader is not familiar with the cited text.

Name: _____ **Date:** _____

Think Sheet

Directions: Write down the main topic of the reading. Next, write questions about the topic in the My Questions column. Write what you already know about the question in the My Thoughts column. After reading, record important ideas in the Text Support/Evidence column.

Main Issue: _____

My Questions	My Thoughts	Text Support/Evidence

Alphaboxes

Background Information

The Alphaboxes strategy, originally developed by Linda Hoyt (2002), offers a systematic way to activate prior knowledge when brainstorming about a topic prior to reading or discussion. Often, when students are asked to think about a given topic or concept, they become fixated on a word or two and have difficulty considering variable meanings or aspects of the concept. The Alphaboxes strategy encourages students to activate their prior knowledge by providing them with an alphabet chart and asking them to fill in related words according to their initial letter. For example, for the book *The Little Engine That Could* by Watty Piper, a student might write *conductor* in the *C* box, *locomotive* in the *L* box, *steam* in the *S* box, *track* in the *T* box, and so on. It is rare that any student is able to think of 26 words related to a topic, starting with any given letter. Instead, this strategy helps students think creatively and activate related knowledge. Furthermore, the creation of a class word list at the end of the activity enables students to acquire, comprehend, and use a greater variety of domain-specific words related to the reading selection.

Grade Levels/Standards Addressed

See page 79 for the standards this strategy addresses, or refer to the Digital Resource CD (standards.pdf) to read the correlating standards in their entirety.

Activity

To begin this activity, conduct a preview of the text as a class. Examine the cover and any illustrations included in the story. Discuss the title and the table of contents or chapter names, if present. As a class, select a main topic or concept that is central to the comprehension of the story, and have students write the name of the topic on the *Alphaboxes* activity sheet (page 97, alphaboxes.pdf). Designate a timeframe and tell students to think of as many words as they can that are related to the topic. Using a document camera to display the activity sheet, demonstrate how to write each word in the box that corresponds to its initial letter. Remind students that the goal of the activity is not to fill as many boxes as possible but rather to activate as much knowledge as possible. Have students work independently to complete the *Alphaboxes* activity sheet during the designated time. Once the time is finished, display the activity sheet again, and ask students to share the words on their individual activity sheets so that you can create a class chart with as many words as possible. Discuss the words as students share them, and clarify the connections with the topic when necessary.

Differentiation

Provide written materials (magazines, books, etc.) relating to the topic for English language learners to scan in order to help identify related words. Challenge above-level students to think of multiple words per letter, and ask them to explain the associations between the words in small groups. Remind below-level students that this is a pre-reading activity and the emphasis is on brainstorming and activating prior knowledge. Encourage them to write down any words that come to mind and not to worry about spelling or grammar on this particular pre-reading assignment.

Alphaboxes (cont.)

Grades 1–2 Example

Topic: *The Very Hungry Caterpillar* by Eric Carle

A	B butterfly birds	C cocoon change crawl	D dirt
E eggs eat	F forest	G green grass garden	H
I insect	J	K	L leaves
M moth	N nibble	O outside	P pretty
Q	R	S soft squishy stripes	T thread transform
U underneath	V	W	XYZ

Alphaboxes (cont.)

Grades 3–5 Example

Topic: *Little House on the Prairie* by Laura Ingalls Wilder

A ax	B brave	C covered wagons	D difficult
E	F family firewood	G grass garden	H hunting hardship horses
I independent	J	K	L log cabins
M	N Native Americans	O	P prairie pioneers
Q	R	S settlers	T
U	V	W west wells wolves	XYZ

Alphaboxes *(cont.)*

Grades 6–8 Example

Topic: *North By Night: A Story of the Underground Railroad* by Katherine Ayres

A African American	**B** black barns bravery	**C** colored civil rights chain gang	**D** discrimination dangerous distance
E escape	**F** fighting flight families	**G**	**H** hardship hidden
I injustice	**J**	**K**	**L**
M migration	**N** North	**O** opportunity	**P** plantations
Q	**R** race risk	**S** segregation struggle slavery	**T** trouble terrified
U unhappy	**V** violence	**W**	**XYZ**

Alphaboxes (cont.)

Grades 9–12 Example

Topic: *The Good Earth* by Pearl S. Buck

A agriculture arranged marriage addiction	**B** bound feet	**C** China customs concubine	**D** destiny dynasty
E earth	**F** farming	**G** generations	**H** hard work
I infanticide	**J**	**K**	**L** luck lotus
M	**N**	**O** opium	**P** poverty peasants
Q	**R** rural respect of elders	**S** society slaves	**T** toil traditions
U	**V**	**W** work	**XYZ**

Name: _____ **Date:** _____

Alphaboxes

Directions: Fill in the boxes with words related to the main topic. Write each word in the box underneath its initial letter. Try to think of as many words as possible.

Topic: _____

A	B	C	D
E	**F**	**G**	**H**
I	**J**	**K**	**L**
M	**N**	**O**	**P**
Q	**R**	**S**	**T**
U	**V**	**W**	**XYZ**

Points of Confusion

Background Information

In order to develop the ideal learning environment, teachers must create a setting where students feel safe and valued. According to Maria (1990), a "climate of risk taking encourages children to make predictions and ask questions about what they are reading—both necessary strategies for effective comprehension" (63). The Points of Confusion strategy seeks to address this need by providing students with a way to identify confusing words and topics without calling attention to the fact that they do not understand in front of their peers. In this strategy, students first scan the new story or text selection, looking for words or phrases that they think might be confusing to "someone else" in the class. Then, the class works together to clarify the confusing words or concepts, thereby activating prior knowledge through a collective experience. At the end, students record their new knowledge about the highlighted words or concepts. By implementing this strategy, each student has an opportunity to activate his or her prior knowledge, identify areas of confusion in a safe, non-embarrassing manner, and determine the meaning of unknown words and concepts prior to reading the text.

Grade Levels/Standards Addressed

See page 79 for the standards this strategy addresses, or refer to the Digital Resource CD (standards.pdf) to read the correlating standards in their entirety.

Activity

To begin this activity, allow students to preview the text selection. In younger grades, the teacher may choose to read a preview or summary of the text aloud to the class. Once students have scanned the material, ask them to preview it again, this time looking or listening for key words or concepts that might be confusing to their peers. Each student can also note points that he or she personally find confusing, but the emphasis should be on identifying concepts that students think might confuse their classmates in order to remove any sense of embarrassment associated with admitting a lack of understanding. Have students note these confusing words and concepts on the *Points of Confusion* activity sheet (page 101, pointsconfusion.pdf). Next, display the activity sheet with a document camera, and ask students to share their ideas so that you can compile a list of challenging words and concepts for the class. Have students record the additional concepts on their own charts and discuss each topic as a class. During the discussion, students should take notes on each word or phrase in the corresponding column on the activity sheet. At the end, each student should have a completed activity sheet, with accurate notes about important ideas, concepts, and vocabulary words for the upcoming reading selection.

Differentiation

For English language learners, conduct the text preview in a small group setting to encourage participation and help highlight potentially confusing topics and words. Students reading below grade level will benefit from conducting the preview with a partner. Let these students choose their own partners so they will be more likely to share their areas of uncertainty or confusion. Challenge above-level students by having these students provide explanations and definitions for the confusing words and topics.

Points of Confusion (cont.)

Grades 1–2 Example

Text: *No Roses for Harry!* by Gene Zion

Confusing Words and Concepts	Clarifying Notes
stitch	a loop of thread in fabric
wool	the material that comes from spinning the hair of animals, such as sheep and goats
How are sweaters made?	most sweaters are made by knitting
drooped	to hang downward, often as a sign of weakness or sadness
What do birds use to make their nests?	Birds use twigs, sticks, and pieces of grass or plants to make their nests. They also collect other materials. They collect bits of fur, string, and fabric from the environment to add to their nests.

Grades 3–5 Example

Text: *Charlie and the Chocolate Factory* by Roald Dahl

Confusing Words and Concepts	Clarifying Notes
colossal	gigantic or huge
poverty	having little or no money; living very poorly
greed	selfishly wanting more of something
vices	a moral fault; something one does for pleasure that is not morally acceptable
How do factories work?	A factory is a building where something is produced. Often, there are a series of machines, connected by conveyor belts, where each performs a separate operation on the product to make it into its desired form.

Points of Confusion (cont.)

Grades 6–8 Example

Text: *The Lord of the Flies* by William Golding

Confusing Words and Concepts	Clarifying Notes
savagery	uncivilized, cruel, violence
conch shell	large, spiral-shaped shell
instinct	a natural and automatic response to something
civilization	a high level of technological and cultural development; having refined manners or tastes
allegory	using fictional characters to represent truths about humankind; a story with a hidden political or moral meaning

Grades 9–12 Example

Text: *Heart of Darkness* by Joseph Conrad

Confusing Words and Concepts	Clarifying Notes
imperialism	the control of one country over another; starting around 1900, many developed countries (such as Britain) took a great interest in colonizing and influencing other, less developed countries
hypocrisy	pretending to believe in attitudes or principles that one does not truly accept as true or right
immutable	not able to change
lurid	horribly fierce or savage
sepulchre	a place of burial

Points of Confusion

Directions: Record confusing words and concepts in the column on the left. In the right column, write notes to help you clarify and understand these words and concepts.

Text: _____

Confusing Words and Concepts	Clarifying Notes

Using Prediction and Inference Overview

Using Predictive Strategies

Closely related to assessing and building on prior knowledge is using predictive strategies to enhance reading comprehension. As the National Reading Panel (2000) has found in its analysis of reading research, prior knowledge affects a reader's comprehension by creating expectations about the content. This directs the reader's attention to the most important and relevant parts of the text, which enables the reader to infer from and elaborate on what is being read. As a result, the reader is able to fill in missing or incomplete information in the text. When drawing on prior knowledge and using prediction skills, the reader taps into the pre-existing mental structures, or schemata, to construct memory representations. Because these mental structures already exist, the reader is easily able to use, recall, and reconstruct the information in the text at a later time.

What Is Prediction?

Making predictions can be described simply as the ability to guess at what will happen and then read to see how things turn out. However, true predicting is not mere guesswork for successful readers. Readers rely heavily on their prior knowledge on a topic to determine their predictions. They use their prior knowledge to create a framework for understanding new material, and as they read, they determine whether their predictions were correct. We can call their predictions "educated guesses," but as Frank Smith (2004) asserts in *Understanding Reading: A Psycholinguistic Analysis of Reading and Learning to Read*, prediction simply means that the uncertainty of the reader is reduced to a few probable alternatives.

What makes good predictors good readers? Students who have encountered the information before, who are familiar with text patterns, and who can guess the missing word are better readers. If the predictions are accurate, the process of reading is much more fluent, flexible, and effective.

Prediction and the Investigative Process

Using predictive strategies is much like the processes that geographers, economists, and political scientists employ. Those who work in social studies-related fields spend much of their time making predictions. Geographers make predictions about and draw inferences from maps, historical documents, surveys, journals, photographs, etc. Economists make predictions about future trends based on market reports, stock history, world events, and natural disasters. Political scientists use Gallup Polls, historical trends, and government reports to make predictions.

Social scientists form a hypothesis or a theory, which is a possible explanation for what they have observed. Before testing a hypothesis, they must first make predictions. After testing the hypothesis by conducting experiments, they analyze the results and draw conclusions based on those results. Predicting in reading works much the same way. Readers look at their reading material prior to reading; this is called previewing. This gives them clues about what to expect in the reading. Readers look at the title, the pictures, the organization, and the words chosen, and they compare and contrast what they see with what they already know. This enables them to predict what will happen in the reading. Predictions in reading direct the reader's expectations about what they will find in the text.

We all make judgments about what we observe every day. We wake up, look out the window, and see that the sky is dark and cloudy, which usually indicates rain, so we decide to bring an umbrella along with us. We infer from the clouds and dark sky, based on our past experiences with these weather conditions, that

Using Prediction and Inference Overview (cont.)

it is likely to rain. We use inferential thinking when evaluating the information available to predict what will happen next. Social scientists use their observations about events to help forecast or make generalizations about future events.

Making Inferences

Inferential thinking requires readers to read the text carefully, evaluate the information presented, and consider how it is presented in order to determine general facts or minute details, emotions and feelings of characters, information about the author (opinions, point of view, personal history), and implications for and connections to other information. Students must use clues, references, and examples from the text to make inferences. They must also examine the connotative meanings of words used in the text to infer meaning.

What the Research Says

While the connection between prediction and the activation of prior knowledge has been established by researchers, it has primarily focused on the effectiveness of prediction skills with narrative texts. Duke and Pearson (2002) demonstrate that engaging students in prediction behaviors has proven successful in increasing interest in and memory for stories. In fact, in Jane Hansen's study (1981), and Hansen and Pearson's study (1983), the findings show that when students were encouraged to generate expectations about what characters might do based on their own experiences in similar situations, their reading comprehension was superior. They also performed better when reading similar stories independently. When teachers presented students with oral previews of stories, and turned these into discussions and predictions, story comprehension increased.

The National Reading Panel (2000) includes the following predicting activities as valuable procedures for improving reading comprehension: having students preview the text by examining the structure, the visuals, the organization, and the content; having students answer pre-reading questions about the text in order to make predictions about the content based on the students' prior knowledge; having students search the text and using what they know to answer inferential questions about the text; and encouraging students to compare their lives with situations in the text, either prior to or during the reading.

Developing predicting skills in students helps them set their purpose for reading, increases their motivation to read, instills curiosity, and heightens their motivation to learn (Ryder and Graves 2003).

Using Prediction and Inference Overview (cont.)

Standards Addressed

The following chart shows the correlating standards for each strategy in this section. Refer to the Digital Resource CD (standards.pdf) to read the correlating standards in their entirety.

Strategy	McREL Standards	Common Core State Standards
Picture Prediction	Grades 1–2 (5.2) Grades 3–5 (5.1, 5.2) Grades 6–8 (5.1) Grades 9–12 (5.1)	Grade 1 (RL.1.7, RL1.10) Grade 2 (RL.2.7, RL.2.10) Grade 3 (RL.3.7, RL.3.10) Grade 4 (RL.4.7, RL.4.10) Grade 5 (RL.5.7, RL.5.10) Grade 6 (RL.6.7, RL.6.10) Grade 7 (RL.7.7, RL.7.10) Grade 8 (RL.8.7, RL.8.10) Grades 9–10 (RL.9-10.7, RL.9-10.10) Grades 11–12 (RL.11-12.7, RL.11-12.10)
Text and Subtext	Grades 3–5 (5.3) Grades 6–8 (7.5) Grades 9–12 (7.5)	Grade 3 (RL.3.1, RL.3.10) Grade 4 (RL.4.1, RL.4.10) Grade 5 (RL.5.1, RL.5.10) Grade 6 (RL.6.1, RL.6.10) Grade 7 (RL.7.1, RL.7.10) Grade 8 (RL.8.1, RL.8.10) Grades 9–10 (RL.9-10.1, RL.9-10.10) Grades 11–12 (RL.11-12.1, RL.11-12.10)
Wordsplash	Grades 3–5 (5.3) Grades 6–8 (5.1) Grades 9–12 (5.2)	Grade 3 (RL.3.10) Grade 4 (RL.4.10) Grade 5 (RL.5.10) Grade 6 (RL.6.10) Grade 7 (RL.7.10) Grade 8 (RL.8.10) Grades 9–10 (RL.9-10.10) Grades 11–12 (RL.11-12.10)

Using Prediction and Inference Overview (cont.)

Strategy	McREL Standards	Common Core State Standards
Preview	Grades 1–2 (7.2) Grades 3–5 (7.6) Grades 6–8 (7.4) Grades 9–12 (7.1)	Grade 1 (RL.1.10) Grade 2 (RL.2.10) Grade 3 (RL.3.10) Grade 4 (RL.4.10) Grade 5 (RL.5.10) Grade 6 (RL.6.10) Grade 7 (RL.7.10) Grade 8 (RL.8.10) Grades 9–10 (RL.9-10.10) Grades 11–12 (RL.11-12.10)
Inference Investigation	Grades 3–5 (6.8) Grades 6–8 (6.9, 6.10) Grades 9–12 (6.9)	Grade 3 (RL.3.1, RL.3.10) Grade 4 (RL.4.1, RL.4.10) Grade 5 (RL.5.1, RL.5.10) Grade 6 (RL.6.1, RL.6.10) Grade 7 (RL.7.1, RL.7.10) Grade 8 (RL.8.1, RL.8.10) Grades 9–10 (RL.9-10.1, RL.9-10.10) Grades 11–12 (RL.11-12.1, RL.11-12.10)
Character Inferences	Grades 1–2 (6.2, 6.4) Grades 3–5 (6.5, 6.8) Grades 6–8 (6.4, 6.10) Grades 9–12 (6. 4, 6.9)	Grade 1 (RL.1.1, RL.1.3, RL.1.10) Grade 2 (RL.2.1, RL.2.3, RL.2.10) Grade 3 (RL.3.1, RL.3.3, RL.3.10) Grade 4 (RL.4.1, RL.4.3, RL.4.10) Grade 5 (RL.5.1, RL.5.3, RL.5.10) Grade 6 (RL.6.1, RL.6.3, RL.6.10) Grade 7 (RL.7.1, RL.7.3, RL.7.10) Grade 8 (RL.8.1, RL.8.3, RL.8.10) Grades 9–10 (RL.9-10.1, RL.9-10.3, RL.9-10.10) Grades 11–12 (RL.11-12.1, RL.11-12.3, RL.11-12.10)

Picture Prediction

Background Information

It is important to guide students to closely examine any pictures in a narrative selection prior to reading to formulate some expectations about what they will learn. Students seem naturally drawn to the colorful pictures in fiction books, but they need to develop inferential thinking so that they can more accurately predict the content of the reading. Teachers draw or gather images related to the reading selection to present to students. After presenting the images, the teacher asks students to predict how the pictures are related to one another and to generate a list of words and concepts associated with the pictures. Students then try to anticipate the content of the reading selection because the better they are at anticipating the content, the more effective and fluent their reading comprehension will be. As students read the selection, they check to see how the images are related to the new information, allowing them to more efficiently incorporate new knowledge into their existing schema. Additionally, through their predictions, students understand how specific aspects of a text's illustrations contribute to the development of the story's elements, such as character, plot, setting, etc. Moreover, students are more motivated to read when they have determined the purpose of a reading task.

Grade Levels/Standards Addressed

See page 104 for the standards this strategy addresses, or refer to the Digital Resource CD (standards.pdf) to read the correlating standards in their entirety.

Activity

After carefully examining the reading selection, draw or gather three to six images directly relevant to the content, and arrange them in the desired order. Either place the images on the *Picture Prediction* activity sheet (page 109, pictureprediction.pdf), and distribute them to small groups or individual students, or project the images on a large screen for the class to view. As students view the images, ask them to consider how the images are related to one another and predict the content of the reading. Place students in small groups, and ask them to generate a list of words or concepts associated with the pictures and the inferred topic of study. Have groups present their words and concepts as you write them on the board. Ask students to look over all of the words and try to generate any words that were not mentioned. As students tackle the reading selection, ask them to consider how the pictures are related to content and the new information they encounter. As an extended activity to encourage metacognitive skills, students can write reflectively about their predictions, how they related to the pictures, and what they learned from the reading. They should consider the process as a whole.

Differentiation

English language learners may have difficulty generating words related to the pictures, so it may help to have a list of words handy for them. To increase the challenge, the list might include words unrelated to the picture in addition to words relevant to the topic of study. Below-level students will work best in the small-group setting. Above-level students will enjoy the challenge of the activity, particularly if they have a different set of images related to the topic of study to work with.

Picture Prediction *(cont.)*

Grades 1–2 Example

from *Lin Yi's Lantern: A Moon Festival Tale+* by Brenda Williams

Words: lantern, light, paper, market, buying, rice, moon, trading

My Prediction: A little boy is going to buy something at a market. He needs a paper lantern to light the way because it is nighttime.

Grades 3–5 Example

from *Fantastic Mr. Fox* by Roald Dahl

Words: fox, farmer, mean, farm, chickens, catch, steal, eat

My Prediction: I think the reading will be about a fox that wants to steal and eat the mean farmer's chickens.

Picture Prediction *(cont.)*

Grades 6–8 Example

from *11 Birthdays* by Wendy Mass

Words: birthday, balloons, celebration, friends, boy, girl, cycle, circle, arrows, around and around, repeating

My Prediction: Two friends are celebrating a birthday, but something keeps repeating.

Grades 9–12 Example

from *Old Man and the Sea* by Ernest Hemingway

  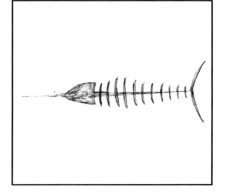

Words: fish, marlin, strong, fast, fisherman, boat, fishing rod, hook, bait, skeleton, dinner

My Prediction: The fisherman struggles to catch a large fish and then eats it.

Picture Prediction

Directions: Write down any words that you think of when you look at the pictures. Think about what you will be reading, and write down what you think the reading will be about.

Words

_____

_____

My Prediction

_____

_____

Text and Subtext

Background Information

When students make inferences while reading, they make connections to what they already know, to other information they have read, and to their general knowledge of the world around them. They take what they "see" and infer information that is not explicitly stated in the reading. Students are generally taught inferential reasoning when reading fiction (Hoyt 2002). Fiction provides an excellent foundation for teaching inference because the reader must use information presented in the text to learn about the thoughts, attitudes, actions, and properties of fictional characters, settings, and situations. As Hoyt (2002) points out, "With adequate modeling, readers can infer from even so little as a sentence and experience the power of reading beyond what is stated."

Teachers can begin the explicit instruction of inferential reasoning by allowing students to interpret body language, facial expressions, pictures in reading books, photographs, and short predictable stories. After much practice, students can extrapolate information to demonstrate insight on the topic of study.

Grade Levels/Standards Addressed

See page 104 for the standards this strategy addresses, or refer to the Digital Resource CD (standards.pdf) to read the correlating standards in their entirety.

Activity

Begin the activity with teacher modeling and demonstration. Conduct a read aloud of the reading selection for students. When finished, model for students how to restate the information from the text in their own words by thinking aloud and writing your thoughts on the board. Then, have students write their own summaries of the text on the *Text and Subtext* activity sheet (page 112, textsubtext.pdf). Next, have students look back through the text to find a quote that supports their summary and record it on the graphic organizer. Ask students to study the two statements and then explain what information they can infer. Students should look at word choice, sentence structure, and details. When students use inference, they are also identifying the subtext. Guide students in using their inferring skills to identify subtext and then record their thoughts in the subtext section on the activity sheet. After students identify the subtext, hold a class discussion to further explore meaning and implications of the subtext.

Differentiation

Teaching inference can be tricky, so it is best to provide individual instruction for both English language learners and below-level students. All students will benefit from heterogeneous grouping for this activity. It is important for English language learners to have adequate modeling for this activity. Make sure that the reading selection is at an appropriate level for below-level students. Above-level students may need little instruction and may prefer to work independently.

Text and Subtext *(cont.)*

Grades 3–5 Example

Restate the reading selection in your own words

The narrator's grandmother said good night to them because their mother was not there to do it.

> **Quote from the reading**
> "Mom still hadn't come upstairs when we went to bed, so once again, Granny said good night." (Freeman 66)

Subtext

The narrator is disappointed by his mother's frequent absences at bedtime.

Grades 6–8 Example

Restate the reading selection in your own words

The shadow of Mr. Morrison covered him (Kaleb Wallace) as the two men stood close together for a second. Then, Mr. Morrison turned away from Kaleb Wallace and looked into the truck.

> **Quote from the reading**
> "Mr. Morrison's long shadow fell over him and for a breathless second, Mr. Morrison towered dangerously near him. But as the fear grew white on Kaleb Wallace's face, Mr. Morrison turned without a word and peered into the truck." (Taylor 225)

Subtext

Mr. Morrison scared Kaleb Wallace by his physical presence, but instead of hurting him, he turned away towards the truck.

Grades 9–12 Example

Restate the reading selection in your own words

She realized she had many thoughts and feelings she had never shared with Jody.

> **Quote from the reading**
> "She found that she had a host of thoughts she had never expressed to him, and numerous emotions she had never let Jody know about." (Hurston 68)

Subtext

Janie was growing more distant from Jody and did not feel the ability or desire to communicate with him on a personal level.

Text and Subtext

Directions: After completing the reading, explain what the selection says in your own words. Find a quote that supports your explanation. Then, write down what the subtext is.

Restate the reading selection in your own words

_____

_____

_____

_____

Quote from the reading

_____

_____

_____

_____

Subtext

_____

_____

_____

_____

Wordsplash

Background Information

Wordsplash is a vocabulary activity created by W. Dorsey Hammond, a professor of education at Salisbury University. Wordsplash generates interest on a topic, draws on students' prior knowledge, and asks them to make predictions about how words are related to each other and to the topic (Hammond and Nessel 2011). Prior to assigning a reading task, the teacher selects grade-appropriate words and concepts from the article or text. The words should be placed randomly on a page. Students then examine the words and work either individually or in a group to predict the relationships between the words and the topic being studied. Students write down statements in which they explain the relationships. Once the statements are generated, students read the text and check the accuracy of their predictions. This activity helps students read and comprehend literature by enabling them to anticipate what they will encounter in the reading material. Wordsplash allows students to see that they already know something about the topic being studied. Even if students' predictions are inaccurate, they establish a framework for learning new information from the reading by making a personal connection to it.

Grade Levels/Standards Addressed

See page 104 for the standards this strategy addresses, or refer to the Digital Resource CD (standards.pdf) to read the correlating standards in their entirety.

Activity

After carefully reading the text, select key words and important concepts from the literature selection for students to use for this activity. Limit the number of words to no more than 10. Next, prepare a *Wordsplash* activity sheet (page 116, wordsplash.pdf) in which the words appear randomly on the page. Place students in groups or direct them to work individually to write a short paragraph that explains how the words and concepts work together. After students have finished writing, hold a brief discussion about their predictions. Then, allow students to read the text to see if their predictions were accurate. Prompt them to compare and contrast their paragraphs with the material in the reading. Have students share their predictions and findings with the class. Extend the activity by asking students to write a reflective paragraph about the process.

Differentiation

If some words on the *Wordsplash* activity sheet are not easily understood by English language learners or below-level students, be sure to provide definitions for them. Read the words aloud to students and provide visuals if possible to aid in their understanding of the vocabulary. Group your above-grade-level students homogeneously and have them create their own wordsplash list of words to work on.

Wordsplash (cont.)

Grades 3–5 Example

from *Breaking Stalin's Nose* by Eugene Yelchin

Soviet Union   Communist party

Stalin

capitalism   dream

political youth group

disrupt

desire   secret police

Wordsplash summary

The story takes place in the Soviet Union. Stalin is the leader of the Communist party at this time and capitalism is considered bad. The main character is a child who desires to join the communist political youth group. Then, the secret police come and disrupt this dream.

Grades 6–8 Example

from *The Chosen* by Chaim Potok

orthodox   religious

Hasidic

yeshiva   sect

different

rivalry

baseball

Wordsplash summary

The main characters are from different religious Jewish sects. They both are from orthodox Jewish families, but one is Hasidic. They go to different yeshivas, but both play baseball and their teams have a rivalry.

Wordsplash *(cont.)*

Grades 9–12 Example

from *A Farewell to Arms* by Ernest Hemingway

World War I

lieutenant

army

nurse

desertion

tension

love

Italy

Wordsplash summary

A lieutenant in World War I falls in love with a nurse in Italy. The tension of this love makes him consider desertion from the army.

Wordsplash

Directions: After examining the words below, write a few sentences or a paragraph using the words.

Wordsplash summary

_____

_____

_____

_____

_____

Preview

Background Information

An effective pre-reading activity that prepares students for reading is a Preview. As the name implies, a Preview is a short summary or excerpt—usually five to ten minutes long—that the teacher reads aloud to students before they begin a reading task. Students can read Previews silently, but research shows that they are more effective when read aloud and followed by a discussion with predicting activities (Neuman 1988). By providing students with a Preview, teachers activate and build on students' background knowledge, establish a purpose for reading, and give students the opportunity to discuss or question information prior to reading (Ryder and Graves 2003). The best Previews connect the text material to students' lives and experiences, provide students with an overall summary, establish a context and purpose for the reading task, and ask questions that stimulate thinking. This strategy improves a student's ability to read and comprehend literature by stimulating his or her curiosity and increasing student's motivation to read. Previews, if written correctly, help students understand the reading material and orient their thinking on the topic of study.

Grade Levels/Standards Addressed

See page 105 for the standards this strategy addresses, or refer to the Digital Resource CD (standards.pdf) to read the correlating standards in their entirety.

Preparation

Ryder and Graves (2003) suggest the following steps when constructing the Preview. Carefully review the reading material and establish the learning objectives. Note the important concepts, people, and events, and define the main ideas. When constructing the introductory statement, consider how to make the information relevant and useful to students. End the introduction with a question that draws on students' prior knowledge. Next, write a summary that includes the main ideas and supporting details in the order they appear in the reading. Emphasize the information in the beginning of the reading, and do not give away any resolution or conclusions. In the end, construct purpose-setting questions that stimulate interest in the topic.

Activity

When presenting the Preview to students, familiarize yourself with what you have written so that the presentation is fluid and interesting. Inform students that you are about to introduce a section of reading to them and begin the Preview. Point out other things such as illustrations that students should consider as they read to help them comprehend the material.

Differentiation

Speak slowly and clearly, use intonation, volume, and pauses, rephrase statements and questions, and repeat key concepts to help English language learners understand better. Carefully assess the prior knowledge of below-level students so that you can more effectively construct the preview to link to their background knowledge and prior experiences. Ask above-level students open-ended questions to be explored through further independent research or reading.

Preview (cont.)

Grades 1–2 Example

We are about to read a book called *A Diary of a Wombat*. In the book, an Australian wombat writes about her daily life in her diary. She figures out that she has new human neighbors. What types of things do you think a wombat might write in a diary? What do you think animals think about with the people they meet?

from *A Diary of a Wombat* by Jackie French

Grades 3–5 Example

Can you imagine what it feels like to move to entirely new town where you do not know anyone or have any friends? This is what happens to a 10-year-old girl named Opal in the book *Because of Winn-Dixie* by Kate DiCamillo. In this book, Opal moves to Florida with her father and befriends a stray dog named Winn-Dixie. Winn-Dixie helps Opal in many different ways as she settles into her new life in Florida. What kind of obstacles do you think Opal faces when she moves to Florida? How do you think a stray dog can help a young girl?

from *Because of Winn-Dixie* by Kate DiCamillo

Grades 6–8 Example

We are going to read a book called *Hatchet* by Gary Paulsen. I think you will really enjoy this book because it is about a 13-year-old boy, Brian, and his struggle to survive in the woods by himself. How many of you have ever gone camping? What are some of the challenges you face when you are camping? What kind of equipment did you have to help you overcome those challenges? Now imagine that you are alone with no equipment at all. How do you think you could survive in the woods? What type of personality traits or characteristics do you think would help you survive in this situation?

from *Hatchet* by Gary Paulsen

Grades 9–12 Example

The next novel we are going to read is *One Flew Over the Cuckoo's Nest* by Ken Kesey. This novel chronicles the story of life inside a mental hospital. This particular ward is governed by an exceedingly strict nurse, Nurse Ratched, who uses fear and violence to control the patients. One day a new, boisterous patient, McMurphy, enters the ward and begins to change things. He stands up to Nurse Ratched and provides hope, leadership, and inspiration for the other patients in the ward. What role do you think individuality plays in a mental hospital? Who should hold the power in a mental institution? Once McMurphy assumes a leadership role, what are his responsibilities to his followers?

from *One Flew Over the Cuckoo's Nest* by Ken Kesey

Inference Investigation

Background Information

Fictional literature provides the ideal basis for teaching the skill of inference because it offers more possibilities for a wider variety of interpretation than do informational texts (Moreillon 2009). In order to make an inference, a person must take information provided by another source, interpret it in light of his or her own experiences, and reach a conclusion about how it makes sense. According to Judy Moreillon (2009), "By definition, inference requires that each reader construct a meaning that makes the text a reflection of her experience" (77). The Inference Investigation strategy enables students to collect textual evidence explicitly stated in the literature, combine this information with their own background knowledge, and make an inference that integrates these two pieces of material.

Grade Levels/Standards Addressed

See page 105 for the standards this strategy addresses, or refer to the Digital Resource CD (standards.pdf) to read the correlating standards in their entirety.

Preparation

Prior to beginning the activity, locate a simple, wordless cartoon in a newspaper or magazine. Websites for students may also be good resources for appropriate cartoons. The cartoon should be short (3–6 frames) and simple enough for the students to understand independently.

Activity

Begin the activity by displaying a cartoon strip without words using a document camera, and ask students to explain what is occurring in the cartoon. Hold a discussion about how they came to their conclusions since the cartoon does not contain any words. Point out to students that they combined their prior knowledge and experiences with the new evidence presented in the cartoon to make inferences about the cartoon. Distribute a text passage or reading selection, and explain that good readers make inferences when they read, too. Display the *Inference Investigation* activity sheet (page 122, inferinvestigation.pdf), and demonstrate how to make an inference. To begin, read the first few sentences of the text, noting the key words or phrases in the Word Clues column on the activity sheet, adding notes about your personal experience or prior knowledge in the Experience column. Then, discuss your thought process aloud as you think through how to combine the information in these two columns to summarize your inference. Once students understand how to use the strategy, direct them to read the rest of the text and complete their own activity sheet. Discuss students' inferences as a class.

Differentiation

The skill of inference can be challenging for both English language learners and below-level students because it often requires the reader to understand nuanced meanings of the words. Preview any challenging vocabulary for these students before reading, and make sure the reading selection is accessible to them, as well. It may also be helpful to highlight or underline some of the passages or phrases to be used in the Word Clues column, and allow these students to complete the Experience and Inference columns independently. Above-level students may learn this strategy quickly and be able to complete the activity independently. To challenge them, provide a more difficult text selection that includes less obvious inferences.

Inference Investigation (cont.)

Grades 3–5 Example

Word Clues	Experience	Inference
there was a loud crash from the baby's room, followed by the sound of crying	babies often cry when something wakes them up unexpectedly	someone or something was making noise in the baby's room
the boy shuddered and walked inside when he observed the humid air and big, dark clouds in the sky	that is usually how the weather is before a thunderstorm	the boy is afraid of thunderstorms
the puppy cast his eyes to the ground and slunk under the table when we returned home	I like to hide and avoid eye contact when I know I have done something wrong	the puppy got into mischief while he was home alone
the sun cast long shadows on the ground	shadows grow longer as the sun gets lower in the sky	the sun is about to set and it will be dark soon

Grades 6–8 Example

Word Clues	Experience	Inference
the tribe worked diligently to store food and supplies during the autumn	plants and animals are more scarce during the winter	the tribe depends on their stored food and supplies to help them survive the winter
the girls hesitated to enter the classroom when they saw they had a substitute teacher	sometimes substitute teachers can be really strict	the girls were worried they would get in trouble with the strict substitute teacher
his dog refused to eat his dinner and paced the floor instead	animals sometimes sense danger before humans	something dangerous was about to happen
he walked away instead of joining the basketball game when he noticed he was the only freshman there	it can be difficult or embarrassing when something makes you different from everyone else	he did not think he was good enough to play with the older basketball players and did not want to embarrass himself

Inference Investigation *(cont.)*

Grades 9–12 Example

Word Clues	Experience	Inference
she stayed up all night studying for the exam so she could prove her father wrong	I study hard when I want to do well on an exam	her father assumed she would not do well on the exam
the farmer's hands were brown and callused	skin gets more brown from being in the sun and calluses form to protect the skin from injury or abrasions	the farmer frequently worked very hard in the sun for long hours
even though she said she would come, her mom still called to make sure she was on her way	I like to double-check things when I am not sure of something	her mom did not trust that her daughter would be true to her word
she left the hairdryer balanced precariously on the edge of the bathtub	a hairdryer that is plugged in can cause electrocution if it falls into a bathtub with water	she was acting dangerously or carelessly

Name: _____ Date: _____

Inference Investigation

Directions: After reading the text selection, record words, phrases, or sentences from the text in the Word Clues column. Note your personal experience or prior knowledge in the Experience column, and then combine the information in these two columns to make an inference in the Inference column.

Word Clues	Experience	Inference

Character Inferences

Background Information

Authors frequently rely on inference as a tool for character development in fictional literature. The characters in a fictional story are unknown to the reader at the beginning of the story, so the author often spends a great deal of time developing the characters' personalities, opinions, and attitudes to make them believable and interesting for the reader. By providing readers with the information necessary to make inferences about fictional characters, the author allows each reader to personalize the book's characters through his or her own experiences. Students' inferences about the characters in the story enable them to describe the characters in depth, including the characters' traits, motivations, feelings, and thoughts. Furthermore, the ability to distinguish an inference from a conclusion drawn directly from the text enables students to comprehend how personal experiences affect a reader's interpretation of the text. As the reader infers more information about a story's characters, he or she is better able to make predictions and draw more accurate conclusions about the characters and the text.

Grade Levels/Standards Addressed

See page 105 for the standards this strategy addresses, or refer to the Digital Resource CD (standards.pdf) to read the correlating standards in their entirety.

Activity

For this activity, students focus exclusively on the use of inference in character development. Before beginning the activity, review what students already know about character development, and remind them that an inference is made by combining information from the text with students' personal prior knowledge or experiences. Emphasize the difference between an inference and a conclusion drawn directly from material stated explicitly in the text. Display the *Character Inferences* activity sheet (page 126, characterinfer.pdf) with a document camera, and model your thought process as you read a paragraph from the text and complete the diagram. Once students feel comfortable with the strategy, have them read the rest of the text independently and complete their own individual *Character Inferences* activity sheets. Upon completion, ask students to share their character inferences with the rest of the class, and record these inferences on the board. At the end, review the compilation of inferences, and work together as a class to write a summary of the characters.

Differentiation

Below-level students will benefit from scaffolding to complete this activity. Provide extra assistance by identifying sections of the text that require the reader to make inferences about the characters and allow these students to add their own personal knowledge and complete the inference. To challenge above-level students, encourage them to identify as many character inferences as possible. For English language learners, make sure they understand the meaning of the relevant vocabulary words and allow them to work with a partner to identify the text prompts containing inferences.

Character Inferences (cont.)

Grades 1–2 Example

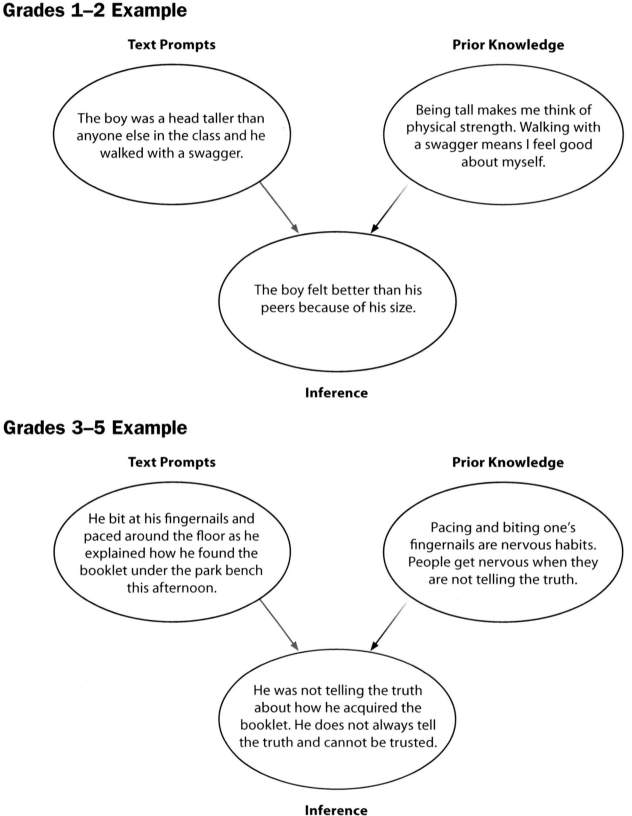

Text Prompts

The boy was a head taller than anyone else in the class and he walked with a swagger.

Prior Knowledge

Being tall makes me think of physical strength. Walking with a swagger means I feel good about myself.

The boy felt better than his peers because of his size.

Inference

Grades 3–5 Example

Text Prompts

He bit at his fingernails and paced around the floor as he explained how he found the booklet under the park bench this afternoon.

Prior Knowledge

Pacing and biting one's fingernails are nervous habits. People get nervous when they are not telling the truth.

He was not telling the truth about how he acquired the booklet. He does not always tell the truth and cannot be trusted.

Inference

Character Inferences *(cont.)*

Grades 6–8 Example

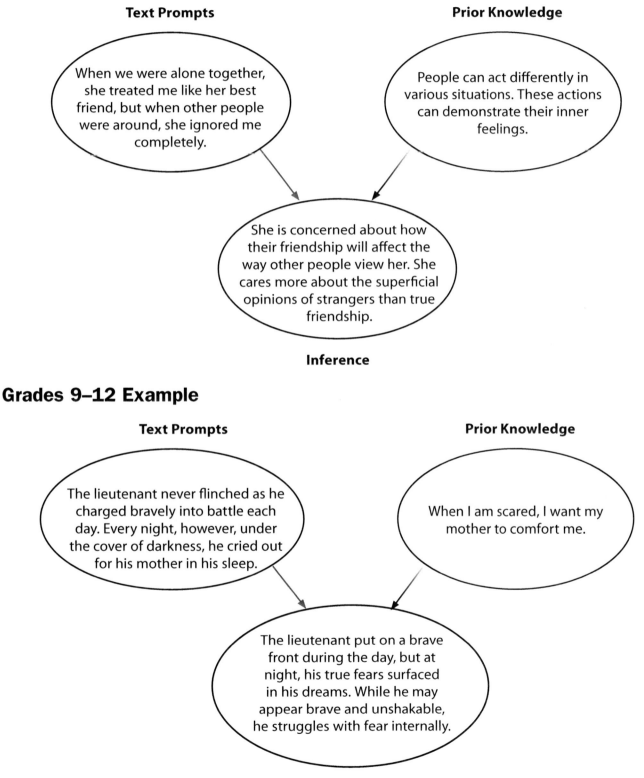

Text Prompts

When we were alone together, she treated me like her best friend, but when other people were around, she ignored me completely.

Prior Knowledge

People can act differently in various situations. These actions can demonstrate their inner feelings.

She is concerned about how their friendship will affect the way other people view her. She cares more about the superficial opinions of strangers than true friendship.

Inference

Grades 9–12 Example

Text Prompts

The lieutenant never flinched as he charged bravely into battle each day. Every night, however, under the cover of darkness, he cried out for his mother in his sleep.

Prior Knowledge

When I am scared, I want my mother to comfort me.

The lieutenant put on a brave front during the day, but at night, his true fears surfaced in his dreams. While he may appear brave and unshakable, he struggles with fear internally.

Inference

Character Inferences

Directions: Read the text selection and identify an area where the author requires you to make an inference about a character. Record the information provided by the text, your prior knowledge or experiences, and the inference you can draw from this information.

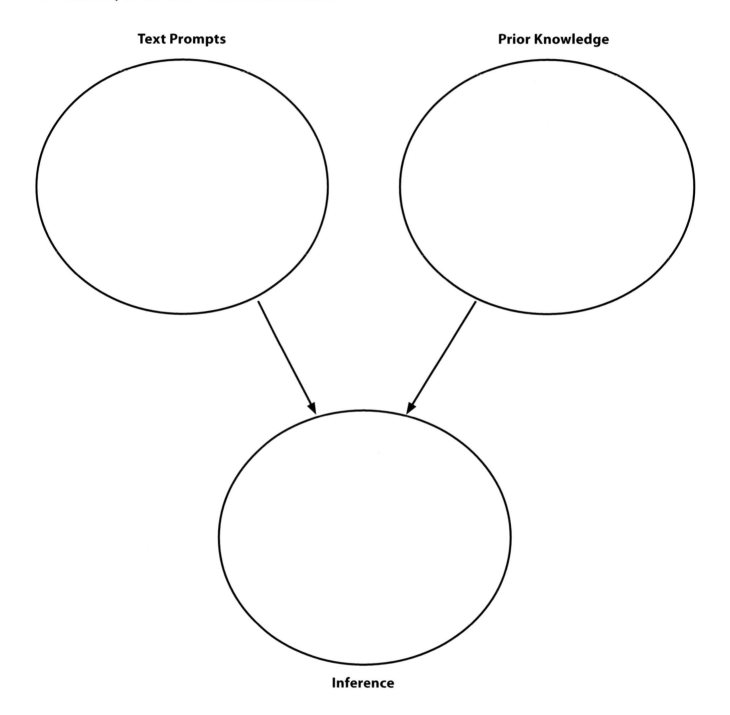

Text Prompts

Prior Knowledge

Inference

Using Think-Alouds and Monitoring Comprehension Overview

Metacognitive Thinking

The knowledge of and control over one's ability to think and learn is referred to as *metacognition*. In other words, metacognition is thinking about thinking. To be metacognitive is to be able to reflect on one's own thinking processes; it includes knowing about oneself as a learner, about the tasks one attempts, and about the techniques one uses to understand the world, reading material, and oneself. Researchers include in the definition of metacognition the word *control* because self-awareness also includes self-monitoring and regulating of one's thinking. Readers use metacognition to plan how they will read, to predict what will happen in the reading, to check for accuracy in their predictions, to monitor their comprehension, to evaluate their progress, to remediate when difficulties arise, and to revise their strategies for learning when necessary (Baker 2002).

It is well accepted in the reading research community that metacognition plays an important role in reading comprehension. Furthermore, metacognition is firmly established in theories of reading and learning. Reading researchers have long acknowledged that highly skilled readers monitor their comprehension while they are reading (Block and Pressley 2003). Good readers are aware of the thinking processes involved in reading. They establish a goal or purpose before they read, and they can adjust their goal while reading. They reflect on the author's purpose before, during, and after reading. Essentially, good readers can identify the elements of a passage that are confusing, and they can select a strategy to figure out what they do not understand. Most importantly, they can talk about what it is they are doing as they read.

Poor readers do not have such self-awareness as they read, and as a result, they have difficulty articulating their thought processes. They have trouble identifying the source of their struggle. Research demonstrates that they cannot become proficient unless their teachers can demonstrate and model for them how to think while they are reading (Block and Israel 2004).

Based on the research it has reviewed, the National Reading Panel (2000) concludes that metacognition and comprehension monitoring should be fostered in comprehension instruction. Therefore, students must have opportunities to develop and enhance metacognitive skills to meet the demands of understanding print material. Numerous studies provide solid evidence that comprehension monitoring skills of good and poor readers alike can be enhanced through direct instruction. The development of metacognitive skills in students should begin with direct teacher explanations and modeling of reading comprehension strategies, but it develops more fully when students practice using comprehension strategies as they read (Pressley 2002a). Michael Pressley (2002a) points out that it is especially helpful if students can practice and are given opportunities to explain how they use the strategies and reflect on the use of strategies over the course of a semester.

Using Think-Alouds and Monitoring Comprehension Overview (cont.)

What Is a Think-Aloud?

Think-alouds, also known as mental modeling (Ryder and Graves 2003), are strategies to verbalize a teacher's thoughts aloud to students while reading a selection orally. As teachers talk about their thoughts, they model the process of comprehension for the students and focus on the reasoning involved while reading. Think-alouds allow readers to stop periodically, reflect on the thinking they do to understand a text, and relate these processes orally for the benefit of the listeners. Teachers use this technique to help students verbalize their thoughts while reading so that they can duplicate the process later when reading independently. Research demonstrates that the metacognitive awareness involved in think-aloud strategies significantly increases students' scores on comprehension tests, adds to students' ability for comprehension monitoring, and improves students' skill in selecting fix-up strategies to overcome comprehension struggles while they read (Block and Israel 2004).

Think-alouds are used in conjunction with other reading comprehension strategies during instruction. Teachers should employ think-alouds as they model how to use a reading comprehension strategy at appropriate points in the reading process. Think-alouds differ from explanation because they occur when the teacher is actually using a reading comprehension strategy while reading. Modeling is a much more effective method for teaching reasoning than explanation because the strategy used is much clearer to students.

The think-aloud is a teaching technique that comes easily to teachers who are metacognitive themselves in that they are very aware of their own thinking processes as they read. One of the characteristics of highly effective comprehension teachers is their own understanding of their metacognitive thinking. Skilled comprehension teachers take the time to understand their thoughts. As they read, they scrutinize the reading materials, record what ideas come to mind as they read, pay attention to which areas may cause confusion, consider which fix-up strategies they can use, develop questions and answers about what they are reading, and summarize the content in a variety of ways, among a number of other activities. Obviously, teachers who involve their own metacognitive thinking as they develop lessons are doing a tremendous amount of work. One of the reasons teachers do not teach think-aloud strategies is because they feel it is difficult to do (Block and Israel 2004; Baker 2002).

While teaching students to become more aware of their understanding while reading, the goal is to go beyond teaching students how to think about their thinking. Metacognition should not be promoted as a goal in itself, taught in isolation, but rather as a tool that is integrated with comprehension instruction (Baker 2002).

Traditionally, there has been a tendency among educators to focus on word recognition and vocabulary development in the primary grades and focus on comprehension skills in the upper grades. As Pressley (2002b) points out, this view has been increasingly rejected in favor of developing comprehension skills during the primary grades with the expectation that such instruction will hopefully affect students dramatically in the short term and lead to the development of better comprehension skills over the long term.

Using Think-Alouds and Monitoring Comprehension Overview *(cont.)*

How to Construct a Think-Aloud

The steps for developing think-alouds are as follows (Readence, Bean, and Baldwin 2000):

- Select a short passage. The passage should be somewhat difficult so that when you explain your thinking and reasoning, it will make sense and be useful to the students. If the passage is too easy, the students will lose interest.

- Think about the comments you can make for the think-aloud based on students' experiences. Since the material is not difficult for you, you need to prepare the think-aloud to model the metacognitive skills that will benefit the students.

- Prior to beginning the think-aloud, explain to students what you will be doing. Be explicit so that they know what to expect and what they should be learning from listening to you.

- As you read the passage to students, pause and insert your comments, as necessary. Pause after you make each comment so that students have enough time to process your thinking strategies. It may be difficult for them to follow another person's train of thought, so allow adequate time for processing.

- When you are finished, encourage students to ask you questions about how you think or about the think-aloud strategy.

Think-Aloud Activities

The think-aloud activities for grades 1–2, grades 3–5, and grades 6–8 come directly from those presented in Cathy Collins Block and Susan Israel's "The ABCs of Performing Highly Effective Think-Alouds" except for the Determine Word Meanings Think-Aloud. The think-aloud activities for grades 9–12 are original samples designed to mirror the think-aloud activities developed by Block and Israel (2004).

Monitoring Comprehension

An important part of comprehension instruction is teaching readers the importance of monitoring their understanding of what they are reading and helping them develop the tools to do so (Neufeld 2005). However, Paul Neufeld (2005) points out that teaching students how to monitor their understanding is only part of the process. Students must be able to figure out what to do (which strategy to use) when they have a comprehension breakdown. Students should be able to ask themselves questions to check their own understanding. Examples of questions include *Do I understand what I just read? What parts were confusing or unclear?* In addition, students should be able to ask and answer journalistic-type questions as they monitor their own understanding of text. Questions of this type might include *who, what, where, when, why,* and *how*. Readers should be able to generate a summary of a text as a way to monitor their own comprehension, and if they struggle to write a summary, this is a clear sign that there is a comprehension breakdown.

Using Think-Alouds and Monitoring Comprehension Overview *(cont.)*

Proficient readers act in the following ways as they monitor their reading for meaning (Keene 2002):

- They know when text makes sense, when it does not, what does not make sense, and whether the unclear portions are critical to their overall understanding of the piece.

- They identify when text is comprehensible and recognize the degree to which they are understanding it. They identify ways in which a text becomes gradually more understandable by reading past an unclear portion or by rereading parts of the whole text.

- They are aware of the processes readers can use to make meaning clear. They check, evaluate, and revise the evolving interpretation of the text while reading.

- They identify confusing ideas, themes, or surface elements (words, sentence or text structures, graphs, tables, and so on) and can suggest a variety of different means to solve the problems readers may encounter.

- They are aware of what they need to comprehend in relation to the purpose for reading.

- They learn how to pause, consider the meanings in text, reflect on understandings, and use different strategies to enhance understanding. Readers best learn this process by watching proficient readers think aloud and by gradually taking responsibility for monitoring their own comprehension as they read independently.

Using Think-Alouds and Monitoring Comprehension Overview *(cont.)*

Fix-Up Strategies

When students begin to understand the nature of their comprehension breakdown, they must determine what kind of clarification they need and use a fix-up strategy to solve the problem. When readers struggle through a section of text, they must evaluate the strategies they know to determine which one will work best to understand the text. They also must determine whether it is necessary to completely understand the portion of the text that is causing them trouble. Fix-up strategies used by the most expert readers include rereading parts or all of the text, scanning or looking ahead to preview information, pausing and connecting information to what the reader already knows, examining other resources on the same topic, and seeking support from more knowledgeable readers (Neufeld 2005). In addition, proficient readers use the six major systems of language (graphophonic, lexical, syntactic, semantic, schematic, and pragmatic) to solve reading problems (Keene 2002). They ask the following questions when they are not comprehending:

- Does this word, phrase, sentence, or passage make sense?

- Does the word I'm pronouncing sound like language?

- Do the letters in the word match the sounds I'm pronouncing?

- Have I seen this word before?

- Do the pictures give me a clue about what the sentence says?

- Is there another reader who can help me make sense of this?

- What do I already know from my experience and the context of this text that can help me solve this problem?

- How can I find the main idea?

- How can I figure out what the words imply?

Ellin Oliver Keene (2002) also asserts that proficient readers know a wide range of problem-solving strategies and can make appropriate choices in a given reading situation (i.e., skip ahead or reread, use the context and syntax, sound it out, speak to another reader, consider relevant prior knowledge, read the passage aloud, and so on).

Using Think-Alouds and Monitoring Comprehension Overview (cont.)

Standards Addressed

The following chart shows the correlating standards for each strategy in this section. Refer to the Digital Resource CD (standards.pdf) to read the correlating standards in their entirety.

Strategy	McREL Standards	Common Core State Standards
Overview the Text Think-Aloud	Grades 1–2 (5.7) Grades 3–5 (5.8) Grades 6–8 (5.4) Grades 9–12 (5.3)	Grade 1 (RL.1.10) Grade 2 (RL.2.10) Grade 3 (RL.3.10) Grade 4 (RL.4.10) Grade 5 (RL.5.10) Grade 6 (RL.6.10) Grade 7 (RL.7.10) Grade 8 (RL.8.10) Grades 9–10 (RL.9-10.10) Grades 11–12 (RL.11-12.10)
Preparing for the Topic Think-Aloud	Grades 1–2 (5.7) Grades 3–5 (5.8) Grades 6–8 (5.4) Grades 9–12 (5.3)	Grade 1 (RL.1.2, RL.1.10) Grade 2 (RL.2.2, RL.2.10) Grade 3 (RL.3.2, RL.3.10) Grade 4 (RL.4.2, RL.4.10) Grade 5 (RL.5.2, RL.5.10) Grade 6 (RL.6.2, RL.6.10) Grade 7 (RL.7.2, RL.7.10) Grade 8 (RL.8.2, RL.8.10) Grades 9–10 (RL.9-10.2, RL.9-10.10) Grades 11–12 (RL.11-12.2, RL.11-12.10)
Look for Important Information Think-Aloud	Grades 1–2 (5.7) Grades 3–5 (5.8) Grades 6–8 (5.4) Grades 9–12 (5.3)	Grade 1 (RL.1.2, RL.1.10) Grade 2 (RL.2.2, RL.2.10) Grade 3 (RL.3.2, RL.3.10) Grade 4 (RL.4.2, RL.4.10) Grade 5 (RL.5.2, RL.5.10) Grade 6 (RL.6.2, RL.6.10) Grade 7 (RL.7.2, RL.7.10) Grade 8 (RL.8.2, RL.8.10) Grades 9–10 (RL.9-10.2, RL.9-10.10) Grades 11–12 (RL.11-12.2, RL.11-12.10)

Using Think-Alouds and Monitoring Comprehension Overview (cont.)

Strategy	McREL Standards	Common Core State Standards
Activate Prior Knowledge Think-Aloud	Grades 1–2 (5.7, 7.4) Grades 3–5 (5.8, 7.6) Grades 6–8 (5.4, 7.4) Grades 9–12 (5.3)	Grade 1 (RL.1.10) Grade 2 (RL.2.10) Grade 3 (RL.3.10) Grade 4 (RL.4.10) Grade 5 (RL.5.10) Grade 6 (RL.6.10) Grade 7 (RL.7.10) Grade 8 (RL.8.10) Grades 9–10 (RL.9-10.10) Grades 11–12 (RL.11-12.10)
Determine Word Meanings Think-Aloud	Grades 1–2 (5.7, 7.4) Grades 3–5 (5.5, 5.8) Grades 6–8 (5.4) Grades 3–5 (5.2, 5.3)	Grade 1 (RL.1.10, L.1.4, L.1.5) Grade 2 (RL.2.10, L.2.4, L.2.5) Grade 3 (RL.3.10, L.3.4, L.3.5) Grade 4 (RL.4.10, L.4.4, L.4.5) Grade 5 (RL.5.10, L.5.4, L.5.5) Grade 6 (RL.6.10, L.6.4, L.6.5) Grade 7 (RL.7.10, L.7.4, L.7.5) Grade 8 (RL.8.10, L.8.4, L.8.5) Grades 9–10 (RL.9-10.10, L.9-10.4, L.9-10.5) Grades 11–12 (RL.11-12.10, L.11-12.4, L.11-12.5)
Predict Think-Aloud	Grades 1–2 (5.7) Grades 3–5 (5.8) Grades 6–8 (5.4) Grades 9–12 (5.3)	Grade 1 (RL.1.10) Grade 2 (RL.2.10) Grade 3 (RL.3.10) Grade 4 (RL.4.10) Grade 5 (RL.5.10) Grade 6 (RL.6.10) Grade 7 (RL.7.10) Grade 8 (RL.8.10) Grades 9–10 (RL.9-10.10) Grades 11–12 (RL.11-12.10)

Using Think-Alouds and Monitoring Comprehension Overview *(cont.)*

Strategy	McREL Standards	Common Core State Standards
Ask Questions Think-Aloud	Grades 1–2 (5.7) Grades 3–5 (5.5, 5.8) Grades 6–8 (5.4) Grades 9–12 (5.3)	Grade 1 (RL.1.1, RL.1.10) Grade 2 (RL.2.1, RL.2.10) Grade 3 (RL.3.1, RL.3.10) Grade 4 (RL.4.1, RL.4.10) Grade 5 (RL.5.1, RL.5.10) Grade 6 (RL.6.1, RL.6.10) Grade 7 (RL.7.1, RL.7.10) Grade 8 (RL.8.1, RL.8.10) Grades 9–10 (RL.9-10.1, RL.9-10.10) Grades 11–12 (RL.11-12.1, RL.11-12.10)
Make Inferences Think-Aloud	Grades 1–2 (6.4) Grades 3–5 (6.8) Grades 6–8 (6.9, 6.10) Grades 9–12 (6.9)	Grade 1 (RL.1.1, RL.1.10) Grade 2 (RL.2.1, RL.2.10) Grade 3 (RL.3.1, RL.3.10) Grade 4 (RL.4.1, RL.4.10) Grade 5 (RL.5.1, RL.5.10) Grade 6 (RL.6.1, RL.6.10) Grade 7 (RL.7.1, RL.7.10) Grade 8 (RL.8.1, RL.8.10) Grades 9–10 (RL.9-10.1, RL.9-10.10) Grades 11–12 (RL.11-12.1, RL.11-12.10)

Overview the Text Think-Aloud

Background Information

Cathy Collins Block and Susan Israel (2004) note the importance of modeling what expert readers think before they read a large section of text. The Overview the Text Think-Aloud (Block and Israel 2004) uses mental modeling for students to demonstrate connections that readers make prior to actually reading and shows them how to activate prior knowledge on a given topic. Teachers need to model for students how to examine the pictures, writing style, organization, genre characteristics, and other qualities in order to preview the text prior to reading because these actions improve comprehension. The activation of prior knowledge contributes to students' abilities to make inferences from the text, determine word meanings, and make connections with other texts while they read the text.

Grade Levels/Standards Addressed

See page 132 for the standards this strategy addresses, or refer to the Digital Resource CD (standards.pdf) to read the correlating standards in their entirety.

Activity

Present a selection of text that you enjoyed personally and describe to students what attracted you to it, how you knew you would like the topic, how many times you have read something on the subject or by the same author, etc. Explain that the use of visuals and the qualities of this author's writing style, such as the genre, the density of the language or ideas, the sentence and paragraph length, the level of vocabulary, the organization, etc., can help you understand the text. Hold up the reading selection and begin a think-aloud. Refer to the think-alouds on page 136 as samples.

Differentiation

Use the reading material as a concrete example for English language learners. It is best to share the first reading selection with a document camera so that you can point to different sections. Repeat and rephrase key concepts and key vocabulary for English language learners as you think aloud. Be sure to show below-level students how to identify the table of contents and chapter titles (if present). Use visual cues, as they may not be familiar with the organizing features of the text. Above-level students should be invited to share their thinking in small groups and explain their thinking processes as much as possible.

Overview the Text Think-Aloud (cont.)

Grades 1–2 Example

Let's look at this book (story, paragraph, etc.). I wonder what it is going to be about. I can read the title. I've read other things about this topic before, and I liked those books. I have read another book by this same author. I liked it a lot. That means this book is probably good, too. I wonder if I can read all the words in this book. I love to look at the pictures in books, too. I wonder if this book has lots of pictures or if it is mostly words. Let me see. Next, I am going to check to see if there are chapter titles or picture captions on the pages. I think this book is going to be about….

Grades 3–5 Example

Before you start reading something new, take a look at the book carefully. Think about the topic and how much you want to learn about it. Read the title and the name of the author. Think about if you enjoyed reading a book by the same author or on the same subject. Look over the text to see if you can understand all of the words easily. Decide if the text has too many pictures or too much writing. Check over the table of contents, headings, and chapter titles. Think about what the text is going to be about.

Grades 6–8 Example

Before you start reading a text, consider how much you want to learn about a topic. Read the title and author to see if you have enjoyed reading anything about that subject or that author. Skim the text to see if it contains too many difficult words for you to understand and read comfortably. Decide if the reading has too many pictures, too little information, or information you already know. Check over the table of contents, picture captions, and chapters to think about what will be covered in the selection.

Finish by reminding students that they will develop the skill to automatically complete an effective overview every time they choose a book, which will help them understand and enjoy their reading more.

Grades 9–12 Example

Before you start reading a text, you can get a good idea about the subject by reading the title and thinking about the topic. What do you know about the author? What does it make you think about? Reflect on what you hope to learn from the reading. Also consider what you already know about the topic and how you hope to tie that information in with the new ideas in the literature. Consider the physical text itself. Does it look like something you will be able to read? Does it look too easy or short? Does it look like something you will enjoy reading? Read over any headings or chapters in the text to gather clues about the content. Try to make predictions about what type of story you think the text will contain.

Finish by reminding students that they will develop the skill to automatically complete an effective overview every time they choose a book, which will help them understand and enjoy their reading more.

Preparing for the Topic Think-Aloud

Background Information

Block and Israel (2004) express the need for students to learn how to think about a topic prior to reading. It is important for teachers and proficient readers to model for students how to think about the purpose and main ideas as they begin to read a selection for the first time. Closely examining the first few paragraphs increases students' comprehension because they can more rapidly identify the types of concepts that will reappear in a book. The early sentences in a text often provide important details that allow the reader to determine central ideas or themes of a text. A solid understanding of the key details enables students to accurately recount the story and to identify the main idea, moral, message, or lesson in the literature. They can also predict more reliably how main ideas and detail sentences will be connected and what meaning will be revealed in later detail sentences.

Grade Levels/Standards Addressed

See page 132 for the standards this strategy addresses, or refer to the Digital Resource CD (standards.pdf) to read the correlating standards in their entirety.

Activity

Tell students that when they begin reading a piece of fiction, they should think about the purpose and main ideas and pay particular attention to all details in the first few pages. Explain that these pieces of information are used to help the reader determine the central ideas or themes of a story. Tell students to familiarize themselves with the author's train of thought during the first few pages so they can align their thinking in the same direction. Before students begin reading, hold up the text and say:

When I begin to read a story, I read the first few pages to put details together, identify if the author puts his or her main ideas as the first or last sentence of paragraphs, and find out what kinds of details this writer uses to describe a main point. By thinking these thoughts, I can more quickly follow the author's train of thought.

Afterward, read the first few paragraphs. Describe how you identify those sentences that are main idea statements and what kinds of details the author uses. Tell students that most authors put the most important or main idea statement either as the first or last sentence in a paragraph. If it is the first sentence, it usually introduces the topic of that paragraph and all remaining sentences describe details about that topic. If it is the last sentence, it usually ties all the details in the prior sentences together and is a more general summary statement.

By reading the first few paragraphs, students can determine which type of detail statement will be used in that selection. Once students can identify the sentences that contain the central ideas or themes, they can use the key details to analyze and summarize the development of the main idea.

Preparing for the Topic Think-Aloud *(cont.)*

Next, repeat the Preparing for the Topic Think-Aloud with a different reading selection to demonstrate how to begin thinking about the topic and the author's train of thought within the first few pages. Discuss how different authors have different styles and patterns of writing about the same subject. Examine the detail statements in depth and discuss the determination of the main idea of the text. Finally, ask students to describe their thought processes as they read the opening of another fiction selection.

Differentiation

Use the reading material as a concrete example for English language learners. It is best to share the first reading selection with a document camera so that it can be referred to. Repeat and rephrase key concepts and key vocabulary for English language learners as you think aloud. Invite and encourage below-level students and the rest of the class to share all of their thinking—even their struggling, negative thoughts—by modeling this for them. Invite above-level students to share their thinking with the class and explain their processes as much as possible, particularly when they run into difficulties.

Look for Important Information Think-Aloud

Background Information

Block and Israel (2004) note that expert readers know how to pay greater attention to important sentences, and they know how to ignore the minor details that may distract them from their goal of overall comprehension. By learning how to identify the important information in a text, students can determine the main idea and key details of the story. They can also use this skill to accurately summarize the story by including only the important information and excluding superfluous details. Block and Israel (2004) present the following activity to assist students in learning how to locate the most important information in a reading selection after watching the process modeled by their teacher.

Grade Levels/Standards Addressed

See page 132 for the standards this strategy addresses, or refer to the Digital Resource CD (standards.pdf) to read the correlating standards in their entirety.

Activity

Hold up the reading selection and turn to a chapter students have not yet read. Then, begin a think-aloud. Refer to the think-alouds on page 140 as samples.

Ask students to follow along as you read the next paragraph. Have them work in pairs to identify the clues that point out the most important idea or sentence in that paragraph. Help them summarize the important information in order to determine the main idea and key details of the story. Continue asking students to perform Look for Important Information Think-Alouds as a whole group, in small groups, in pairs, and individually until the class can do it independently. Monitor students individually as they read silently.

Differentiation

Place the key phrases *for example, for instance, such as,* and *to illustrate* on the board to help English language learners identify them while reading. Make sure to rephrase and repeat key concepts and words for English language learners. Below-level students will benefit from having the selection shared with a document camera so that they can follow the instructions very closely. It may be necessary to provide above-level students who are expert readers with a more challenging reading selection.

Look for Important Information
Think-Aloud *(cont.)*

Grades 1–2 Example

At the beginning of a reading selection, the author usually tells you how to find the most important information. The author says certain words more than once. Sometimes the author says the same thing more than once. Sometimes the author gives examples. If you can find the author's big idea, then you can find the most important information faster. Notice how the most important thing to learn is right here *(point to a sentence that contains a key idea and describe how you know it is important)*.

Grades 3–5 Example

At the beginning of a chapter or a book, the author gives clues to help you find the most important information. The author repeats important words and restates important ideas more often than others. The most important idea is usually followed by certain phrases such as *for example*, *for instance*, or *to illustrate*. Also, when you know where the author generally puts the main ideas in the paragraphs, it is much easier to find the most important points. For example, in this section, the author's most important points appear here in this paragraph *(point to a sentence containing a key idea and describe how you know it is important)*.

Grades 6–8 Example

At the beginning of a chapter or book, the author reveals clues to help you locate and understand the most important information. The author repeats certain words and restates some ideas more frequently than others. Another clue is that the most important idea is often followed by a sentence that gives an example or contains the words *for example*, *for instance*, or *to illustrate*. Also, when you identify where the author places the main ideas in paragraphs, you can find the most important points more quickly. For instance, in this reading selection, the author's most important points appear here in this paragraph *(point to a sentence containing a key idea and describe how you know it is important)*.

Grades 9–12 Example

At the beginning of a reading selection, the author usually provides clues to help the reader identify the main idea or key points of the text. The author often highlights the main idea by restating it several times using different terminology. Most writers also provide examples to illustrate the key points. When you see phrases like *for example* or *to illustrate*, you know that the author is providing you with support for the main idea. Once you have identified where in the text the author generally puts the main idea, it will help you highlight the key points and supporting evidence. For example, in this paragraph, the main idea appears here *(point to main idea and discuss how you identified it)*.

Activate Prior Knowledge Think-Aloud

Background Information

As reading researchers assert, the best readers activate their prior knowledge and background experiences prior to reading (Duke and Pearson 2002). In doing so, they make it possible for new information that they encounter to be organized in an accessible locale within their schemata. Struggling readers need guidance and modeling via the think-aloud technique so that they can see how expert readers make connections between what they already know and what they are learning. This technique helps them improve their ability to read and comprehend different types of literature by making connections when they are reading independently.

Grade Levels/Standards Addressed

See page 133 for the standards this strategy addresses, or refer to the Digital Resource CD (standards.pdf) to read the correlating standards in their entirety.

Activity

Select a section of text for students to read. After they have read about four pages, interrupt students and begin a think-aloud. Refer to the think-alouds on page 142 as samples.

Using a document camera to display a single page of text, point to specific sentences in which you connect relevant prior knowledge. Demonstrate how you activate your similar personal experiences and how you eliminate irrelevant or inaccurate prior knowledge. Read a sentence and describe an event from your personal experience that connects to the new information in that statement. Make the connections perfectly clear to students. Ask the class to practice and discuss activating prior knowledge. Have each student perform the think-aloud in small groups, then pairs, and finally in one-on-one conferences.

Differentiation

It is important that think-alouds be performed very slowly and that the words be enunciated very clearly for English language learners. Choose your words carefully and try to explain your thinking in a number of ways. Below-level students should have the task modeled for them in their small groups by students who are reading at grade level. This will lower their anxiety levels for conducting their own think-alouds. While it may seem ideal to have above-level students model their thinking during reading for the rest of the class, do this with care. Some students may feel intimidated by the skills demonstrated. Be sure to focus on creating an atmosphere of mutual respect for think-alouds to incorporate above-level students' skills effectively. Group above-grade-level students homogeneously and have them share this think-aloud with each other.

Activate Prior Knowledge Think-Aloud (cont.)

Grades 1–2 Example

When you listen to someone read or when you read by yourself, you can think about what you know about the topic. What things have you heard about the topic? What have you done or seen that is related to the topic? You could stop paying attention, but you might miss something important. Good readers pay close attention to what is being read. They stop and they think about what they know about the topic. They think about what they have seen or done in their own lives. I am going to show you how I think about what I know as we continue to read the next page.

Grades 3–5 Example

After reading the first few pages of any reading material, you can continue to read carefully and think about things you have learned or experiences you have had that are very similar to the information in the reading. Or, you can let your mind wander rather than concentrate on the words in the reading. Good readers follow along with the words, pausing briefly to recall background knowledge or similar experiences they have had in their lives. Let me show you how I activate my prior knowledge as we continue to read the next page.

Grades 6–8 Example

What you know about a topic prior to reading about the topic is very important. After you begin reading, it is very important to think about your experiences and knowledge that are related to the information in the reading. You could just let your mind wander instead of concentrating on the words and details, but that wouldn't help you much. Good readers follow the author's words closely, and they pause to recall their background knowledge or similar experiences they've had in their lives. Let me show you the connections I make to what I already know as we continue to read the next page.

Grades 9–12 Example

When you're reading, it is very important to connect the new information you're learning with your prior knowledge about the topic. Ask yourself, "What do I already know about this topic?" Sometimes it is easy to let your mind wander when reading, but good readers always maintain concentration on the text and focus on the content of the reading. Pausing to connect the information in the reading with your own prior knowledge is an effective way to gain new understanding from the text and to help you remain focused while reading. Let me demonstrate how I connect my own personal experiences with the text as we continue reading.

Determine Word Meanings Think-Aloud

Background Information

Most students resort to skipping over words that they do not understand when they are reading. Looking up unknown words in the dictionary creates such an interruption for most readers that it causes them to disconnect from the reading. They lose their place and train of thought during the process and end up rereading a large selection of the text.

In fictional literature, it is common for writers to use unusual, domain-specific words that students have never encountered before. It is important that students have a variety of strategies from which they can choose to determine or clarify the meaning of unknown words. Writers usually provide clues within the context of the story that help readers figure out the meanings of those words. It is important to teach students how to use the different types of context clues to decipher the meaning of unknown words. Using context clues effectively helps students develop better fluency and speed when reading, which encourages more pleasure reading and increases standardized test scores.

Grade Levels/Standards Addressed

See page 133 for the standards this strategy addresses, or refer to the Digital Resource CD (standards.pdf) to read the correlating standards in their entirety.

Types of Context Clues

Many types of context clues are worthy of direct instruction to improve reading comprehension during instruction:

Apposition or Definition Clues—Authors often provide synonyms or definitions of difficult words to help the reader understand the reading material. By relating unknown words to words with similar, but not identical meanings, the author provides clues to the word's meaning within the context of the story. Usually, the definition or synonym is signaled to the reader by a comma, dash, parentheses, or words and phrases such as *or, is called, which means, who is, called, which is, that is,* and *in other words.*

Example: She had a querulous attitude—she complained all the time.

Example Clues—Writers provide examples that illustrate and clarify difficult to understand concepts or words. The example usually appears in the same sentence as the new word or in sentences that come before or after the word. Students can use the context clues provided in the example to determine or clarify the meaning of a new word or concept. The signal phrases for examples are *such as, including, for instance, to illustrate, are examples of, other examples,* and *for example.*

Example: She always acted in a benevolent manner. For example, she often gave to charitable organizations.

Contrast Clues—Writers sometimes indicate the meanings of unknown or difficult words by relating them to their opposites, or antonyms. By creating a relationship between a word and its antonym, the author provides clues to the meaning of the unknown or difficult word. Signals for opposition include *although, even though, yet, but, however, on the other hand,* and *in contrast.*

Determine Word Meanings Think-Aloud *(cont.)*

Example: In contrast to my gregarious older brother, my younger brother is shy and introverted.

Modifier Clues—Sometimes modifiers (words that describe another word), such as adjectives, adverbs, or relative clauses, contain clues to a word's meaning. Relative clauses begin with *who, which, that, whose,* or *whom* and often explain or extend an idea or word in the main part of a sentence.

Example: The prodigy, who patented his first invention at age 12, frequently left me speechless.

Repetition Clues—Writers often repeat difficult words in familiar and new situations so that readers can figure out the meaning of the unknown words using their prior knowledge.

Example: The mercenary felt no personal attachment to the cause for which he fought. In fact, the mercenary only worked for his wages.

Suggested Meaning Clues—When a sentence contains no specific clue words or explanations, the ideas in the sentence often suggest the meaning of unknown words. Students should study the sentence as a whole and try to determine or clarify the meaning of the unknown word by asking questions about the information in the sentence. Students can draw on their prior knowledge and experience to help them decipher the meaning of the word.

Example: The detective felt a high degree of trepidation as he stepped onto the crime scene.

Activity

Prior to reading from a fictional text, ask students to locate any words they do not recognize or do not understand. Write the words on the board. Read the text aloud with students. When you come to the word in question, say the following:

This is a word I don't know. There are a few things I can do to help me determine or clarify the meaning of this unknown word. First, I need to reread the sentence to see if I can figure it out. No, that didn't help. I'll try to read some sentences before and after the word to see if that might give me some clues. Are there any context clues? If not, maybe I can figure out the meaning by looking at the root word. Have I ever seen this word in another situation or book? What do I remember about it? I have read about this topic before. Let me think of things I remember about this topic to give me some clues.

Be sure to let students know that they do not have to go through all of the questions you model for them as you try to figure out the meaning of the word. They need to question themselves until they find a possible answer. Encourage students to use context clues to identify the meaning of the words they have selected. Encourage them to check the dictionary to determine the precise meanings of key words and phrases. This will give them more confidence in using context clues.

Determine Word Meanings Think-Aloud *(cont.)*

Variation

Students in grades 1–2 may not be able to read with great fluency, but they can still use context clues to decipher the meaning of unknown words. Teach them to use the following prompts for figuring out unknown words (Robb 2003):

- Did that sound right?
- Find the part that was not right.
- Take a good look at the beginning, middle, and end of the word.
- Does what you say match the letters you see?
- Can you think of another word it looks like?
- Can you say the word in chunks or syllables?
- Does the word have a prefix? What is it?
- Does the word have a suffix? What is it?
- Can you say what's left of the word?

Differentiation

English language learners will benefit from one-on-one instruction with context clues during the explicit instruction phase. Below-level students should be paired with strong readers during guided instruction and guided practice for modeling purposes and to provide extra support. It may be necessary to select an alternate section of the text for this activity for English language learners and below-level students. Above-level students should be assigned to read a section of text appropriate for their reading level and encouraged to participate in the discussion of how to decipher unknown words so that their expert decoding skills can benefit the whole class when modeled.

Predict Think-Aloud

Background Information

Researchers have established that expert readers revise their understanding and predict as they read (Block and Pressley 2003). Making predictions allows students to create a purpose for reading because they read to find out if their predictions are correct. These predictions may pertain to the characters, plot, conflict, or resolution in the story. It is effective for students to learn how to revise their predictions by watching and listening to their teacher model for them in the Predict Think-Aloud (based on Block and Israel 2004).

Grade Levels/Standards Addressed

See page 133 for the standards this strategy addresses, or refer to the Digital Resource CD (standards.pdf) to read the correlating standards in their entirety.

Activity

Read a small section of text. Make some predictions about what might happen. To explain how to make accurate predictions, pause and describe what was in the text that helped you to make your prediction. Keep reading and deliver a Predict Think-Aloud. Refer to the following think-aloud as a sample:

My prediction is X. I have come to this prediction because the author left clues to tell me what would happen. The author used certain words and repeated phrases. Here are the questions that I asked myself while I was reading so that I could make predictions:

- *What clues did the author give me?*

- *What did I already know that helped me to make a correct prediction?*

- *What did I miss that caused my prediction to be wrong?*

Over the course of a few weeks, ask students to practice adding to, or changing, what they think to make predictions while they read.

Differentiation

It is essential to model this think-aloud for English language learners because they may struggle to articulate how they came to their predictions. Slow the speech rate; choose appropriate words to describe the scene to the reader; and use appropriate volume, intonation, and pauses to aid students in understanding the meaning. Below-level students should have a predictable text to work with as they learn how to monitor their own reading comprehension and determine the number of questions to ask for clarification of what they do not understand.

Ask Questions Think-Aloud

Background Information

Asking students questions about what they have read has long been a staple of education. Teachers traditionally check for students' successful comprehension through questioning. There is no doubt that students need to have the skills to answer questions successfully, but to do that, they should know how to generate and anticipate the questions worthy of asking. Reading researchers agree that expert readers ask and answer questions of themselves as they read to monitor their understanding of the material. Students should learn to ask and answer questions such as *who, what, where, when, why,* and *how* to comprehend the key details of the text. Research shows that when students learn to generate questions about the text as they read, their overall comprehension improves (Duke and Pearson 2002). The Ask Questions Think-Aloud (Block and Israel 2004) is designed to assist students to check the validity of their ideas, to clarify their thinking, or to signal that they need to reread or read ahead.

Grade Levels/Standards Addressed

See page 134 for the standards this strategy addresses, or refer to the Digital Resource CD (standards.pdf) to read the correlating standards in their entirety.

Activity

As students are reading a section of text independently, begin a think-aloud. Refer to the think-aloud samples in this lesson.

Read aloud more of the text to determine if students' thinking is correct. Ask students to use the same thought processes as they read the text silently from that point. Meet with students individually and assess their abilities to ask questions by asking them to pause and describe their thinking as they read.

Differentiation

English language learners may struggle to find the words to describe their thinking. It may help to have a list of words, phrases, or sentence frames available that are associated with think-alouds. Above-level students and below-level students can use a reading selection that is appropriate for their reading levels, otherwise they may have too much or too little to consider when thinking about their struggles to understand the material.

Grades 1–2 Example

Sometimes when I read, I don't understand. When I don't understand, I ask questions. I ask, *What don't I understand? Is it a word I don't recognize? Can I break the word into chunks that I can recognize? Why doesn't the sentence make sense to me? Do I need to reread the sentence to see if I can figure it out, or should I read ahead to see if I can figure it out later? Can I look at the pictures to get a better idea of what it means?* After that, I ask myself questions like a journalist. *Who or what is the main idea? What is happening? Where? When? Why?*

Ask Questions Think-Aloud (cont.)

Grades 3–5 Example

Sometimes when I read, I get confused. When I don't understand something, I stop and ask myself questions. I ask, *What don't I understand? Is it a word? Is it the way this sentence connects to the previous sentence? Is the sentence confusing? Is it a bigger idea than the one that occurred before? Is the sentence so long that I need to go back and reread, or should I go ahead and see if I can figure it out later?* After I ask myself questions like these, I can find the reason for my confusion and add whatever thoughts I need to read on with understanding. At that point, I can begin to ask myself questions so that I can summarize and remember what I have read. I ask myself, *What is important? What is happening? Who or what is involved? Where is it happening? When is it happening? How does it happen? Why is it important?*

Grades 6–8 Example

Sometimes when I read, I come across sections that are confusing. Whenever I don't understand a word or a sentence, I remember that I need to stop and ask questions. I ask *What is it about this sentence that I don't understand? Is it a word? Is it the string of ideas connecting this sentence to the previous sentence? Is the sentence unclear? Is it a bigger idea than the one that has occurred before? Is the sentence so long that I need to go back and reread, or should I read ahead to get more context clues?* Once I have asked myself questions like these, I can find the reason for my confusion and add whatever thoughts I need to continue reading with understanding. I also need to ask myself questions so that I can summarize what I have read. I ask myself, *What is important? What is happening? Who or what is involved? Where is it happening? How does it happen? Why is it important?*

Grades 9–12 Example

It is easy to get confused when you are reading and one important way to monitor your own understanding is to stop and ask questions. Ask yourself questions about what part of the text is confusing you. *Did I not understand a word or multiple words? Did I lose my place and forget what I already read? Is it a whole sentence, or even the whole paragraph, that I'm having trouble understanding? Is there something about the structure of the paragraph or the main idea that I don't understand?* By asking yourself these questions, you'll understand the source of your confusion which will enable you to get clarification and gain understanding before you continue reading. Asking yourself questions throughout a reading also allows you to assess your own learning and retain information so you can summarize the information. Questions such as *What are the key points? What is happening and to whom? How do these events occur? Why is this important? What have I learned?* will help you monitor your learning and understanding of the text.

Make Inferences Think-Aloud

Background Information

Research indicates that a student's interest level in the reading material is positively associated with reading comprehension (Maria 1990). In other words, the more interest a student has in the text, the better he or she is able to comprehend it. Furthermore, recent research also suggests that it is inference generation that links personal interest with reading comprehension (Clinton and Van Den Broek 2012). In order to draw an inference from the text, a student must connect the words in the story with his or her prior knowledge and experience and draw a conclusion based on combining these two sets of information. It is this connection that builds interest and facilitates comprehension. However, the ability to draw inferences from the text does not come easily to all students and the Make Inferences Think Aloud is designed to explicitly explain and teach this strategy.

Grade Levels/Standards Addressed

See page 134 for the standards this strategy addresses, or refer to the Digital Resource CD (standards.pdf) to read the correlating standards in their entirety.

Activity

As students are reading a section of text independently, begin a think-aloud. Refer to the think-alouds on page 150 as samples.

After introducing the Make Inferences Think-Aloud strategy, read another text selection aloud and work together as a class to analyze it and talk through the inference strategy. Then, have students read through another selection independently and discuss the inferences they made in groups. Circulate to each group during the discussion portion and make sure all students comprehend the activity.

Differentiation

One key to differentiating this strategy is ensuring that all readers are using an appropriate text. English language learners will benefit from a text with familiar vocabulary and below-level students will need a text that they can easily access when reading independently. Above-level students will benefit from a more challenging text with multiple options to draw complex inferences. Above-level students may have difficulty verbalizing their thinking because the inference-making thought process may come automatically to them. However, it is important to challenge these students to analyze their own thought processes both to help the rest of the students and to build metacognitive awareness.

Make Inferences Think-Aloud (cont.)

Grades 1–2 Example

Sometimes it is important to draw inferences while you are reading. You make an inference when you connect what you are reading with your own experiences or knowledge and make a conclusion or judgment based on this information. For example, you may be able to infer more about a character in the book if you think about the people you know in your life that are similar to the fictional character in the story. Now I'm going to read the following passage aloud and show you how I connect this reading to my own life and use this information to draw an inference from the text.

Grades 3–5 Example

When you are reading, it is important to think about how the text relates to your own life. Sometimes you can make a connection between the text and your prior knowledge that allows you to draw a conclusion not explicitly stated in the story. This is called making an inference. In order to do this, ask yourself, *Does this character/setting/situation remind me of anything in my own life? If so, what did I learn from my experience that I can apply to the story? What conclusions or judgments can I make based on this information?* Now I'm going to read the following passage aloud and show you how to think through drawing an inference from the text.

Grades 6–8 Example

Have you ever encountered a character or situation in a fictional story that reminded you of something in your own life? Were you able to apply your prior knowledge or experiences to make conclusions about what you read in the text? If so, you made an inference. Inferences occur when you connect the material in the text with your prior knowledge and make a judgment or conclusion based on combining these two pieces of information. Now I'm going to read the following passage aloud and show you how I connect this reading to my prior knowledge in order to draw an inference from the text.

Grades 9–12 Example

Drawing inferences from the text is an important skill to learn in order to develop good reading comprehension. You make an inference when you connect what you are reading with your own experiences or knowledge and make a conclusion or judgment based on this information. By combining these two pieces of information, you learn something not explicitly stated in the text. Sometimes it is helpful to ask yourself questions in order to draw an inference. For example, you might ask yourself, *Do the characters in this story remind me of anyone from my own life? Have I ever been in a similar situation as the characters in this story? What do I already know about the characters/setting/ situation in this book?* Once you have gathered this prior knowledge, ask yourself, *Based on what I read in the book and my prior knowledge about the situation, what conclusions can I make?* These conclusions are your inferences about the story. To demonstrate this process, I'm going to read the following passage aloud and tell you about my thought processes so that you can understand how I draw an inference based on the text and my prior knowledge.

Questioning Overview

Questioning in Language Arts

Socrates said, "I have no answers, only questions." Thinking and learning are essentially extensions of questioning. Questioning is an integral part of the thinking process, and therefore, it is an essential element of learning. Students must develop their abilities to question in order to become successful problem-solvers, critical thinkers, and decision-makers. However, when young readers are asked questions by teachers, others, or themselves, they have difficulty answering them well (National Reading Panel 2000).

Perhaps the most prominent activities in a language arts classroom are teacher questioning and answering the questions located in the literary text after the students have completed the reading. Obviously, question answering is an important feature of the classroom, but teachers should not limit its use for assessment purposes. While most of the questions to which students respond involve factual bits of information, these types of questions do not promote the development of learning about larger concepts. Questions that promote and emphasize the application of knowledge rather than the recall of facts help students to develop reasoning abilities (Ryder and Graves 2003). Questions should be used to engage the students in the reading and help them apply their prior knowledge and cultural experiences to the reading.

Questioning Should…

The teacher's goals in using questions to promote understanding include the following (Ryder and Graves 2003, 147):

Develop Interest and Motivate Students to Learn—Provocative questions can generate student interest in the topic to become more actively involved.

> *Example:* Does the main character have sinister motives? How do you know?

Highlight Lesson Content—Questions can be used to point out important information, concepts, and ideas in the reading that are relevant to the learning objectives.

> *Example:* What impact does the setting have on the story?

Integrate Lesson Content with What Students Have Studied and What They Already Know—Questions should allow students to apply previously learned material to the content of a particular reading as well as applying their prior knowledge on the topic to the question.

> *Example:* Considering the other novels you have read, how does this setting in particular compare and impact the character's decisions?

Structure High-Level Understanding—Questions should be sequenced in a way that encourages students to apply information to other situations or contexts. By focusing their attention on key concepts, then relating the concepts to a critical thinking question, students are given a scaffold to support higher-order thinking.

> *Example:* Why do the character's decisions make sense according to the time and place in which he or she lives?

Questioning Overview (cont.)

Promote the Integration of Students' Knowledge, Values, and Cultural Background with Learning Objectives—Learning becomes more relevant and meaningful when students are encouraged to draw on their knowledge and background. Students should be encouraged to construct meaning using their values, knowledge, and cultural perspective because in doing so they contribute to a richer and more stimulating environment.

> *Example:* In our unit on friendship, we have examined a number of friendships between characters. In what ways did these characters prove their loyalty to one another? How does this compare with how people show their loyalty today?

Types of Questions

While the purpose of questioning is to improve understanding, developing questions is an arduous task that requires the teacher to consider different cognitive levels of understanding information. Some questions can be answered easily because they are simple, factual questions. Other questions require great consideration and require the reader to integrate new information being learned with prior knowledge in order to formulate generalizations (Ryder and Graves 2003). While some educators classify questions into a few main categories (literal, interpretative, applied, open-ended), there are many other types of questions commonly asked of students about reading on standardized tests. These types of questions ask students to understand or use: main ideas, author's purpose, details, sequence, inference/prediction, literary techniques, fact/opinion, reading strategies, location of information/text organization, conventions, characterization, cause/effect, and vocabulary. Other researchers categorize questions within the framework of Bloom's Taxonomy. These levels, begin with the most superficial and end with the most complex: remembering, understanding, applying, analyzing, evaluating, and creating.

The Direct Instruction of Questioning

The goal of direct instruction of the question-answering strategy is to help teach readers how to become independent, active readers who can employ reading comprehension strategies to improve their understanding of the text. The National Reading Panel (2000) examined a number of studies on the effects of question-answering instruction and determined that students need question-answering instruction while reading so that they can learn and remember more from a text. The National Reading Panel found that direct instruction of the question-answering strategy leads to an improvement in answering questions after reading passages and in selecting strategies for finding answers in the text. Students should learn the steps to follow when answering questions and learn what to do when they cannot answer a question.

Questioning Overview (cont.)

Steps to Answering Questions

Students follow a series of steps, either consciously or unconsciously, in order to respond to the questions asked of them. In the direct instruction of question-answering techniques, it is important to teach students the steps to follow. These steps include (Cotton 1988):

- Examining the question

- Deciphering the meaning of the question

- Looking back in the text to find the answer

- Formulating a response internally (thinking)

- Generating a response externally (saying, writing)

- Revising the response (based on the teacher's probing, discussion, and other feedback)

What the Research Says

General investigations on the role of classroom questioning have revealed several important conclusions (Cotton 1988). Instruction that includes posing questions during reading is more effective in producing achievement gains than instruction without questioning students. Furthermore, students perform better on test items previously asked as discussion questions than on items to which they have not been previously exposed. In addition, questions posed orally during classroom discussion are more effective in fostering learning than are written questions. Also, questions that highlight the important components of the reading result in better comprehension than questions that do not.

It is important to note that the placement and timing of questions have also proved to have an impact on student comprehension and achievement. Research shows that asking questions frequently during class discussion has a positive impact on students' ability to learn new information.

Think Time and Wait Time

Researchers on questioning strategies also indicate that both *think time* and *wait time* impact student achievement. Think time is the amount of time the teacher allows to elapse after posing a question and before the student begins to speak. Wait time refers to the amount of time a teacher waits after a student has stopped speaking before saying anything.

Questioning Overview *(cont.)*

Increasing both think and wait times during oral questioning results in (Cotton 1988):

- Improving student achievement and retention of information
- Increasing the number of higher-level thinking responses in students
- Increasing the length of student responses
- Increasing the number of unsolicited responses
- Decreasing students' failure to respond to questions
- Increasing the amount and quality of evidence students offer to support their inferences
- Increasing the contributions made by students who do not participate much when wait time is shorter
- Expanding the variety of responses offered by students
- Decreasing student interruptions
- Increasing student-to-student interactions
- Increasing the number of questions posed by students

Self-Questioning

While students should be expected to successfully answer questions about the reading posed by their teachers, researchers have found that engaging students in the process of generating questions about the text as they read improves their ability to comprehend (Duke and Pearson 2002). Students should be actively engaged in asking questions during reading, and the classroom should be such that students are encouraged to ask questions. Without training, young readers are not likely to question themselves, nor are they likely to use questions spontaneously to make inferences. Research shows that when readers are taught how to generate questions, they better engage in the text by asking questions that lead to the development of better memory representations. The goal is to teach students to self-question while reading. If readers ask *why, how, when, where, which,* and *who* questions, it is possible for them to integrate sections of the text, which thereby improves comprehension and memory for what is read, and enables them to gain a deeper understanding of the text. Question generation is a metacognitive skill and increases the students' awareness of whether or not they understand what they are reading.

The National Reading Panel (2000) cites research that focuses on the metaanalysis of 30 studies that instructed students how to generate questions during reading. These studies demonstrated that there is strong empirical and scientific evidence that reading comprehension is benefited by instruction of question generation during reading in terms of memory and answering questions based on text as well as integrating and identifying main ideas through summarization.

Questioning Overview (cont.)

Standards Addressed

The following chart shows the correlating standards for each strategy in this section. Refer to the Digital Resource CD (standards.pdf) to read the correlating standards in their entirety.

Strategy	McREL Standards	Common Core State Standards
Previewing the Text through Questioning	Grades 1–2 (5.2) Grades 3–5 (5.3)	Grade 1 (RL.1.7, RL.1.10) Grade 2 (RL.2.7, RL.2.10) Grade 3 (RL.3.7, RL.3.10) Grade 4 (RL.4.7, RL.4.10) Grade 5 (RL.5.7, RL.5.10)
Scaffolding Reader Questions	Grades 1–2 (8.2) Grades 3–5 (8.2) Grades 6–8 (8.2) Grades 9–12 (8.2)	Grade 1 (RL.1.1, RL.1.7, RL.1.10) Grade 2 (RL.2.1, RL.2.7, RL.2.10) Grade 3 (RL.3.1, RL.3.7, RL.3.10) Grade 4 (RL.4.1, RL.4.7, RL.4.10) Grade 5 (RL.5.1, RL.5.7, RL.5.10) Grade 6 (RL.6.1, RL.6.7, RL.6.10) Grade 7 (RL.7.1, RL.7.7, RL.7.10) Grade 8 (RL.8.1, RL.8.7, RL.8.10) Grades 9–10 (RL.9-10.1, RL.9-10.7, RL.9-10.10) Grades 11–12 (RL.11-12.1, RL.11-12.7, RL.11-12.10)
Coding the Text	Grades 1–2 (8.2) Grades 3–5 (8.2) Grades 6–8 (8.2) Grades 9–12 (8.2)	Grade 1 (RL.1.2, RL.1.10) Grade 2 (RL.2.2, RL.2.10) Grade 3 (RL.3.2, RL.3.10) Grade 4 (RL.4.2, RL.4.10) Grade 5 (RL.5.2, RL.5.10) Grade 6 (RL.6.2, RL.6.10) Grade 7 (RL.7.2, RL.7.10) Grade 8 (RL.8.2, RL.8.10) Grades 9–10 (RL.9-10.2, RL.9-10.10) Grades 11–12 (RL.11-12.2, RL.11-12.10)
ReQuest	Grades 3–5 (8.2) Grades 6–8 (8.2) Grades 9–12 (8.2)	Grade 3 (RL.3.10) Grade 4 (RL.4.10) Grade 5 (RL.5.10) Grade 6 (RL.6.10) Grade 7 (RL.7.10) Grade 8 (RL.8.10) Grades 9–10 (RL.9-10.10) Grades 11–12 (RL.11-12.10)

Questioning Overview (cont.)

Strategy	McREL Standards	Common Core State Standards
Beat the Teacher	Grades 3–5 (8.2) Grades 6–8 (8.2) Grades 9–12 (8.2)	Grade 3 (RL.3.10) Grade 4 (RL.4.10) Grade 5 (RL.5.10) Grade 6 (RL.6.10) Grade 7 (RL.7.10) Grade 8 (RL.8.10) Grades 9–10 (RL.9-10.10) Grades 11–12 (RL.11-12.10)
Questioning the Author	Grades 3–5 (8.2) Grades 6–8 (8.2) Grades 9–12 (8.2)	Grade 3 (RL.3.2, RL.3.6, RL.3.10) Grade 4 (RL.4.2, RL.4.6, RL.4.10) Grade 5 (RL.5.2, RL.5.6, RL.5.10) Grade 6 (RL.6.2, RL.6.6, RL.6.10) Grade 7 (RL.7.2, RL.7.6, RL.7.10) Grade 8 (RL.8.2, RL.8.6, RL.8.10) Grades 9–10 (RL.9-10.2, RL.9-10.6, RL.9-10.10) Grades 11–12 (RL.11-12.2, RL.11-12.6, RL.11-12.10)
Character Interview	Grades 1–2 (8.2) Grades 3–5 (8.2) Grades 6–8 (8.2) Grades 9–12 (8.2)	Grade 1 (RL.1.3, RL.1.10) Grade 2 (RL.2.3, RL.2.10) Grade 3 (RL.3.3, RL.3.10) Grade 4 (RL.4.3, RL.4.10) Grade 5 (RL.5.3, RL.5.10) Grade 6 (RL.6.3, RL.6.10) Grade 7 (RL.7.3, RL.7.10) Grade 8 (RL.8.3, RL.8.10) Grades 9–10 (RL.9-10.3, RL.9-10.10) Grades 11–12 (RL.11-12.3, RL.11-12.10)
Character Preview	Grades 1–2 (8.2) Grades 3–5 (8.2)	Grade 1 (RL.1.3, RL.1.10) Grade 2 (RL.2.3, RL.2.10) Grade 3 (RL.3.3, RL.3.10) Grade 4 (RL.4.3, RL.4.10) Grade 5 (RL.5.3, RL.5.10)
Question Hierarchy	Grades 3–5 (8.2) Grades 6–8 (8.2) Grades 9–12 (8.2)	Grade 3 (RL.1.1, RL.1.6, RL.1.10) Grade 4 (RL.4.1, RL.4.6, RL.4.10) Grade 5 (RL.5.1, RL.5.6, RL.5.10) Grade 6 (RL.6.1, RL.6.6, RL.6.10) Grade 7 (RL.7.1, RL.7.6, RL.7.10) Grade 8 (RL.8.1, RL.8.6, RL.8.10) Grades 9–10 (RL.9-10.1, RL.9-10.6, RL.9-10.10) Grades 11–12 (RL.11-12.1, RL.11-12.6, RL.11-12.10)

Previewing the Text through Questioning

Background Information

One way to stimulate students to ask questions is by previewing the text's pictures and illustrations before reading the text. Picture books serve as the foundation of fiction in early childhood and children delight in examining, discussing, and asking questions about a book's illustrations. Even once they graduate to chapter books, students still acquire a great deal of information about a story through the pictures presented on a book's cover, page, and chapter headings. Previewing the Text through Questioning (Hoyt 2002) is an effective pre-reading activity that enables students to develop questioning skills while also activating prior knowledge and making predictions. Before the class reads the book together, the teacher guides students as they look at each picture included in the reading selection. The teacher marks an important image in the text with a sticky note and asks students to begin on that page rather than at the beginning of the selection. As students focus on developing questions about the pictures, they activate their prior knowledge on the topic. They use prediction skills to predict answers to their own questions, and they are encouraged to reflect on the accuracy of their question-answering abilities after reading in order to help them develop stronger metacognitive skills. As they mature, students learn to analyze how their picture predictions helped them surmise information about the book's meaning, tone, setting, characters, and other story elements.

Grade Levels/Standards Addressed

See page 155 for the standards this strategy addresses, or refer to the Digital Resource CD (standards.pdf) to read the correlating standards in their entirety.

Activity

Determine the reading selection to be introduced to students. Invite students to preview the book by looking at all of the pictures as a class. Model the strategy by thinking aloud as you examine the pictures and encourage students to share their thoughts. Ask students to choose the picture that they believe is most important and have them explain their choice. Have students develop questions about the picture and the reading selection, and write these on sticky notes.

Point out moments during the question generating when students are relying on their prior knowledge. Encourage them to predict the answers to their questions. Summarize the questions and students' answers for the class and then ask students to read the selection or read it to them. Have students reflect on their pre-reading questions and answers by asking them to identify which questions they answered correctly during the preview, why they were able to answer the questions, and which questions they discovered answers to. Discuss how their picture predictions helped them learn about the book's characters, setting, meaning, and tone even before they read the words.

Students can use the *Previewing the Text through Questioning* activity sheet (page 160, previewingquestioning.pdf) to preview the reading in small groups and then independently. Stop students before they complete the reading to share and discuss their questions and the possible answers. Ask them to justify and explain their predictions.

Previewing the Text through Questioning (cont.)

Differentiation

English language learners may need to have the text read aloud to them as they complete the activity independently or in small groups. It may help to allow below-level students to complete the handout orally, and have a classmate write down students' answers. Encourage above-level students to develop higher-level questions before they read so that they can look into causes, experiences, and facts to draw a conclusion or make connections to other areas of learning.

Grades 1–2 Example

Previewing Questions	
As I previewed the images, my questions were:	**Possible answers:**
Why are the other animals laughing at the giraffe?	The other animals are laughing at the giraffe because he does not have anyone to dance with.
Does the cricket help the giraffe?	The cricket plays music for the giraffe so he can practice dancing.
How does the giraffe feel after he dances at the end?	The giraffe feels proud.

After-Reading Questions
What were the questions about that I answered correctly during the preview?
I answered the questions about the giraffe's feelings correctly.
Why was I able to answer the questions correctly?
I saw the looks on the giraffe's face. I thought about my own feelings and facial expressions.
What questions can I now answer after reading?
How did the giraffe learn to dance? What did the other animals think after they saw the giraffe dance at the end? How did the giraffe beat his fear and embarrassment?

from *Giraffes Can't Dance* by Giles Andreae

Previewing the Text through Questioning *(cont.)*

Grades 3–5 Example

Previewing Questions	
As I previewed the images, my questions were:	**Possible answers:**
Who is the woman that the little boy is kissing?	I think the boy is giving his mother a kiss.
Why is her torso brown?	I think her torso is brown because she is turning into chocolate.
Why is the boy holding a brown apple?	The boy is holding a brown apple because he thinks it is magic and will stop his mom from turning into chocolate.

After-Reading Questions
What were the questions about that I answered correctly during the preview?
I correctly guessed that the boy is giving his mom a kiss and that the mom's torso is brown because she is turning into chocolate.
Why was I able to answer the questions correctly?
I thought about my family and I know that the only women I kiss are my mom, grandmother, and aunts.
I know that chocolate is brown and the title of the book is *The Chocolate Touch* so I guessed that the brown color on the mom is chocolate.
What questions can I now answer after reading?
Why is the mom turning into chocolate? Does she stay chocolate forever? Why is the boy not turning into chocolate? Is the chocolate touch a good thing?

from *The Chocolate Touch* by Patrick Skene Catling

Name: _____ Date: _____

Previewing the Text through Questioning

Directions: Before you begin reading, preview the text and write down your questions and possible answers. After reading, write your answers to the reflection questions.

Previewing Questions	
As I previewed the images, my questions were:	**Possible answers:**
_____	_____
_____	_____
_____	_____
_____	_____

After-Reading Reflections

What were the questions about that I answered correctly during the preview?

_____

_____

_____

Why was I able to answer the questions correctly?

_____

_____

_____

What questions can I now answer after reading?

_____

_____

_____

_____

_____

Scaffolding Reader Questions

Background Information

It is essential to encourage students to verbalize and record their questions when developing questioning skills to improve reading comprehension. This helps readers anticipate questions in the future and develop their reasoning skills. When students are young, teachers can help readers formulate and record their questions, but as they become more fluent readers, they can record their own questions. The Scaffolding Reader Questions strategy (Hoyt 2002) enables students to develop questions before, during, and after reading. The teacher should model how to construct questions during each of the reading phases to make the process clear. If desired, the teacher can guide students to ask questions about particular aspects of the reading, such as characters, setting, or theme, or leave the activity open-ended and allow them to generate any type of question about the text.

Grade Levels/Standards Addressed

See page 155 for the standards this strategy addresses, or refer to the Digital Resource CD (standards.pdf) to read the correlating standards in their entirety.

Activity

Distribute the *Scaffolding Reader Questions* activity sheet (page 166, scaffoldingreader.pdf). Before students begin reading a particular selection, ask them to conduct a preview in which they look at the title, table of contents, headings, key vocabulary, pictures, and other elements. Have students create questions based on the preview. Be sure to highlight how the book's illustrations (if present) contribute to their generation of questions about the elements of the story.

Have students share their questions with the entire class and explain how the preview directly led them to their questions. Next, instruct students to begin reading the selection. During guided reading, pause and ask them to record important items worthy of noting. For the older students, make sure to emphasize the importance of referring explicitly to the text when recording the things they noticed. Before students continue reading, they must record questions that will allow them to further their understanding and learning on the topic. Finally, ask students to record questions that the reading did not address but that they want to find the answers to.

Differentiation

English language learners will benefit from having the process modeled for them. They may need a list of words to help them complete the activity. Provide extra time for below-level students to produce questions. Be sure to write down and display the questions students generate based on their previews with a document camera or the board for the class to review and use as a guide. Above-level students should be encouraged to ask higher-level thinking questions to make connections to other topics and areas of learning.

Scaffolding Reader Questions *(cont.)*

Grades 1–2 Example

Before-Reading Questions	
Based on my preview of…	**My questions are:**
title	How does the family collect all the money in the jar?
pictures	What happened during the fire?
During-Reading Questions	
While I was reading, I noticed…	**My questions are:**
The mom, the grandma and the girl all put money in the jar.	Does the little girl have a father?
The neighbors were very kind and giving when they moved into their new apartment after the fire.	Did the neighbors have extra furniture they could afford to give the girl's family? Or did they buy them new furniture?
After-Reading Questions	
I still wonder about…	**My questions are:**
how much the chair cost	How did my family save enough money to buy furniture when we moved into our new house?
the missing sofa	Is the family in the story going to keep saving for a sofa and another chair?

from *A Chair for My Mother* by Vera B. Williams

Scaffolding Reader Questions (cont.)

Grades 3–5 Example

Before-Reading Questions	
Based on my preview of…	**My questions are:**
pictures	Why is Ferdinand by himself in the flowers?
title	What made him jump up into the air in surprise?
key words	Why is he sitting in the bull ring while a matador waves a cape in front of him?
During-Reading Questions	
While I was reading, I noticed…	**My questions are:**
The other bulls would fight with each other all day.	Did the other bulls fight with each other so they would look strong and ferocious?
The other bulls wanted to be picked to go to the bullfight.	Why did the other bulls want to be picked to go to the bullfight?
The job of the Banderilleros, Picadores and Matadors at the bullfights was to make the bulls mad by sticking them with pins, spears, and swords.	Do the Banderilleros, Picadores and Matadors enjoy making the bulls mad?
After-Reading Questions	
I still wonder about…	**My questions are:**
Spanish bullfights	How did bullfights become a Spanish tradition?
Ferdinand's fate	Was Ferdinand allowed to live happily ever after in his peaceful pasture even though he was considered a failure at the bullfight?

from *The Story of Ferdinand* by Munro Leaf

Scaffolding Reader Questions *(cont.)*

Grades 6–8 Example

Before-Reading Questions	
Based on my preview of…	**My questions are:**
cover illustration	Is the girl going to survive the storm?
book jacket summary	Is that a wild wolf in the boat with her?
title	Is the girl lonely on the island by herself?

During-Reading Questions	
While I was reading, I noticed…	**My questions are:**
Karana lived alone with her brother on the island before he was killed by feral dogs.	How did her brother's presence and subsequent death affect her ability to survive by herself?
She formed strong bonds with the animals on the island.	Did Karana's bonds with the animals compensate for her lack of human friendship?
Karana had several chances to leave the island before she actually chose to leave.	Why did Karana choose to stay on the island when she had an opportunity to leave?
	Why did she choose to leave when she did?

After-Reading Questions	
I still wonder about…	**My questions are:**
Karana's loneliness	Was it only through the friendship of Rontu, and later Tutok, that Karana realizes how lonely she is?
her experience once she leaves the island	Did Karana ever regret her decision to leave the island?

from *Island of the Blue Dolphins* by Scott O'Dell

Scaffolding Reader Questions *(cont.)*

Grades 9–12 Example

Before-Reading Questions	
Based on my preview of...	**My questions are:**
book cover	Do the man and the woman in the illustration have a relationship with each other?
title	Does the title describe traits of the book's characters?
second column text	Does pride lead to prejudice or vice versa?
During-Reading Questions	
While I was reading, I noticed...	**My questions are:**
Darcy judges Elizabeth based on her social standing.	Will Darcy be able to look beyond social standing to see Elizabeth's true virtues?
Lady Catherine tries to control Darcy, her nephew.	How much influence does Lady Catherine really have over Darcy's actions?
The Bennett sisters are extremely concerned about their social reputation.	Can one sister's decisions regarding love influence the marriageability of the other sisters?
After-Reading Questions	
I still wonder about...	**My questions are:**
Elizabeth's initial impressions of Mr. Darcy	Will Elizabeth be able to abandon the prejudices she initially formed through her first impressions of Mr. Darcy, or will they continue to haunt her even after they get married?
Lydia's decision to elope	How will Lydia's elopement affect the lives of her other sisters in the future?

from *Pride and Prejudice* by Jane Austen

Scaffolding Reader Questions

Directions: Before you read, preview the text and write down your questions. While you read, take notes of what you notice in the text and write down your questions. After reading, write down what questions you still have about the topic.

Before-Reading Questions	
Based on my preview of…	**My questions are:**
_____	_____
_____	_____
_____	_____
_____	_____
_____	_____

During-Reading Questions	
While I was reading, I noticed…	**My questions are:**
_____	_____
_____	_____
_____	_____
_____	_____

After-Reading Questions	
I still wonder about…	**My questions are:**
_____	_____
_____	_____
_____	_____
_____	_____

Adapted from Linda Hoyt's *Make It Real* (Portsmouth, NH: Heinemann, 2002), 125.

Coding the Text

Background Information

It is essential for students to self-monitor as they read so that they can check their understanding and use fix-up strategies, if needed. Coding the Text is an activity that helps students to generate questions about the text and develop their metacognitive skills. The activity teaches students how to deal with areas of confusion when reading. The teacher performs a think-aloud when introducing the activity so that students have a model for completing the task. During Coding the Text, students use sticky notes to mark the moments in the reading that are confusing, things they want to know more about, and new or important information. This strategy not only helps students clarify their points of confusion, but also enables them to identify information that can be used to understand central ideas or themes from the literature.

Grade Levels/Standards Addressed

See page 155 for the standards this strategy addresses, or refer to the Digital Resource CD (standards.pdf) to read the correlating standards in their entirety.

Activity

Write the codes on the board that students should use to make notes about the reading.

?	*I am confused/I don't understand*
M	*I want to learn more about this*
*	*This is important*
N	*New information*
C	*Connection*
TH	*Theme of the text*
AHA	*Big idea in the text*

Emergent readers should be limited to the first two codes while more fluent readers can use more codes. Distribute sticky notes to students and instruct them to place the notes in the text and code the text as they read. After students code the text, instruct them to generate questions based on the codes they have created. Share the questions in a classroom discussion in which students attempt to answer the questions and generate more.

Differentiation

English language learners may benefit from hearing the reading selection read aloud as they follow along. Below-level students should use only three codes as they read, as too many might overwhelm them. Above-level students should be encouraged to explain why they placed the codes in the locations they did; push them to generate higher-order thinking questions.

ReQuest

Background Information

The ReQuest activity (Manzo 1969) boosts students' reading comprehension by modeling how to ask their own questions about their reading. When students ask questions of themselves while reading, they learn how to monitor their own understanding of the text and they have better comprehension as a result. The ReQuest activity can be used with individuals, small groups, or the whole class. It is an interactive questioning technique that increases students' motivation to read and facilitates independent and proficient reading skills.

Grade Levels/Standards Addressed

See page 155 for the standards this strategy addresses, or refer to the Digital Resource CD (standards.pdf) to read the correlating standards in their entirety.

Activity

Choose a reading selection that contains many challenging new ideas or topics for students. First introduce the ReQuest activity by modeling its use. Use examples from a reading selection previously read by students. Begin by reading the first paragraph of the text aloud. Then, ask and answer questions about the contents of the passage. Model for students how you formulate your answers and try to use examples, if possible, in your answers. Ask students to read the next section of the text. Limit this section to no more than a paragraph or two in length. Instruct students to take turns in asking you questions about what they read, and answer the questions as you modeled for them previously. Ask students to continue reading the next section of the text, and inform them that you will be asking them questions about the section and they will be answering your questions. Continue to alternate between student-generated questions and teacher-generated questions until the entire passage is read. Remind students to ask questions of themselves as they read because in doing so they can monitor their understanding and improve their comprehension.

Differentiation

Preteach English language learners the reading assignment in advance so that class time is review. Provide ample think- and wait-time throughout the activity. It is usually helpful to give English language learners a vocabulary list to assist them with the reading material. Write the questions asked and the answers provided on the board or display them with a document camera for below-level students to study. Type up the questions and answers and distribute them to use as a study guide. Above-level students should be encouraged to ask challenging questions that go beyond the material in the reading. They can find the answers through independent research.

Beat the Teacher

Background Information

Beat the Teacher (Hoyt 2002) is another questioning strategy that helps students develop strong questioning skills in order to enhance their reading comprehension. As students read the text, they generate questions that they pose to the teacher. The activity motivates students to try to stump their teacher with their questions. Their goal is to ask a question the teacher cannot answer about the assigned reading. The activity increases student motivation to read and reread in their quest to stump the teacher, and in the process of generating challenging questions, they must listen to and pay attention to the teacher's answers.

Grade Levels/Standards Addressed

See page 156 for the standards this strategy addresses, or refer to the Digital Resource CD (standards.pdf) to read the correlating standards in their entirety.

Activity

Assign a reading selection to students to complete in small groups or paired reading. Instruct students to read the selection closely and with great care. Explain that the goal is to generate very challenging questions that the teacher cannot answer about the reading. Read the selection silently as students are reading and writing questions, and stop often to write your own questions about the text. When the time for reading and question generation is complete, take a seat in the front of the room, and have students ask their questions about the text in an orderly fashion. Ask one student to record the questions and answers so that you can give them to students to review later.

To challenge students further and create a competition, the activity can be modified to engage students in question answering. Every time the teacher answers a question correctly, students must answer a teacher question, and points are tallied on the board for correct answers.

Differentiation

Provide English language learners with plenty of time to generate questions. It may help to give them the reading assignment the day before or an audio version of the text so that they can have adequate time to process the information. Have students write down the questions they pose and the answers you give on the board or display them with a document camera so that below-level students can see them. Model how you examine a question and formulate your answer through detailed think-alouds. Above-level students should be encouraged to find the answers to any questions posed that you cannot answer.

Questioning the Author

Background Information

Questioning the Author (Beck et al. 1997) is an activity that helps students to understand, analyze, and elaborate on an author's meaning and intent as they read a text. The purpose of Questioning the Author is to engage readers beyond the factual, surface-level information and to help them understand the ideas and concepts represented in the literature. This strategy also allows students to understand that a text represents an author's ideas and attitudes and enables them to compare their personal point of view with that of the book's narrator and author. By generating and answering questions directed to the author of a story, this strategy helps students comprehend how the narrator's point of view does not always represent an author's point of view.

In this strategy, teachers probe students' understanding through a series of questions called *queries*. Queries encourage students to work together during student-to-student interactions to construct meaning as they read and reflect on the text. Queries help students engage in working with the ideas in literature. They are used when students are engaged in reading a short passage rather than at the conclusion of a longer reading. Most teachers use conventional questioning associated with reading (Who? What? Why?), but queries are purposefully open-ended to encourage multiple answers and divergent thinking (Clark and Graves 2005).

To help students along, ask the following types of questions during Questioning the Author (Clark and Graves 2005; Ryder and Graves 2003; Beck, et al. 1997; Lenski, Wham, and Johns 1999):

Initiating Queries—For identifying ideas:

- What is the author trying to say here?
- What is the author's message?
- What is the author talking about?

Follow-Up Queries—For connecting ideas in the text to construct meaning:

- What do you think the author means in this sentence?
- Why do you think the author says that now, right here?
- How does that connect with what the author has already told us?
- Does that make sense with what the author told us before?
- Did the author explain it clearly?
- Does the author explain why?
- How did the author work that out for us?
- Is there anything missing?
- What do we need to find out?

Grade Levels/Standards Addressed

See page 156 for the standards this strategy addresses, or refer to the Digital Resource CD (standards.pdf) to read the correlating standards in their entirety.

Questioning the Author *(cont.)*

Preparation

Carefully read through the text selection to identify the most important concepts and ideas. Develop the questions to present to students based on important themes you find compelling. Break up the reading selection into smaller segments that will be read and then discussed by students. Develop the queries that focus on essential ideas and concepts in the reading and on each of the text segments to be presented.

Activity

Inform students that they will be taking a different approach to reading in the activity. Tell them that they will be reading a series of short segments of text. Once they have finished reading one segment, they will hold a class discussion about its meaning. Explain to students that a person wrote the text, and that in order to understand the author's intentions or purpose, it helps to discuss the text and the possibilities of meaning in detail. Direct students to read the first segment of the text. When they are finished, ask the class to initiate queries on the list in relationship to the reading. Encourage students to answer and respond to one another's questions and comments and to use the text to support their positions. An alternative approach is to have the teacher or several students take turns acting the part of the author. Have the "author" sit in front of the class and endeavor to answer the queries posed by the rest of students about his or her work. Make sure to distinguish between the author's point of view in the text and students' personal points of view. Then, direct students to read the next segment of the text and ask them the follow-up queries in relationship to the reading. Have students discuss the meaning of the passage with the class.

Differentiation

English language learners will need the reading broken up into small enough sections so that they can effectively focus their attention. Each passage should involve a limited number of ideas and concepts to reduce the chances that below-level students will have trouble understanding the text. Above-level students may prefer to work independently or in a small homogenous group.

Character Interview

Background Information

Unlike nonfiction, fictional literature relies heavily on innovative and detailed character development to engage the reader and communicate a story. An accurate understanding of a story's characters is necessary for students to be able to proficiently and independently read and comprehend fictional literature. The Character Interview strategy fosters a deeper understanding of the characters in a fictional text by asking students to take on the traits of the character in order to generate and answer questions from his or her point of view. By adopting a character's point of view, students gain insight into a given character's opinions, personality traits, motivations, feelings, and relationships. More than simply acting like the character as one would do in a play, the task of asking and answering questions forces students to truly analyze the character and adopt his or her perspective.

Grade Levels/Standards Addressed

See page 156 for the standards this strategy addresses, or refer to the Digital Resource CD (standards.pdf) to read the correlating standards in their entirety.

Preparation

Before beginning the activity, familiarize students with different types of questions they can ask the character. For younger students, it may be helpful to provide them with a list of questions and have them choose questions from the list. Older students should be encouraged to write their own questions. Caution students that they need to choose questions that are related to the text so that the student acting as the character has a basis for answering the question. Encourage students to pick questions that will reveal new or different information about the character rather than factual questions explicitly stated in the text. There are a wide variety of questions that can be asked. Use the following list as sample questions or starting points for developing additional questions to ask:

- What are your goals?
- What are the obstacles you must overcome to reach these goals?
- What is your biggest fear?
- What is your most treasured possession?
- What is your greatest regret?
- What is your greatest achievement?
- What makes you sad?
- Who are the important people in your life? Why?
- Who are your heroes? Who are your enemies?
- What is your most unique quality?

Character Interview *(cont.)*

Activity

After reading a story or text selection, hold a brief class discussion about the story's characters and decide which character the class would like to interview. Then, distribute the *Character Interview* activity sheet (page 176, characterinterview. pdf) to students. Ask students to work in pairs or small groups to generate questions that they would like to ask the chosen character and record them in the Interview Questions column. Select a student volunteer or assign a student to act as the chosen character. This student should sit in front of the class for the interview or another visible location. Allow the other students to ask the character questions and have them record the character's answers in the Character Responses column. If the student acting as the character needs help answering a question, he or she can ask for guidance from the teacher or the rest of the class. If the character gives a response that the other students disagree with, ask students and the character to reference the text to refer to details and examples in order to support or refute the character's point of view.

Differentiation

Provide English language learners with a list of questions from which they can choose. Review the questions with them before starting the activity so that they will feel comfortable choosing and asking questions during the interview. For below-level students, assess story comprehension before beginning the activity and answer any questions they might have about the text. A thorough understanding of the story will allow these students to develop better interview questions for the character. Guide above-level students to craft more complex questions that get at the theme and other main ideas in the text. Above-level students should also be encouraged to act as the character so that they will be challenged to answer the class's questions from the character's point of view.

Character Interview (cont.)

Grades 1–2 Example

Text: *Violet the Pilot* by Steve Breen

Character: Violet

Interview Questions	Character Responses
Why don't you have any friends except your dog, Orville?	I just have different interests than the other kids. They think I'm strange because I like to build mechanical things instead of play with dolls and tea sets.
How did it feel when the mayor gave you a medal?	It felt great! I was really disappointed that I missed the airshow, but getting the medal of valor more than made up for it.
What will your next project be?	Right now I'm working on building a solar-powered airplane that I can fly around the world.

Grades 3–5 Example

Text: *Number the Stars* by Lois Lowry

Character: Annemarie

Interview Questions	Character Responses
How did the German occupation of Copenhagen affect your daily life?	The Germans made everyone afraid. We weren't allowed to run in the streets and there was a strict curfew. The adults were always worrying and whispering. We weren't allowed to act like children.
How did you feel about pretending that Ellen was your sister to fool the Germans?	I was happy that we could help Ellen and her family, but I was scared too. Pretending that Ellen was my sister put my whole family in danger. I'm glad that I could help my best friend, though.
Why did you decide to wear Ellen's Star of David pendant at the end of the story?	I wanted to wear the pendant to remind myself of Ellen until she returns. It also reminded me of what it was like during the war and what the Germans did to us. Some people just wanted to forget the whole war, but I think it is important to remember.

Character Interview (cont.)

Grades 6–8 Example

Text: *Hatchet* by Gary Paulsen

Character: Brian

Interview Questions	Character Responses
What was your main concern while you were living by yourself in the wilderness?	Most of the time, I was worried about food. Finding enough to eat was always a concern although it got better once I figured out how to catch fish. I also worried about having enough wood for the fire.
Did you ever lose hope that you would be rescued?	When the plane flew by me and did not hear me, I was very devastated. I started to lose hope and give up. I lost my will to survive.
How did it feel after you were rescued?	At first, I couldn't believe it. I thought the rescue plane was a figment of my imagination. Once I got back to civilization, it was hard to adjust. The whole experience seemed unreal. Eventually I got used to being home though and I'm very happy I was rescued.

Grades 9–12 Example

Text: *How the Garcia Girls Lost Their Accents* by Julia Alvarez

Character: Carlos (father)

Interview Questions	Character Responses
Do you regret your decision to agitate against Trujillo's regime?	No, I don't regret it although it certainly affected my family's future. I stood up for what I believed in. I don't always agree with the choices my family has made since coming to the U.S., but I wouldn't change our decision to leave the Dominican Republic.
How has your cultural assimilation experience differed from that of your daughters'?	When I came to New York, I was already a grown man with an established profession. It was difficult to reestablish my professional reputation in a new country. Also, since I'm older, it is harder for me to see the benefits of change. Mostly I would just prefer it if my daughters adhered to Dominican traditions, rather than acquiring American ones.
What bothers you most about your daughters' assimilation into American society?	I think the thing that bothers me most is their interactions and relationships with men. In the Dominican Republic, interactions between unmarried women and men are very formal and there is always a chaperone present. In America, my daughters do whatever they like with whomever they like. I don't think it is a good way to live your life.

Name: _____ **Date:** _____

Character Interview

Directions: Note the character that the class will be interviewing on the line below. Record your interview questions and the character's responses in the corresponding chart columns.

Text: _____

Character: _____

Interview Questions	Character Responses

Character Preview

Background Information

The previewing strategies used to activate prior knowledge for informational texts, such as scanning the text for bold words, subheadings, charts, and illustrations, are not as effective with fictional literature because many literary texts do not include these types of readily apparent comprehension aids. However, schema activation and development regarding literary elements, such as theme, plot, and characters, can greatly enhance students' ability to read and comprehend fictional literature (Gambrell et. al 2007; Irvine 2007, as quoted in Hedgcock and Ferris 2009). The Character Preview strategy is specifically designed to allow students to activate and gain prior knowledge about a fictional story's characters prior to reading the book by developing and answering questions about the characters.

Grade Levels/Standards Addressed

See page 156 for the standards this strategy addresses, or refer to the Digital Resource CD (standards.pdf) to read the correlating standards in their entirety.

Preparation

Thoroughly read through the text selection and designate one character on which the class should focus. Prepare a brief summary of the character so you will be adequately prepared to answer students' questions about him or her.

Activity

Read the class a one- or two-sentence description of the character and explain that students will be asking questions to learn more about this character before reading the story. Discuss the various types of questions they might want to ask such as questions about physical description, family, friends, location, favorite possessions, strengths, weaknesses, etc. Ask each student to write one question on a small sheet of paper, and collect students' questions in a bowl. Have students take turns blindly selecting a question from the bowl and reading it aloud while you do your best to answer the questions from the character's perspective. Time permitting, allow students to write additional questions based on the new information they have learned and answer another round of questions. At the end of the activity, summarize the information they learned about the character on the board or with a document camera. Refer back to this information as you read and conduct follow-up activities.

Differentiation

Encourage above-level students to develop more complex questions that will reveal a broader range of information about the character. You may also want to enlist their help with recording and summarizing the class's information at the end of the activity. Provide English language learners with a list of questions from which they can choose. Have them practice reading and answering questions with a partner before beginning the activity with the whole class. Below-level students will benefit from a list of question categories (physical description, personality, etc.) from which to choose so they can consider a wider variety of question possibilities.

Question Hierarchy

Background Information

Most teachers are familiar with Bloom's Taxonomy of Educational Objectives, a question framework designed to help differentiate between various levels and types of questions (Bloom et al. 1956, as cited in Buehl 2009). By using Bloom's Taxonomy, as well as the updated version by Lorin W. Anderson, David R. Krathwohl, and Benjamin S. Bloom (2001), educators can generate better and more meaningful questions that truly help to assess students' comprehension. In addition to using Bloom's Taxonomy to assess student learning, this tool can also be used to enhance comprehension by teaching students how to develop deeper, more meaningful questions themselves. This strategy strives to improve students' reading comprehension by challenging them to think metacognitively about different types of questions and to create and ask more complex, higher-level questions about the text.

Grade Levels/Standards Addressed

See page 156 for the standards this strategy addresses, or refer to the Digital Resource CD (standards.pdf) to read the correlating standards in their entirety.

Activity

Begin the lesson by displaying the *Question Hierarchy* activity sheet (page 182, questionhierarchy.pdf) with a document camera. Explain to students that they are going to be learning about different types of literary questions, and at the end of the lesson, they will be responsible for creating assessment questions that will be used to evaluate the class's understanding of a fictional text selection. Review the *Question Hierarchy* activity sheet with students, making sure to thoroughly discuss each type of question by reviewing the category's objectives and providing examples. Note that the question categories are hierarchical because they go from relatively simple, factual questions to complex, more involved questions that require higher-level thinking. Next, read a sample text passage aloud and practice developing different types of questions for each category as a class. Once you feel that students have a firm grasp of the question categories, have them read the fictional text selection for the lesson independently and complete their own *Question Hierarchy* activity sheet. Once they complete the chart, hold a class discussion to review the different types of questions and allow students to share their own examples. Finally, collect students' activity sheets and use students' questions to develop a comprehension assessment for the text.

Differentiation

Before beginning the lesson, review difficult vocabulary terms such as *hierarchy*, *analyze*, *evaluate*, and *apply* with English language learners to facilitate comprehension of the *Question Hierarchy* activity sheet. Provide English language learners and below-level students with additional examples of questions for each category so they have adequate reference material to develop their own questions. Challenge above-level students to generate higher-level questions.

Question Hierarchy (cont.)

Grades 3–5 Example

Text: *Sarah, Plain and Tall* by Patricia MacLachlan

Question Type	Question Objective	Assessment Questions
Remembering	to help the reader remember the story's elements, such as characters, setting, and sequence of events	Who is Sarah Wheaton? What time of year does the story take place? Where does Sarah come from? Where does the Whitting family live?
Understanding	to help the reader understand what the author is communicating about the characters, situation, conflict, etc.	Why are the children worried? How does Jacob Whitting feel about Sarah Wheaton? How does Caleb feel when Sarah goes to town?
Applying	to help the reader use the text in a meaningful way, including connections to one's own life	Why might the author have the dogs love Sarah? How does this story relate to your own life?
Analyzing	to enhance the reader's understanding of the text, especially through the analysis of literary devices	What role does the season play in the story? Why did the author choose that season? What is the significance of the beach dunes in the story?
Evaluating	to critically examine the story, including the influences of the author's attitude and perspective	What emotions does the author reveal through the story? How do you think the author's personal background of growing up on a prairie affected how she wrote the story?
Creating	to create new knowledge about the author's intentions, the theme, or personal implications	How does the author express themes of loss and abandonment? What is she trying to tell the reader about the role of love?

Question Hierarchy (cont.)

Grades 6–8 Example

Text: *Wonder* by R. J. Palacio

Question Type	Question Objective	Assessment Questions
Remembering	to help the reader remember the story's elements, such as characters, setting, and sequence of events	Who are the first kids that August meets at his new school? Why has he never attended public school before? What are August's interests outside of school?
Understanding	to help the reader understand what the author is communicating about the characters, situation, conflict, etc.	Who are the important figures in August's life and why? Why does August decide to attend public school for the first time in 5th grade? How do August's parents feel about August going to a mainstream school?
Applying	to help the reader use the text in a meaningful way, including connections to one's own life	Do you know anyone like the character of Julian in the story? Why is Julian so mean to August? How can you relate to August's experiences in school?
Analyzing	to enhance the reader's understanding of the text, especially through the analysis of literary devices	What is the significance of Halloween for August? What is the meaning of August's bad experience on Halloween this year?
Evaluating	to critically examine the story, including the influences of the author's attitude and perspective	Why did the author choose to have multiple narrators? What do these various points of view make the reader understand or feel about August?
Creating	to create new knowledge about the author's intentions, the theme, or personal implications	How do you think you will feel the next time you encounter someone with a physical abnormality? What are the societal implications of this book?

Question Hierarchy (cont.)

Grades 9–12 Example

Text: *The Things They Carried* by Tim O'Brien

Question Type	Question Objective	Assessment Questions
Remembering	to help the reader remember the story's elements, such as characters, setting, and sequence of events	When does this story take place? Who are the soldiers that lose their lives in the book? Who is Linda?
Understanding	to help the reader understand what the author is communicating about the characters, situation, conflict, etc.	What are the various relationships between O'Brien and the other characters in the book? How do the characters' feelings for one another change over the course of the book?
Applying	to help the reader use the text in a meaningful way, including connections to one's own life	What are the characters' feelings about the war? How does war affect human relationships?
Analyzing	to enhance the reader's understanding of the text, especially through the analysis of literary devices	What is the significance of the book's title? How does the author use the motif of storytelling in this book?
Evaluating	to critically examine the story, including the influences of the author's attitude and perspective	How does the author feel about the war? How do these feelings affect his book? How does the author communicate feelings of loneliness and isolation through his writing?
Creating	to create new knowledge about the author's intentions, the theme, or personal implications	What purpose does this book serve for the author and the reader? How has this story changed your thinking about the war and its implications?

Name: _____ **Date:** _____

Question Hierarchy

Directions: After reading the story, write at least one question for each category. Make sure your questions relate directly to the text and accomplish the goal of each category.

Text: _____

Question Type	Question Objective	Assessment Questions
Remembering	to help the reader remember the story's elements, such as characters, setting, and sequence of events	
Understanding	to help the reader understand what the author is communicating about the characters, situation, conflict, etc.	
Applying	to help the reader use the text in a meaningful way, including connections to one's own life	
Analyzing	to enhance the reader's understanding of the text, especially through the analysis of literary devices	
Evaluating	to critically examine the story, including the influences of the author's attitude and perspective	
Creating	to create new knowledge about the author's intentions, the theme, or personal implications	

Adapted from Doug Buehl's "Taxonomy Self-Questioning Chart for Literary Fiction" (Newark, DE: International Reading Association, 2009).

Summarizing Overview

The Challenge of Summarizing

Reading research indicates that summarizing is a skill that is difficult for students to learn (Duke and Pearson 2002), but it offers tremendous benefits to readers. Summarizing improves readers' abilities to locate the main ideas and supporting details, identify and omit unnecessary details and redundant material, remember what is read, analyze text structure and see how ideas are related, generalize details, clarify meaning, take notes, and rethink what they have read so that they can process it more deeply.

Summarizing is, to a certain extent, like a scientific process. When students summarize their reading, they distill large sections of text, extract the most essential information, and then create a coherent, more concise text that relates the same information as the original text. In order to effectively summarize, readers must be able to identify the main idea and differentiate important information from less important information in order to stress the most vital parts and minimize less relevant details.

When expert readers tackle a text, they stop periodically to summarize what they have read as a way to monitor their own comprehension and processing of the text. They mentally "put together" or reconstruct what they have read so far so that they can continue to process the text when they continue reading.

When summarizing, students pay much closer attention to what is read. They spend more time on reading and trying to understand what they are reading. This enables them to integrate ideas and generalize from the text information.

Condensing text so that the substance of a reading selection is in brief form is no easy task and often leads to artificial, awkward language and organization. Reading experts suggest that reading comprehension is further improved by revising summaries so that they sound more natural when read because students will remember the information better. Students remember revised summaries better because they are written in their own words. Reading research indicates that students are more successful at synthesizing information if they put the information in their own words. When students translate the ideas they have read into their own words, they can more easily retrieve that information to accomplish a learning task. Students must use their own words to form connections across the concepts and relate the concepts to their own prior knowledge and experiences.

> **How to Summarize**
>
> - Keep it brief
>
> - Hit the big ideas
>
> - Mention some important supporting details
>
>   (adapted from Hoyt 2002)

Summarizing Overview (cont.)

The Steps in Summarizing

Students need to remember three important elements to summarize effectively. Students must keep the information in their summaries brief, identify the most important ideas, and mention some supporting details. A synthesis of the steps provided by reading researchers (Duke and Pearson 2002) is as follows:

- Delete unnecessary material.

- Delete redundant material.

- Provide a name for categories or list of details.

- Identify and use the author's main ideas.

- Select or construct a topic sentence.

Instructing students to follow these steps when summarizing gives them a framework, exercises their metacognitive skills, and improves their overall ability to comprehend reading materials.

The Main Idea

One of the skills involved in summarizing and retelling is locating the main idea. In order to summarize, students must be able to identify the key concepts or chief topic of a passage, a paragraph, and a sentence. The main idea is the central thought, and because it seems so obvious to skilled readers, it can be overlooked as an important element when teaching students how to summarize. At times, the main topic of the passage is not directly stated but rather is implied. Therefore, students need instruction and practice in locating the main idea, as it is the one idea to which all other sentences in a passage relate.

Quick and Easy Main Idea Activities

The following activities are fast ways to highlight how to locate the main idea (Dechant 1991):

- Instruct students to identify the main idea of specific sentences by underlining key words.

    Example: Let's highlight the main features of the chapter.

- Ask students to locate the topic sentence or the key sentence that best identifies the main idea of a paragraph.

    Example: Which sentence best tells what the character was thinking?

- Have students write a title for a chapter in the book. Have students read a section of the story. Ask students to give the section of the story an appropriate title and then compare it to the actual title used for the chapter.

Summarizing Overview (cont.)

Summarizing vs. Retelling

Is retelling the same as summarizing? Teachers of emergent readers frequently ask students to retell what they have just read, but retelling is different from summarizing. Summarizing forces the reader to condense the information by omitting trivial information. Summarizing involves developing skills in deletion, inference, and making generalizations. Retelling does not involve reducing the text into a more brief statement. When students retell what they have read, they paraphrase information. To teach students how to summarize effectively, they should first build their retelling skills and then move on to condensing information while summarizing.

What the Research Says

The National Reading Panel (2000) analyzed 18 different studies on the direct instruction of summarizing in reading (Trabasso and Bouchard 2002) and revealed that summarization improves readers' comprehension of text. When students are taught how to create summaries, their ability to summarize improves and the quality of their summaries improves. Readers improve the quality of their summaries by identifying main ideas, omitting details, including ideas related to the main idea, generalizing, and removing redundancy. Teachers should train students to summarize automatically as they read so that they are consistently monitoring their comprehension of the text.

Summarizing Overview (cont.)

Standards Addressed

The following chart shows the correlating standards for each strategy in this section. Refer to the Digital Resource CD (standards.pdf) to read the correlating standards in their entirety.

Strategy	McREL Standards	Common Core State Standards
Read, Cover, Remember, Retell	Grades 1–2 (6.2, 6.3) Grades 3–5 (6.3, 6.5, 6.6) Grades 6–8 (6.3, 6.4, 6.9) Grades 9–12 (6.4, 6.6)	Grade 1 (RL.1.2, RL.1.10) Grade 2 (RL.2.2, RL.2.10) Grade 3 (RL.3.2, RL.3.10) Grade 4 (RL.4.2, RL.4.10) Grade 5 (RL.5.2, RL.5.10) Grade 6 (RL.6.2, RL.6.10) Grade 7 (RL.7.2, RL.7.10) Grade 8 (RL.8.2, RL.8.10) Grades 9–10 (RL.9-10.2, RL.9-10.10) Grades 11–12 (RL.11-12.2, RL.11-12.10)
Rank-Ordering Retell	Grades 1–2 (6.2, 6.3) Grades 3–5 (6.3, 6.5, 6.6) Grades 6–8 (6.3, 6.4, 6.9) Grades 9–12 (6.4, 6.6)	Grade 1 (RL.1.2, RL.1.10) Grade 2 (RL.2.2, RL.2.10) Grade 3 (RL.3.2, RL.3.10) Grade 4 (RL.4.2, RL.4.10) Grade 5 (RL.5.2, RL.5.10) Grade 6 (RL.6.2, RL.6.10) Grade 7 (RL.7.2, RL.7.10) Grade 8 (RL.8.2, RL.8.10) Grades 9–10 (RL.9-10.2, RL.9-10.10) Grades 11–12 (RL.11-12.2, RL.11-12.10)
Key Words	Grades 1–2 (6.3) Grades 3–5 (5.2, 6.6)	Grade 1 (RL.1.2, RL.1.10) Grade 2 (RL.2.2, RL.2.10) Grade 3 (RL.3.2, RL.3.10) Grade 4 (RL.4.2, RL.4.10) Grade 5 (RL.5.2, RL.5.10)
Very Important Points	Grades 1–2 (6.3) Grades 3–5 (5.2, 6.6) Grades 6–8 (5.1, 6.9) Grades 9–12 (6.6)	Grade 1 (RL.1.2, RL.1.10) Grade 2 (RL.2.2, RL.2.10) Grade 3 (RL.3.2, RL.3.10) Grade 4 (RL.4.2, RL.4.10) Grade 5 (RL.5.2, RL.5.10) Grade 6 (RL.6.2, RL.6.10) Grade 7 (RL.7.2, RL.7.10) Grade 8 (RL.8.2, RL.8.10) Grades 9–10 (RL.9-10.2, RL.9-10.10) Grades 11–12 (RL.11-12.2, RL.11-12.10)

Summarizing Overview (cont.)

Strategy	McREL Standards	Common Core State Standards
Guided Reading and Summarizing Procedure	Grades 3–5 (5.2, 6.6) Grades 6–8 (5.1, 6.9) Grades 9–12 (6.6)	Grade 3 (RL.3.1, RL.3.2, RL.3.10) Grade 4 (RL.4.1, RL.4.2, RL.4.10) Grade 5 (RL.5.1, RL.5.2, RL.5.10) Grade 6 (RL.6.1, RL.6.2, RL.6.10) Grade 7 (RL.7.1, RL.7.2, RL.7.10) Grade 8 (RL.8.1, RL.8.2, RL.8.10) Grades 9–10 (RL.9-10.1, RL.9-10.2, RL.9-10.10) Grades 11–12 (RL.11-12.1, RL.11-12.2, RL.11-12.10)
Jigsaw	Grades 3–5 (5.2, 6.3) Grades 6–8 (5.1, 6.3, 6.4) Grades 9–12 (6.3, 6.4)	Grade 3 (RL.3.2, RL.3.10) Grade 4 (RL.4.2, RL.4.10) Grade 5 (RL.5.2, RL.5.10) Grade 6 (RL.6.2, RL.6.10) Grade 7 (RL.7.2, RL.7.10) Grade 8 (RL.8.2, RL.8.10) Grades 9–10 (RL.9-10.2, RL.9-10.10) Grades 11–12 (RL.11-12.2, RL.11-12.10)
Chunking Text	Grades 3–5 (5.2, 6.3) Grades 6–8 (5.1, 6.3, 6.4) Grades 9–12 (6.3, 6.4)	Grade 3 (RL.3.2, RL.3.10) Grade 4 (RL.4.2, RL.4.10) Grade 5 (RL.5.2, RL.5.10) Grade 6 (RL.6.2, RL.6.10) Grade 7 (RL.7.2, RL.7.10) Grade 8 (RL.8.2, RL.8.10) Grades 9–10 (RL.9-10.2, RL.9-10.10) Grades 11–12 (RL.11-12.2, RL.11-12.10)
Determining the Theme	Grades 3–5 (5.2, 6.6) Grades 6–8 (5.1, 6.9) Grades 9–12 (6.6)	Grade 3 (RL.3.2, RL.3.10) Grade 4 (RL.4.2, RL.4.10) Grade 5 (RL.5.2, RL.5.10) Grade 6 (RL.6.2, RL.6.10) Grade 7 (RL.7.2, RL.7.10) Grade 8 (RL.8.2, RL.8.10) Grades 9–10 (RL.9-10.2, RL.9-10.10) Grades 11–12 (RL.11-12.2, RL.11-12.10)
SWBST	Grades 1–2 (6.2) Grades 3–5 (5.2, 6.3, 6.5)	Grade 1 (RL.1.2, RL.1.3, RL.1.10) Grade 2 (RL.2.2, RL.2.3, RL.2.10) Grade 3 (RL.3.2, RL.3.3, RL.3.10) Grade 4 (RL.4.2, RL.4.3, RL.4.10) Grade 5 (RL.5.2, RL.5.3, RL.5.10)

Read, Cover, Remember, Retell

Background Information

The Read, Cover, Remember, Retell activity (Hoyt 2002) is an effective approach to help readers who have trouble with reading comprehension because they think that good reading means reading quickly. The technique is modeled for students during a whole class instruction period, and then conducted with pairs of student working together to read the same text. First, one student silently reads a small portion of the text, about the size that he or she could cover with a hand. After reading, the student covers the text, turns to his or her partner, and tries to remember and retell an objective summary of the reading. If the student leaves out any important details, his or her partner can fill in the missing information. The partners then switch roles to read the next section. Gradually, students learn to use this strategy as they read independently.

Grade Levels/Standards Addressed

See page 186 for the standards this strategy addresses, or refer to the Digital Resource CD (standards.pdf) to read the correlating standards in their entirety.

Activity

Model the Read, Cover, Remember, Retell strategy by using the think-aloud technique. Pair students and assign a selection of text for them to read. Instruct one student to begin reading a small portion of the text silently, using the size of the hand to determine how much information to read. After reading, the student covers the text, turns to the partner, and tries to retell it using his or her own words. The partner should evaluate the quality of the retelling, making sure that it remains objective, and fill in any missing information. Students switch roles for the next section of reading. When partners have completed the reading, they can write a summary of the entire reading selection and share it with the class. Use an document camera to evaluate and elaborate on how the summaries can be more effective and concise.

Differentiation

It might help English language learners to have their partners read the section of text aloud to them rather than ask them to read it silently. Below-level students and above-level students should have a text that is appropriate for their levels.

Read, Cover, Remember, Retell

- Read only as much as your hand can cover.

- Cover the words with your hand.

- Remember what you have just read (it is okay to take another look).

- Retell what you have just read in your own words.

Read, Cover, Remember, Retell (cont.)

Grades 1–2 Example

Text: *Stellaluna* by Janell Cannon

Original Text:
Stellaluna learned to be like the birds. She stayed awake all day and slept at night. She ate bugs even though they tasted awful. Her bat ways were quickly disappearing. Except for one thing: Stellaluna still liked to sleep hanging by her feet (Cannon 11).
Student Retell:
Stellaluna stopped acting like a bat. She learned to act like a bird. But she still slept upside down.

Grades 3–5 Example

Text: *Harriet the Spy* by Louise Fitzhugh

Original Text:
Suddenly Harriet screeched in horror. "Where is my notebook?" They all began looking around, but they couldn't find it anywhere. Harriet suddenly remembered that some things had been knocked down before they ran away from the others. She began to run back toward them. She ran and ran, yelling like a banshee the whole way (Fitzhugh 179).
Student Retell:
Harriet is very alarmed when she notices her notebook is missing. She quickly runs back to the others to try to find it.

Grades 6–8 Example

Text: *A Separate Peace* by John Knowles

Original Text:
It seemed clear that wars were not made by generations and their special stupidities, but that wars were made instead by something ignorant in the human heart (Knowles 201).
Student Retell:
The root of all wars is human ignorance.

Grades 9–12 Example

Text: *The House on Mango Street* by Sandra Cisneros

Original Text:
I knew then I had to have a house. A real house. One I could point to. But this isn't it. The house on Mango Street isn't it. For the time being, Mama says. Temporary, says Papa. But I know how those things go (Cisneros 5).
Student Retell:
The narrator wants a real house that will make her proud. The house on Mango Street does not make her proud and she fears they will never live anywhere else.

Rank-Ordering Retell

Background Information

Students need to learn how to evaluate the information in a selection of fictional literature to determine the most important ideas, the moderately important ideas, and the less important ideas to summarize effectively what they have read. Rank-Ordering Retell (Hoyt 2002) assists students in learning to identify the main idea and key supporting details. In the activity, students write down phrases they consider to be important to the topic. These phrases should describe the content of the reading. Students must decide if the phrases can be categorized as the most important, moderately important, or least important concepts in the story. In small groups or as a whole class, students learn how to rank the importance of the information as they justify their placement of the phrases into the different categories. Key details, central messages, and important lessons from the text should always be classified as most important, while less important details and nonessential information should be placed in the moderately important or least important categories.

Grade Levels/Standards Addressed

See page 186 for the standards this strategy addresses, or refer to the Digital Resource CD (standards.pdf) to read the correlating standards in their entirety.

Activity

Distribute strips of paper. As students begin a reading selection, ask them to write down phrases they consider important to the topic. The phrases can be either taken directly from the reading or inferred by students, but all of the ideas should describe the information in the reading. Ask students to use the *Rank-Ordering Retell* activity sheet (page 192, rankordering.pdf) to begin evaluating and sorting the strips into three categories: most important, moderately important, and least important. Instruct them to work with the most important and least important ideas first, as this is the easiest way to evaluate the information. Have students justify their decision to write the phrases in the different categories. Ask students to identify which ideas would be the most helpful if they had to write a summary.

Differentiation

If the content of the reading is completely unfamiliar to English language learners, build their prior knowledge and vocabulary for the topic. Below-level students may have trouble identifying the phrases to sort, so scaffold the task by completing some of the strips for students. Above-level students can extend the activity by defending their answers.

Rank-Ordering Retell *(cont.)*

Grades 1–2 Example

Text: *Owen* by Kevin Henkes

Most important ideas: Owen loves his blanket. He does not want to give it up.
Moderately important ideas: Owen's neighbor thinks he is too old to have a special blanket.
Least important ideas: Owen takes the blanket with him to the dentist.

Grades 3–5 Example

Text: *Horrible Harry and the Ant Invasion* by Suzy Kline

Most important ideas: Harry loves ants and is disappointed when he loses his job as the classroom ant monitor.
Moderately important ideas: Harry thinks of an activity with ant words to impress his teacher and win his job back.
Least important ideas: Mrs. Foxworth, the secretary, is afraid of ants.

Grades 6–8 Example

Text: *The Giver* by Lois Lowry

Most important ideas: Jonas grows very attached to baby Gabriel and tries to save him from being released.
Moderately important ideas: Jonas is the only one in his community that can perceive flashes of color.
Least important ideas: The Giver also used to hear music, something Jonas never experienced.

Grades 9–12 Example

Text: *The Book Thief* by Markus Zusak

Most important ideas: Liesel uses books to help her survive World War II.
Moderately important ideas: Liesel befriends a Jewish refugee, Max, who lives secretly in the basement.
Least important ideas: Liesel never lets her friend, Rudy, kiss her.

Rank-Ordering Retell

Directions: On separate strips of paper, write down important phrases from the text. Then, sort the strips into the categories shown below.

Text: _____

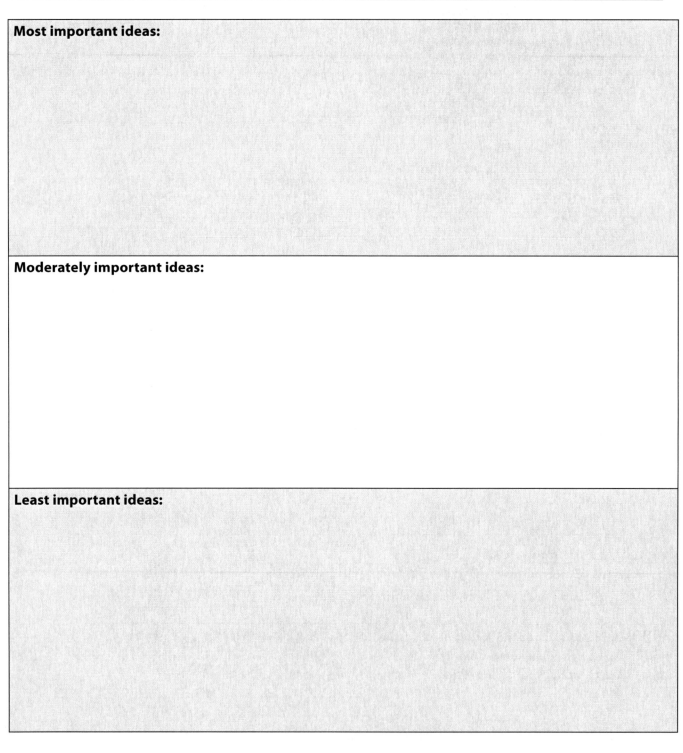

Most important ideas:

Moderately important ideas:

Least important ideas:

Key Words

Background Information

Key Words (Hoyt 2002) is a strategy designed to help younger students learn to summarize by identifying important concepts in small sections of text. In this strategy, students first have to read a short selection of text and then identify one word, the key word, that captures the most important idea or concept to summarize the selection. As students continue reading the selection, they generate a list of words that they can then use to create an overall summary of the text. The strategy is effective because it helps students locate the most important concepts, encourages them to use their own words to create a summary, and forces them to spend more time reading and processing the information than they would if they simply read the text. This introductory strategy is best used with younger students and shorter text selections.

Grade Levels/Standards Addressed

See page 186 for the standards this strategy addresses, or refer to the Digital Resource CD (standards.pdf) to read the correlating standards in their entirety.

Activity

Select a section of text for students to read that is fairly short. Distribute sticky notes, small sheets of paper, or notebook paper. Ask students to read the selection carefully (or conduct a read-aloud or choral reading with primary students) to locate the most important words to summarize the information. Instruct them to write down the most important words in the selection as they read. When students have finished, collect the words or ask students to share the words they selected with the entire class. Make a list of students' words. Discuss the value of each selection and ask students to explain and justify their choices to the class. Demonstrate how to construct an objective summary based on the words students have chosen. Show students how to combine important information, eliminate redundancies, and use their own words so that the summary sounds natural. Introduce the *Key Words* activity sheet (page 194, keywords.pdf) for students to use when constructing their summaries. When students understand the procedure, gradually release the responsibility to them by placing them in pairs to complete the task. With practice, students will use the strategy automatically as they process the text and summarize for clarification.

Differentiation

While English language learners may not struggle to identify the key words in a reading selection, they may struggle to incorporate the words into a cohesive, objective summary. Pair English language learners with other students to work together to create the summary. Below-level students may need the activity scaffolded for them. Select some key words for students when they are working independently so that they can focus their attention on locating other words. Above-level students should be given reading materials that are appropriate for their reading levels.

Name: _____ Date: _____

Key Words

Directions: After closely reading the text, use these transition words to construct your summary based on the important information you selected from the reading. Then, write your summary on a separate sheet of paper.

	Generalizing		
generally	generally speaking	usually	ordinarily
as a rule	as usual	for the most part	

	Adding Details		
also	besides	furthermore	in addition
moreover	again	in fact	for this reason
for example	for instance	and	next
finally	another	such as	

	Comparing and Contrasting		
in contrast	instead	likewise	on one hand
on the other hand	on the contrary	rather	similarly
yet	however	still	nevertheless
neither/nor	but	both	instead

	Sequencing		
at first	first of all	to begin with	in the first place
at the same time	for now	for the time being	the next step
next	in time	in turn	later on
meanwhile	then	soon	later
while	earlier	simultaneously	afterward
in the end	in conclusion		

Very Important Points

Background Information

Identifying the central message and the key details in a selection of reading is integral to summarizing. Students are often expected to summarize without receiving any explicit instruction on how to do so, yet teachers need to model how to gather information prior to writing a summary. In the Very Important Points (VIP) strategy (Hoyt 2002), students place sticky strips on the text to indicate the most important ideas. The tactile or kinesthetic action of placing strips of sticky notes onto the pages of the book increases student involvement and motivation. Students can also use the sticky strips to identify points of interest, points of confusion, key details, a place where the student makes a connection—whatever the teacher or students wish to focus on. Students then discuss the VIPs they select either with partners, in small groups, or as a whole class. They can use the VIPs to help them summarize the reading selection. Students also like the flexibility of the sticky strips. After discussion, they can change their minds and move the sticky strips if they wish, which boosts their confidence.

Grade Levels/Standards Addressed

See page 186 for the standards this strategy addresses, or refer to the Digital Resource CD (standards.pdf) to read the correlating standards in their entirety.

Activity

Select a section of fictional text for students to read. Determine in advance the number of VIPs each student can identify as he or she reads the selection. Distribute the set number of sticky strips (sticky notes that have been cut into thin strips of paper with a sticky end) to each student. Clearly establish the purpose for reading and explain to students what they will be looking for as they read (the most important ideas, unnecessary information, precise details, points of interest, points of confusion, a place that triggers a connection, etc.). Instruct students to place the sticky strips directly on the text. After reading, have students meet with partners or in small groups to discuss the VIPs they selected. Students should then explain and justify their choices and take notes. They may move their sticky strips, if they choose.

Differentiation

Give English language learners adequate time to prepare for defending their sticky strip placement. Below-level students will benefit from limiting the number of sticky strips assigned to them. Otherwise, they may use too many sticky strips. Above-level students should be asked to use the sticky strips for a more complex task, such as identifying moments that trigger a connection. Encourage them to explore the connections in greater depth.

Extension

To make the task more challenging, require students in the small groups to come to a consensus about the location of the sticky strips in a section. Ask students to justify their choices with evidence from the text.

Guided Reading and Summarizing Procedure

Background Information

Transforming the information provided in a reading selection by compressing it into a synopsis is a challenge for many students. The Guided Reading and Summarizing Procedure (Lenski, Wham, and Johns 1999) enables students to summarize independently as they record main ideas and key details, add additional information, correct their initial notes, and then use the information to create a concise summary. The strategy also helps to increase students' abilities to retell stories, self-correct, and organize information.

Grade Levels/Standards Addressed

See page 187 for the standards this strategy addresses, or refer to the Digital Resource CD (standards.pdf) to read the correlating standards in their entirety.

Activity

Provide a fictional text selection for students to read. Tell students that they are going to learn how to summarize what they have read. Explain when summarizing is a useful tool. Direct students to read the selection with the purpose of trying to remember as much as they can. After they have finished reading, ask them to tell you what they remember. List the items on the board or display them with a document camera. Instruct students to reread the selection to see if there is any other information that should be included on the list or any information that needs to be

corrected. Next, evaluate the list as a class to identify the central message of the passage and categorize the information on the list accordingly. Using the organizational structure created by categorizing the information, write a summary for each category of the material as a whole class to model the process for students. Instruct students to omit unnecessary information, combine as much information as possible, and add information to make the summary read naturally and coherently. Record the summary statements at the bottom of the chart. Ryder and Graves (2003) suggest that students and the teacher write the summary for the next category of information individually and compare and contrast students' summaries to that of the teacher. Ryder and Graves (2003) point out that Hayes (1989) suggests the teacher revise his or her summary based on students' alternatives and make a visible record of these changes so the revision process is more concrete for students. As students continue to summarize each category of information, model the revision process in great detail. When students learn how to conduct this strategy independently, they can use the *Guided Reading and Summarizing Procedure* activity sheet (page 200, guidedreadingsummarizing.pdf) to help them construct their objective summaries independently.

Differentiation

English language learners should have the text available to them during the "Details Remembered from Reading" stage of the activity. Below-level students may need someone to read the passage aloud, rephrase sections, and provide explanations. Both English language learners and below-level students should work with partners or in small groups to remember the information and construct the summary. Above-level students may not benefit from the instruction and modeling phase of the activity and can be encouraged to work independently.

Guided Reading and Summarizing Procedure *(cont.)*

Grades 3–5 Example

Text: *Stuart Little* by E. B. White

Details Remembered from Reading	Additions/Corrections
• Stuart has human parents. • Stuart's small size poses constant dangers for him. • Stuart saves Mrs. Little's ring that has fallen down the drain. • He also helps retrieve small objects, like balls, from under the furniture. • Stuart's father is concerned about the mouse hole in the kitchen and wonders if Stuart will ever want to go in it.	• Stuart also helps his family by lifting the sticky piano key. • The mouse hole existed in the house before the Little family moved in.

Main Ideas in Reading
Stuart is an unusual character who seems brave, independent, kind, and helpful. Mr. and Mrs. Little are concerned about the challenges related to having a very small mouse as a son.

Guided Reading and Summarizing Procedure (cont.)

Grades 6–8 Example

Text: *The True Confessions of Charlotte Doyle* by Avi

Details Remembered from Reading	Additions/Corrections
• The story takes place a long time ago. • Charlotte is a 13-year-old girl. • She is traveling from England to America to reunite with her family in Rhode Island. • Her father arranged for her to travel with two other families acting as her guardians. • The other families have children and she is eager to meet them. • She thinks that the journey will be a fun adventure. • Her father gives her a blank journal and instructs her to make daily entries about the voyage.	• The year is 1832. • Charlotte goes to boarding school in England and her parents want her to finish the school year before joining them in Providence.
Main Ideas in Reading	
Charlotte is a brave, but very naive, young girl who thinks her journey to America will be an exciting adventure.	

Guided Reading and Summarizing Procedure *(cont.)*

Grades 9–12 Example

Text: *Fahrenheit 451* by Ray Bradbury

Details Remembered from Reading	Additions/Corrections
• Montag is a firefighter in the future whose job it is to burn books. • Montag likes his job and the rush that comes with seeing things burn. • He always smells like kerosene and says it is his cologne. • Montag has a wife. • Montag meets a young girl, Clarisse, who enjoys doing things not permitted by society, like walking outside, hiking, catching butterflies, and having conversations. • Clarisse questions Montag about his job and his happiness. • Her questions rattle Montag and make him examine his life more critically.	• In their society, it is permitted to walk outside, but only for short amounts of time. • Clarisse and her family are considered strange because they enjoy things like walking and talking. • Clarisse's house is lit up very brightly at night.

Main Ideas in Reading

Until he meets Clarisse, Montag was content with his life.

Clarisse's questions make him assess his life and happiness more closely and he realizes he is actually not happy.

Name: _____ Date: _____

Guided Reading and Summarizing Procedure

Directions: After reading a selected text, write down what you remember in the top left section. Then, reread the text and write down any additional information in the top right section. Finally, evaluate the list and identify the main ideas and details to create an effective summary in the bottom section.

Details Remembered from Reading	Additions/Corrections

Main Ideas in Reading

Jigsaw

Background Information

The Jigsaw strategy, originally developed by Elliot Aronson (1978), is a cooperative learning technique that can be effectively used to teach summarizing skills in the classroom. When compared with students taught by teacher-led approaches and even other cooperative learning methods, research indicates that students using the Jigsaw strategy outperform other students on assessments of reading comprehension (Law 2011). When using the Jigsaw strategy to teach summarizing skills, the teacher assigns different sections of text to small groups of students, and these students work together to read and summarize the information in their assigned text. Next, the teacher forms new groups, being sure that one student representative from the original grouping is included in the new groupings to inform the new group of his or her assigned section, and students take turns teaching the other students in the group the information they initially read and summarized. By using this strategy, students learn to concentrate on the important information and key details from their section of the text so that later they can teach it to their peers. At the completion of the activity, students review the group summaries and collaborate to create an overall summary of the text.

Grade Levels/Standards Addressed

See page 187 for the standards this strategy addresses, or refer to the Digital Resource CD (standards.pdf) to read the correlating standards in their entirety.

Activity

Before beginning the lesson, divide the text into five sections. Separate students into five groups. Give each group a different section to read. Ask students to independently read and summarize the information in the text. Once all the group members have had a chance to read and summarize the text, have students discuss the summaries in their groups and allow them time to revise their summaries so that they reflect the most important information in the text. Have them write their final summaries in the appropriate section on the *Jigsaw* activity sheet (page 202, jigsaw.pdf). Next, regroup students so that one person from each of the original groups is in each new group and that all sections of the text are represented in each group. Ask each member in the new group to teach the other students the information from his or her original text summary. Start with the student that initially read the first section, then proceed to the second section, and so forth. Have the other students take notes on their activity sheets in the appropriate section. After each group member has presented the information from his or her text section, students work together as a group to develop an overall summary of the entire text. The groups share their overall summaries with the class and the teacher reviews the most important points, central messages, and significant themes.

Differentiation

Provide English language learners and below-level students with their text selection the night before so that they have a chance to thoroughly read and comprehend the text before summarizing it for their peers. It may be helpful to read the text sections aloud to below-level students. Both English language learners and below-level students will benefit from the heterogeneous groups used in this strategy. Ask above-level students to demonstrate their thought processes for summarization through think-alouds to help the other students in their groups.

Name: _____ **Date:** _____

Jigsaw

Directions: Read your text selection and record a summary in the appropriate piece of the puzzle. Use the other puzzle pieces to record summaries of the other text sections as your classmates present them. After the pieces are filled, use your summary notes from each text selection to write an overall text summary in the box below.

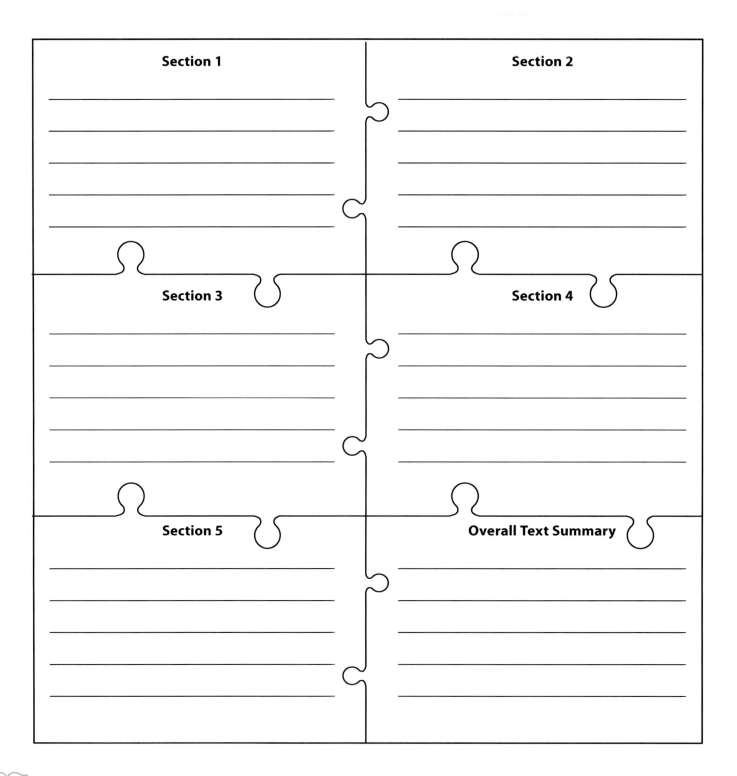

Section 1

Section 2

Section 3

Section 4

Section 5

Overall Text Summary

Chunking Text

Background Information

Research on the strategy of "chunking" text, or breaking the text up into smaller, more manageable sections, indicates that chunking helps improve reading comprehension for a wide range of students, especially below-level students (Casteel 1990). The Chunking Text strategy makes the task of reading less intimidating for struggling readers and also enhances students' ability to identify the exact point of comprehension breakdown during reading. By introducing the skill of summarization into the chunking technique, students learn to review and summarize their learning at predetermined breaks in the text. This strategy asks students to record a short summary for each section of the text and then use these notes to create an overall summary of the entire text selection at the end of the reading. While advanced readers may naturally summarize chunks of text as they read, most readers need to be explicitly taught this strategy in order to improve summarization skills and reading comprehension. This strategy works best for older students tasked with summarizing longer text selections.

Grade Levels/Standards Addressed

See page 187 for the standards this strategy addresses, or refer to the Digital Resource CD (standards.pdf) to read the correlating standards in their entirety.

Activity

Before assigning a fictional text selection for students to read, divide the text into four logical chunks, and clearly delineate these chunks by highlighting, drawing, or using sticky notes to show the beginning and ending of each chunk. Photocopy the text selection and distribute it to students. Then, distribute the *Chunking Text* activity sheet (page 206, chunkingtext.pdf) to students and also display it for students using a document camera. As students follow along, read the first chunk of text aloud, and ask students to summarize the text in the appropriate box on the activity sheet. Encourage students to limit their summaries to one or two sentences per chunk. Discuss students' summaries of the first chunk, reminding them that a summary should be very succinct and only include central ideas, not small details. Record and display a class summary of the first chunk using a document camera. Have students read the rest of the reading selection independently, making sure to stop after each chunk to write a summary. Once students have finished reading and recording, invite them to share their summaries with the rest of the class and discuss and record the summaries for each chunk of text on the class chart. Then, allow students to work with partners or in small groups to use the chunk summaries to create an overall summary of the text. Caution students that the overall summary should not include all of the information from the chunk summaries; they must work together to determine the most important information from these summaries and exclude less relevant details.

Chunking Text *(cont.)*

Differentiation

English language learners and below-level students will benefit from extra time to read and comprehend the text. Make sure that English language learners are familiar with the text's vocabulary, and pre-teach challenging words before the lesson, if possible. During the last phase of the activity, pair struggling readers with more proficient readers and allow them to work together to determine an overall summary of the text. Challenge above-level students by putting word limits on their summary statements. For example, set a limit of 20 words for every chunk summary and 30 words for the overall summary statement. These word limits will encourage above-level students to focus exclusively on the most important information in the text and to critically analyze their work in order to reduce the number of words in each summary.

Grades 3–5 Example

Text: *Superfudge* by Judy Blume, Chapter 1

Chunk 1	Chunk 2
Peter's parents tell him that they are going to have a baby and he is unhappy because he thinks that baby will be just like Fudge, his annoying little brother.	Peter packs a bag so he can run away from home, but his parents talk him into staying until he finishes his dinner.

Chunk 3	Chunk 4
Fudge annoys Peter during dinner by tattling on him and showing off. This reinforces Peter's fear of the baby being like Fudge.	Peter announces that he is running away and Fudge hysterically pleads with him to stay. Peter decides to stay, at least until he can meet the baby.

Overall Summary

Peter gets the surprising news that his parents are going to have a baby and he immediately fears that the baby will be like his annoying younger brother, Fudge. Peter threatens to run away, but eventually he relents and agrees that he will not run away until he can meet the baby.

Chunking Text (cont.)

Grades 6–8 Example

Text: *Little Women* by Louisa May Alcott, Chapter 3

Chunk 1	Chunk 2
Meg excitedly tells Jo that they have been invited to a New Year's Eve party. Jo reluctantly agrees to go.	The girls get ready for the party, but are plagued by problems, including stained gloves, a burned dress and shoes that are too tight. Meg creates a signal system so she can inform Jo if Jo is doing something improper during the party.

Chunk 3	Chunk 4
Jo hides behind a curtain at the party and befriends a boy, Laurie. The two chat and dance together privately.	Meg sprains her ankle and Laurie offers to bring the sisters home in his carriage.

Overall Summary

Jo reluctantly agrees to accompany Meg to a party and, while at the party, Jo befriends Laurie. Meg sprains her ankle and Laurie gives the two sisters a ride home in his carriage.

Grades 9–12 Example

Text: *The Grapes of Wrath* by John Steinbeck, Chapter 2

Chunk 1	Chunk 2
Tom Joad is on his way to his father's farm after being recently released from prison. He hitches a ride with a trucker and the trucker asks Tom about himself.	The trucker tells Tom how the poor farmers are being driven from their farms by landowners and banks.

Chunk 3	Chunk 4
The truck driver worries that he has offended Tom with his questions and he admits that his trucking lifestyle leaves him very lonely.	Tom tells the trucker that he was just released from prison and the trucker assures him that the news does not bother him. Tom gets out of the truck at the road leading to the Joad's farm.

Overall Summary

After being released from prison, Tom hitches a ride to his father's farm with a trucker. The trucker updates Tom on the dire circumstances facing poor farmers in the area and Tom admits his criminal past to the trucker.

Chunking Text

Directions: Carefully read the selected text one chunk at a time. After reading each chunk, stop and summarize the main points in the boxes below. After you have completed the reading, use the chunk summaries to write an overall summary of the text including only the most important information from the story.

Text: _____

Chunk 1	**Chunk 2**
_____	_____
_____	_____
_____	_____
_____	_____
_____	_____

Chunk 3	**Chunk 4**
_____	_____
_____	_____
_____	_____
_____	_____
_____	_____

Overall Summary

_____
_____
_____
_____
_____
_____

Determining the Theme

Background Information

One of the most difficult summarizing skills for students is identifying and describing literary themes in a fictional narrative. In order to develop an effective summary of a literary text, students must accurately recognize the important elements of the story while discarding the superfluous details. However, the skill of determining the theme of a text requires students to take their comprehension to the next level by examining these main ideas and deciphering the hidden message that the author wants to impart to the reader. The Determining the Theme strategy helps students grasp the complex concept of literary theme and teaches them how to identify themes in fictional literature.

Grade Levels/Standards Addressed

See page 187 for the standards this strategy addresses, or refer to the Digital Resource CD (standards.pdf) to read the correlating standards in their entirety.

Activity

To begin the lesson, explain that the theme of a story is the central message, lesson, or moral that the author wants the reader to take away after reading the text. Discuss the differences between a story's plot, main idea, and theme. Next, explain that in order to determine the theme of a story, they must first examine the characters' thoughts and actions to identify the main idea of the story.

Once they understand the main idea, students need to analyze this idea in conjunction with the characters' thoughts and actions in order to figure out the author's message, or theme, of the story. Be sure to mention that some stories have multiple main ideas and themes, but for this activity, students should focus on just one central theme.

Choose a well known fairy tale or fable with an obvious theme such as the *The Little Red Hen* to use as an example. Display the *Determining the Theme* activity sheet (page 210, determiningtheme.pdf) using a document camera. Read the story aloud, discuss the characters' thoughts and actions, agree on the main idea of the story (work ethic), and work together as a class to identify the theme of the story (hard work will be rewarded). Record each step of the process on the class activity sheet.

Once students comprehend the concept of theme and the process used to determine it, provide them with a different fictional text selection, and ask them to read it independently to complete their own *Determining the Theme* activity sheet. If some students are struggling to grasp the concept, you may want to complete the last step, determining the theme from the main idea, as a whole class. Make sure to discuss the story's theme at the end of the activity and review the steps used to determine it so students begin to internalize the process.

Differentiation

Due to the challenging nature of the concept, consider using different texts for each readiness level. For English language learners, use a text with familiar vocabulary so they will be able to put all of their effort toward learning about the theme rather than comprehension of language. Below-level students will benefit from a text appropriate for their reading level. Try to assess story comprehension before beginning the theme activity in order to assure that everyone understands the basics of the story. Above-level students should be encouraged to use a more challenging text with more complex themes.

Determining the Theme (cont.)

Grades 3–5 Example

Text: "The Town Mouse and the Country Mouse" in *Aesop's Fables* by Aesop

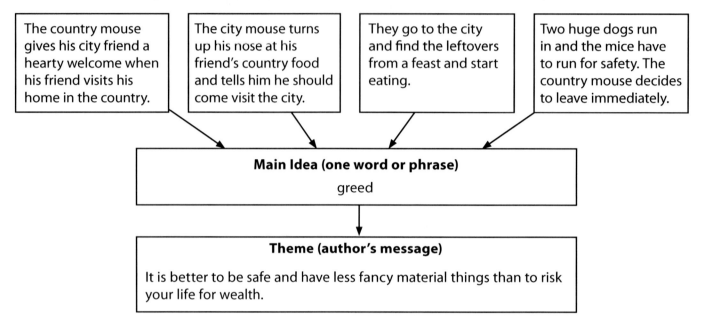

Characters' Thoughts and Actions
(describe what the characters think or do to illustrate main idea)

The country mouse gives his city friend a hearty welcome when his friend visits his home in the country.	The city mouse turns up his nose at his friend's country food and tells him he should come visit the city.	They go to the city and find the leftovers from a feast and start eating.	Two huge dogs run in and the mice have to run for safety. The country mouse decides to leave immediately.

Main Idea (one word or phrase)

greed

Theme (author's message)

It is better to be safe and have less fancy material things than to risk your life for wealth.

Grades 6–8 Example

Text: "The Emperor's New Clothes" in *Hans Andersen's Fairy Tales* by Hans Christian Andersen

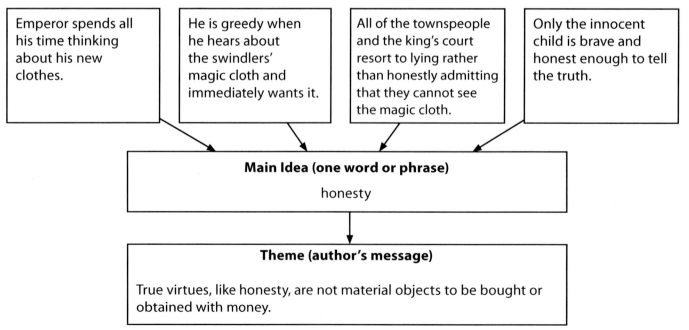

Characters' Thoughts and Actions
(describe what the characters think or do to illustrate main idea)

Emperor spends all his time thinking about his new clothes.	He is greedy when he hears about the swindlers' magic cloth and immediately wants it.	All of the townspeople and the king's court resort to lying rather than honestly admitting that they cannot see the magic cloth.	Only the innocent child is brave and honest enough to tell the truth.

Main Idea (one word or phrase)

honesty

Theme (author's message)

True virtues, like honesty, are not material objects to be bought or obtained with money.

Determining the Theme *(cont.)*

Grades 9–12 Example

Text: *Wuthering Heights* by Emily Brontë

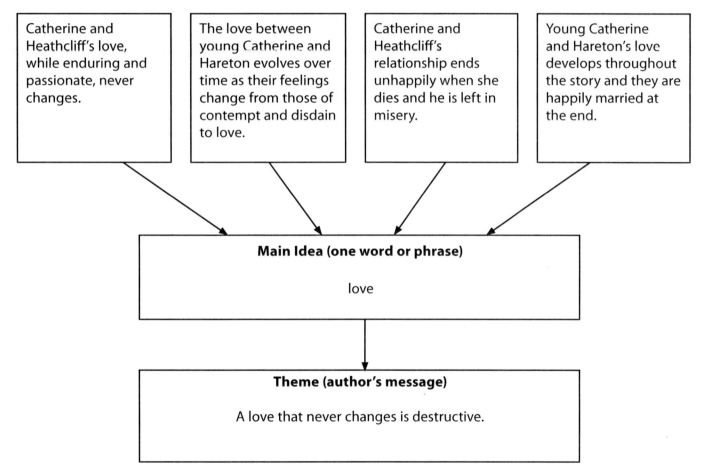

Characters' Thoughts and Actions
(describe what the characters think or do to illustrate the main idea)

Catherine and Heathcliff's love, while enduring and passionate, never changes.	The love between young Catherine and Hareton evolves over time as their feelings change from those of contempt and disdain to love.	Catherine and Heathcliff's relationship ends unhappily when she dies and he is left in misery.	Young Catherine and Hareton's love develops throughout the story and they are happily married at the end.

Main Idea (one word or phrase)

love

Theme (author's message)

A love that never changes is destructive.

Name: _____ **Date:** _____

Determining the Theme

Text:

Characters' Thoughts and Actions
(describe what the characters think or do to illustrate main idea)

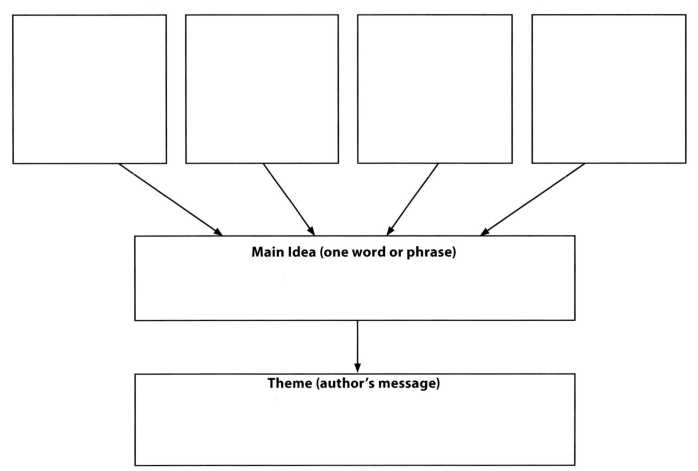

Main Idea (one word or phrase)

Theme (author's message)

SWBST

Background Information

In order to create an accurate summary of a fictional narrative, students must examine the characters in the story and analyze how these characters' actions affect the central conflict in the story. The SWBST strategy is an acronym (Somebody, Wanted, But, So, Then) that helps students remember the critical elements of a story, and enables them to write objective summaries by reviewing and condensing these important elements. This strategy can be used to summarize a story at the end of reading, to record notes for a book report, or even to informally assess students' reading comprehension (Lesesne 2006).

Grade Levels/Standards Addressed

See page 187 for the standards this strategy addresses, or refer to the Digital Resource CD (standards.pdf) to read the correlating standards in their entirety.

Activity

Before reading the text selection, remind students that characters and plot are essential components of a fictional narrative. In a fictional story, the characters interact to resolve or overcome the central conflict. Display the SWBST activity sheet (page 214, swbst.pdf) with a document camera or re-create it on the board. Explain that this strategy is a tool students can use to recall important aspects and key details of a story. Explain how each letter in the acronym SWBST represents an element of the story: S is for "somebody," the W is for "wanted," the B is for "but," the S is for "so," and the T is for "then." Tell students that you are going to read a short story passage aloud and they will work together as a class to complete the SWBST activity sheet. Select a simple text with characters and plot elements that are easy to identify to use to model the strategy. Read the text aloud, stopping periodically to prompt students to identify elements in the story that relate to the components of the acronym. Record these elements and continue to display the activity sheet for the class as you model the process. At the end of the story, review the diagram and complete any missing information. Then, divide students into small groups, and ask them to use the information on the activity sheet to develop an overall summary of the text. Once students comprehend how to use this strategy, distribute a different text and ask them to read it independently—or read it aloud to them—and have them work together to complete their own SWBST activity sheet. Discuss students' diagrams and summaries as a class, and allow them to make additions and corrections where necessary.

Differentiation

Before beginning the lesson, review important literary vocabulary with English language learners in your class. Make sure to include words such as *character*, *plot*, and *conflict* so that they will have a good understanding of the concepts on the SWBST activity sheet. Below-level students need to have a clear understanding of the text before they begin to identify its elements. Provide them with the text the night before so they will have adequate time to read and understand it before beginning the activity. Challenge above-level students to go beyond the elements on the diagram in order to describe the relationships between the characters' actions and the major events and challenges in the story.

SWBST *(cont.)*

Grades 1–2 Example

Text: *The Sneetches* by Dr. Seuss

Somebody	**Describe the characters in the story:** There are Star-Belly Sneetches. There are also Plain-Belly Sneetches.
Wanted	**Describe the characters' goals or desires:** The Plain-Belly Sneetches want stars for their bellies. Then, the Star-Belly Sneetches will not be mean to them anymore.
But	**Describe the conflict or problem in the story:** Sylvester has a machine that can add and remove stars from bellies. The Plain-Belly Sneetches pay Sylvester to add stars. The Star-Belly Sneetches get their stars removed. They want to be different.
So	**Describe what the characters do to overcome or resolve the conflict:** The Sneetches use up all their money. Sylvester leaves. They decide to be nice to all Sneetches. Stars on bellies don't matter.
Then	**Describe the resolution of the story:** The Sneetches become friends and agree to forget about the presence or absence of stars on their bellies.

Story Summary:
The Plain-Belly Sneetches want stars on their bellies. They want to be like the Star-Belly Sneetches. Sylvester has a machine that adds and removes belly stars. The Plain-Belly Sneetches pay to add stars. So, the Star-Belly Sneetches have their stars removed. They wanted to be different. But the Sneetches use up all their money. So Sylvester leaves. But the Sneetches learn to be friends. A star on the belly does not make you better. And no star on the belly does not make you better, either.

SWBST *(cont.)*

Grades 3–5 Example

Text: "The Letter" in *Frog and Toad Are Friends* by Arnold Lobel

Somebody	**Describe the characters in the story:** There is Frog and Toad.
Wanted	**Describe the characters' goals or desires:** Frog wants Toad to be happy.
But	**Describe the conflict or problem in the story:** Toad is unhappy because he waits for the mail every day, but he never receives any letters.
So	**Describe what the characters do to overcome or resolve the conflict:** Frog runs home, writes a letter to Toad, and asks his friend, Snail, to deliver the letter to Toad.
Then	**Describe the resolution of the story:** Frog tells Toad that he will definitely receive a letter soon because Frog wrote him one. Frog and Toad happily wait together for the mail to arrive.

Story Summary:

The characters in this story are two friends, Frog and Toad. Frog wants Toad to be happy, but Toad is very unhappy because he never receives any mail, even though he waits for it every day. Frog runs home, writes a letter to Toad and asks his friend, Snail, to deliver it to Toad. Frog tells Toad that he wrote him a letter. Frog and Toad wait happily together until the letter arrives.

Name: _____ **Date:** _____

SWBST

Directions: After reading the story, complete each box with the relevant information from the text. At the end, combine the information to develop an overall summary of the story.

Text: _____

Somebody	**Describe the characters in the story:** _____ _____ _____
Wanted	**Describe the characters' goals or desires:** _____ _____ _____
But	**Describe the conflict or problem in the story:** _____ _____ _____
So	**Describe what the characters do to overcome or resolve the conflict:** _____ _____ _____
Then	**Describe the resolution of the story:** _____ _____ _____
Story Summary: _____ _____ _____ _____	

© Shell Education

Using Visual Representations and Mental Imagery Overview

Teaching Visual Representation

There are three aspects to how visual representations of text are involved in reading comprehension. Teaching visual representations of text can be accomplished by direct instruction of how to construct mental images during reading. Teaching students to create pictures in their minds as they read improves their reading comprehension. Another aspect involves teaching students how to read, evaluate, and construct the visual material that accompanies informational text. In addition, visual representations of text can take the form of flow charts, mind maps, concept maps, Venn diagrams, etc. One method for students to process reading materials is through the assistance of accompanying graphic organizers. This section focuses on how to use mental imagery to improve reading comprehension, but it also addresses teaching students how to evaluate and create visual materials.

Mental Imagery

The ability to create mental images while reading is called visualization. When readers visualize what they have read in mental images, they create a framework for organizing and remembering the text (Gambrell and Koskinen 2002). In this framework, key images work as triggers for memory storage and retrieval. Several research studies on mental imagery construction demonstrate that the strategy increases readers' memory for text that they imaged and improves their identification of inconsistencies in the reading material (Gambrell and Koskinen 2002). These studies show that mental imagery is integral to improving listening and reading comprehension.

Active Processing

Recent researchers have determined that when students make mental images, they engage in an active information-handling process (Gambrell and Koskinen 2002). Engaging in the text through mental imagery promotes the active processing of the text because the reader must construct meaningful images that link prior knowledge with the information in the text. Researchers are not exactly sure why visualization works as a reading comprehension strategy, but they speculate that when readers construct mental images, they are processing both visual images and print. This causes the reader to put forth greater effort and results in the reader processing the text in much greater depth. As a result of using mental imagery, readers increase their ability to actively integrate the information they learn from the text into their memory. Therefore, using mental images to comprehend text promotes more involved, active processing in readers.

Using Visual Representations and Mental Imagery Overview *(cont.)*

Some Benefits of Visualization

Some of the reasons to teach students to evoke mental images while reading are as follows (Keene and Zimmerman 1997):

- In order to create mental images, students must use all five senses and their emotions, which are linked to their prior knowledge.

- Creating images immerses students in a wealth of rich details. The details are compelling, memorable, and make the text leave a stronger impression.

- Readers who adapt their mental images in response to other readers' mental images are considered more proficient.

Other Benefits of Imagery

Mental imagery can facilitate students in their writing. Creating mental images when reading, developing ideas, and working out details promotes reflection and contemplation. More reflection and contemplation by the writer results in better writing.

Imagery construction also promotes inference skills. Students must infer information provided in their reading as well as in the images they construct or that they view. When students are skilled at using inference as a reading comprehension strategy, they are more strategic readers.

While there is no real evidence to establish that using imagery enhances motivation to read, Linda Gambrell and Patricia Koskinen (2002) suggest that imagery positively affects motivation. They cite a study by Long, Winograd, and Bridge (1989) that found the strength of the images (vividness) was related to reading interest.

Comprehension Monitoring

Using mental imagery also helps readers monitor their comprehension. Gambrell and Koskinen (2002) cite an earlier study by Gambrell and Bales (1986) in which the evidence demonstrated that students who were encouraged to construct mental images while reading performed significantly better at the comprehension-monitoring task than those who did not. Imagery is considered a particularly effective strategy for poor readers because producing images helps them process the text with greater depth.

Using Visual Representations and Mental Imagery Overview *(cont.)*

Steps to Build Imagery Competence and Confidence in Students

Teachers can engage in the following sequence of activities with students to build their skills and confidence in imagery construction (Gambrell and Koskinen 2002):

1. Provide opportunities for students to create images of concrete objects. Have students read a section of the story and close their eyes and form a mental picture of it. Encourage students to compare and contrast their mental images with what others imagined.

2. Provide opportunities for guided imagery of concrete objects. For example, have students make a mental picture of a golden ring. Teachers should provide a guided imagery by refining the picture. *The ring of power has a mysterious written script on it, carefully crafted in Mordor; and it chooses who would be its next possessor.*

3. Encourage students to imagine pictures in their minds and recall familiar objects or scenes. Teachers might ask students to create mental images of a scene from a novel they are reading and then section something familiar around them where that scene could take place. They can later see the movie of the novel and compare and contrast the scenes they imagined with what the movie producer imagined.

4. Provide guided instruction to support students in making images of events and actions. Teachers may begin by asking students to imagine a concrete object (e.g., a ring), but then expand the guided imagery to include movement and action. *See the shiny ring on the ground and pick it up to examine it closely. In a strange way, it begs you to put in on your finger. As soon as you slip the cold ring on, your world turns into a dream.*

5. Develop the use of imagery in listening situations. Have students listen to vivid imagery narratives from various stories. When students read text with illustrations, encourage them to focus on the illustrations and to use them to help make their own images of the events and actions in the stories. For example, when teachers read sections of novels to students, they can conduct a guided imagery of the situations which the characters witnessed.

6. Provide instructions to students to create their own mental images as they read. When students read stories with illustrations, encourage them to focus on the illustrations and to use them to make their own images of the information in the text. Specific instructions can be helpful. *Draw a mental image of the ring of power. What props are in your image that contribute and tell about this special ring and what sets it apart from other rings? Does it glow or give off a vibration? How does it call to and control Bilbo Baggins?*

Using Visual Representations and Mental Imagery Overview (cont.)

Teaching Students to Create Mental Images

Not all teachers feel comfortable with teaching imagery as a comprehension strategy. The skills involved in creating and instructing with the Guided Imagery activity, for example, involve a great deal of creativity. In addition, students may not have engaged in any image-constructing activities in their schooling and may feel somewhat inhibited at first. However, the strategy is extremely effective with students because it helps them to "see" in their mind's eye what it is that they are reading. Once they have mastered the strategy, it becomes second nature. Developing mental image construction skills in students can make reading as natural as watching a movie.

Teachers must model mental image construction for students and provide detailed explanations about generating mental images. The most effective technique to do this is through the Think-Aloud strategy. Teachers verbalize their thoughts about how they construct and use imagery while reading a passage aloud to students. As students become more comfortable with their teacher's imagery, they are encouraged to expand on the teacher's images. Gradually, students are invited to share their own images, and when ready, they are guided to expand on their own images.

The key to developing this skill, as with other reading strategies, is to provide the students with many opportunities to share their images. Teachers and students can help each other to better describe their images. And because mental images are visual representations of words and ideas, it is important to allow students to draw and illustrate their own mental pictures of their reading materials. Sharing their own drawings, explaining them, defending their choices, and comparing them to other illustrations allows for greater understanding of the content in the text.

Some Tips for Using Imagery

Gambrell and Koskinen (2002) suggest the following general guidelines for using imagery:

- Remind students that everyone's images are unique. Students should be encouraged to accept and respect different perspectives. Their prior experience will determine what images they create.

- Encourage students to use the clues in the reading and their background knowledge to form appropriate images to help them understand what they are reading. There are no right or wrong answers when creating images, but students must rely on inference and prior knowledge to be on the right track.

- Use read alouds so students can create images as they listen. Gradually release the responsibility to the students so they can picture the content of the reading in their minds when they read independently.

Using Visual Representations and Mental Imagery Overview (cont.)

How Imagery Is Linked to Visuals

Some of the most important features included in many works of historical fiction and fiction-based literature are visual representations. Photographs, illustrations, drawings, flowcharts, diagrams, graphs, and maps are common in informational texts today because they capture the attention of the reader. Examining visuals is an important skill to develop because the visuals contain so much information. For example, *The Magic School Bus* series by Joanna Cole provides readers with many text clues outside of the written text. Struggling readers need the information provided by visuals to assist them as they decode the text. If instructed to do so, they can learn how to use clues from the visuals to help them to better understand what they are reading. Furthermore, reading researchers have determined that readers who are able to combine their ability to generate mental imagery with attending to illustrations provided in a text better understand what they are reading (Gambrell and Jawitz 1993).

Hoyt (2002) suggests that students should be instructed to analyze visuals that accompany informational text. They should be able to examine the size of photographs, the placement on the page, the caption or title, etc. In essence, it is useful to teach students the elements of layout so that they can develop an awareness of how the layout contributes to the overall reading experience and their ability to comprehend the text.

It is important to heighten the reader's awareness of the visuals because "they make the information come alive" (Hoyt 2002, 136). Teachers bring the visuals into focus for the students so that they can better understand how visuals support the text, how the visuals affect the reader, etc. As Hoyt (2002) points out, many students, particularly those who are not proficient readers, have a tendency to ignore the pictures and diagrams that accompany the text. The task of reading is so arduous for them that they cannot waste time looking at the visuals when they read. These visuals are present to make the job of reading easier for them, so teachers must use visual representations in text as a reading comprehension strategy in the language arts classroom.

Quick and Easy Activities with Visuals:

- Provide students with a variety of visuals that could possibly accompany the reading. Ask them to invent the captions for the visuals. In doing so, the students will synthesize and summarize key concepts and main ideas in a highly condensed form.

- Provide students with stories with no accompanying visuals, and ask them to invent the visuals for the story.

- Have students create comic strips about the content of the reading. Have them work together to explain information in a sequence. Adding humor helps students to engage in the activity.

- Introduce new concepts with a picture book. Picture books help activate prior knowledge before reading and prepare students' schema for adding new information.

Using Visual Representations and Mental Imagery Overview (cont.)

Standards Addressed

The following chart shows the correlating standards for each strategy in this section. Refer to the Digital Resource CD (standards.pdf) to read the correlating standards in their entirety.

Strategy	McREL Standards	Common Core State Standards
Guided Imagery	Grades 1–2 (5.1) Grades 3–5 (5.2) Grades 6–8 (5.2) Grades 9–12 (5.1)	Grade 1 (RL.1.10, SL.1.4) Grade 2 (RL.2.10, SL.2.4) Grade 3 (RL.3.10, SL.3.4) Grade 4 (RL.4.10, SL.4.4) Grade 5 (RL.5.10, SL.5.4) Grade 6 (RL.6.10, SL.6.4) Grade 7 (RL.7.10, SL.7.4) Grade 8 (RL.8.10, SL.8.4) Grades 9–10 (RL.9-10.10, SL.9-10.4) Grades 11–12 (RL.11-12.10, SL.11-12.4)
Talking Drawings	Grades 1–2 (5.1, 6.4) Grades 3–5 (6.8)	Grade 1 (RL.1.7, RL.1.10) Grade 2 (RL.2.7, RL.2.10) Grade 3 (RL.3.7, RL.3.10) Grade 4 (RL.4.7, RL.4.10) Grade 5 (RL.5.7, RL.5.10)
Imagine, Elaborate, Predict, and Confirm	Grades 1–2 (5.2) Grades 3–5 (5.3) Grades 6–8 (5.1) Grades 9–12 (5.2)	Grade 1 (RL.1.10) Grade 2 (RL.2.10) Grade 3 (RL.3.10) Grade 4 (RL.4.10) Grade 5 (RL.5.10) Grade 6 (RL.6.10) Grade 7 (RL.7.10) Grade 8 (RL.8.10) Grades 9–10 (RL.9-10.10) Grades 11–12 (RL.11-12.10)

Using Visual Representations and Mental Imagery Overview (cont.)

Strategy	McREL Standards	Common Core State Standards
Examining Visuals	Grades 1–2 (9.1) Grades 3–5 (9.1) Grades 6–8 (9.1) Grades 9–12 (9.1)	Grade 1 (RL.1.7, RL.1.10) Grade 2 (RL.2.7, RL.2.10) Grade 3 (RL.3.7, RL.3.10) Grade 4 (RL.4.7, RL.4.10) Grade 5 (RL.5.7, RL.5.10) Grade 6 (RL.6.7, RL.6.10) Grade 7 (RL.7.7, RL.7.10) Grade 8 (RL.8.7, RL.8.10) Grades 9–10 (RL.9-10.7, RL.9-10.10) Grades 11–12 (RL.11-12.7, RL.11-12.10)
Plot Sequencing	Grades 1–2 (6.2) Grades 3–5 (6.3) Grades 6–8 (6.3)	Grade 1 (RL.1.2, RL.1.3, RL.1.10) Grade 2 (RL.2.2, RL.2.3, RL.2.10) Grade 3 (RL.3.2, RL.3.3, RL.3.10) Grade 4 (RL.4.2, RL.4.3, RL.4.10) Grade 5 (RL.5.2, RL.5.3, RL.5.10) Grade 6 (RL.6.2, RL.6.3, RL.6.10) Grade 7 (RL.7.2, RL.7.3, RL.7.10) Grade 8 (RL.8.2, RL.8.3, RL.8.10)
Character Portrait	Grades 1–2 (6.2) Grades 3–5 (5.2, 6.5) Grades 6–8 (5.1, 6.4) Grades 9–12 (6.4)	Grade 1 (RL.1.3, RL.1.10) Grade 2 (RL.2.3, RL.2.10) Grade 3 (RL.3.3, RL.3.10) Grade 4 (RL.4.3, RL.4.10) Grade 5 (RL.5.3, RL.5.10) Grade 6 (RL.6.3, RL.6.10) Grade 7 (RL.7.3, RL.7.10) Grade 8 (RL.8.3, RL.8.10) Grades 9–10 (RL.9-10.3, RL.9-10.10) Grades 11–12 (RL.11-12.3, RL.11-12.10)

Guided Imagery

Background Information

Guided Imagery is a comprehension strategy that has a long history in reading and language arts classrooms due to its efficacy in improving reading comprehension. Using this technique, teachers can help students create mental images to anticipate or respond to what they read or hear. This strategy helps teach students how the author uses language to develop important literary aspects of text, such as genre, characters, setting, conflict, meaning, and tone. Teachers should spend ample time preparing a script for the Guided Imagery strategy. These scripts can be presented to the class either before or after completing the reading. To develop the script, teachers should decide on a focus, for example the setting of the story, and then try to engage the five senses through an innovative description of the setting. When the activity is completed, teachers discuss and reinforce with students how creating these images can enhance reading comprehension. This strategy not only fosters reading comprehension by teaching students to create their own mental images while reading, but it also enhances speaking and listening skills when students listen and respond to others' descriptions of their mental images.

Grade Levels/Standards Addressed

See page 220 for the standards this strategy addresses, or refer to the Digital Resource CD (standards.pdf) to read the correlating standards in their entirety.

Activity

After students have developed some skill in mental image construction, begin the Guided Imagery activity (see sample scripts on pages 223–224). Put a note on the classroom door to prevent interruptions, turn off the classroom lights, and close the curtains or blinds. Ask students to get comfortable (they may wish to sit on the floor), close their eyes, relax as much as possible, and listen carefully as you read the script. Suggest the image one sentence at a time, and speak slowly but clearly. Repeat words and phrases, and pause periodically to allow students the opportunity to develop and expand the images they are creating. When you have finished the script, allow students to "wake up" slowly. Ask them to describe and explain their images. Encourage them to speak audibly and include relevant, descriptive details as they communicate their images to the rest of the class. Ask students to tell what they heard, saw, and felt. It may help to have students complete a quickwrite prior to sharing with the class to facilitate a more lively discussion. During the discussion, point out the similarities between their images and the content of the reading selection.

Differentiation

Be sure to speak slowly and enunciate clearly while reading the script to help English language learners understand your words. Make sure the vocabulary and content of the script are not too complex for below-level students. Write the script for below-level students but elaborate for above-level students.

Guided Imagery *(cont.)*

Grades 1–2 Example

Setting

Close your eyes and imagine that you are in the desert. The hard-packed dirt is warm under your bare feet and the sun blazes overhead. The land is flat and brown for as far as you can see. A lizard skitters by and disappears behind a rock. A tall saguaro cactus towers overhead and a bird pokes its head out of a hole in the cactus. Silence surrounds you.

Grades 3–5 Example

Characters

Close your eyes and imagine that you are just about to enter your new school for the first time. The first kid you meet is Dave. Dave stands several inches taller than you and his brown hair hangs unevenly over his eyes. When the principal introduces you, you immediately glance down and notice that one of his shoes is missing a shoelace and the other shoe has a hole where you can see his sock poking through. His torn jeans look like they might fall down over his narrow hips at any point. When he makes eye contact with you, he immediately drops his gaze back to the ground.

Grades 6–8 Example

Suspense

Close your eyes and imagine that you are going scuba diving in the ocean. The sun glistens brightly overhead and the turquoise water beckons invitingly. As you begin to submerge, you notice the brilliant colors of the underwater world. Brightly-colored coral covers the rocks to your left and tiny, iridescent fish flit back and forth in the sunlight. You dive deeper and the water grows darker as the sunlight fails to penetrate the water. In the distance you spot a bright shape and you start to follow it, losing sight of the boat above you. As you start to take another breath from your oxygen tank, you notice a strange wheezing noise coming from the tank. You quickly inhale, but the oxygen flows slowly and your lungs start to burn. You immediately start to swim towards the surface, but you are disoriented. In your panic, your heart pounds faster and you struggle to pull in any oxygen at all. You see the surface in the distance, but it still seems very far away and you don't know if you can make it.

Guided Imagery (cont.)

Grades 9–12 Example

Emotion

Close your eyes and imagine that you have been stranded on an island by yourself for a long time. Suddenly you catch sight of a plane in the distance and you realize, as it starts to descend, that it has come to rescue you. Your heart starts to pound excitedly in anticipation and your thoughts buzz frenetically inside your head. Can this be real? You've dreamed of this day for so long! You want to run and jump and yet you remain motionless, watching the plane's slow descent. Suddenly you are overcome with fear. What if this is your imagination? What if you've truly gone crazy in your isolation? Part of you wants to run away and hide. This is the only home you've known for so long. You glance down at your primitive attire and you start to blush, thinking about your appearance. Again, you want to hide, but you feel the tug of loneliness and know that you crave human contact. Finally you get up and quickly start to gather your few meager possessions as your emotions threaten to overwhelm you. Tears blur your vision and you laugh aloud as the plane touches down.

Talking Drawings

Background Information

One way to activate students' prior knowledge and generate interest in a topic is through the Talking Drawings activity (McConnell 1993, as cited by Wood 2002). Research shows that motivating students to create images before, during, and after reading is an effective method for improving reading comprehension. Prior to reading in the Talking Drawings activity, students create a mental picture initiated by the teacher. They draw what they imagined, and they share their drawings with the entire class. The teacher compiles all of the shared information in a semantic map on the board or shares it with a document camera. After reading the selection using their mental images, students repeat the process and discuss what they have learned after comparing and contrasting their two pictures. Students then discuss how the story's text and illustrations each contributed to an increase in comprehension as displayed by the new knowledge present in students' second drawings.

Grade Levels/Standards Addressed

See page 220 for the standards this strategy addresses, or refer to the Digital Resource CD (standards.pdf) to read the correlating standards in their entirety.

Activity

Instruct students to close their eyes and allow their minds to form mental pictures on a topic you have selected. When students are finished picturing, ask them to draw what they see, using labels to depict locations, people, objects, etc. After they finish their drawings, place students in pairs to share their drawings and talk about what they drew and why. Encourage them to ask their partners questions about their drawings. Meet as a whole class and use a document camera to display all of the information students generated in the *Talking Drawings* activity sheet (page 228, talkingdrawings. pdf). Instruct students to read the text selection with their pictures in mind. After reading, ask them to make another drawing to show what they have learned from reading the text and examining the illustrations. Once they have completed their second drawings, ask each student to compare their two drawings, and note the differences on the activity sheet. Then, have them discuss their pictures with their partners and ask questions about their partners' pictures. Encourage students to note how they came across the new information included in their second drawings. For example, did they read it in the text, see it in an illustration, or infer it from something else in the story?

Differentiation

English language learners should be encouraged to label their first picture in their native language. They can add the words in English later. Below-level students should be placed in homogenous groups to reduce anxiety. Above-level students should be encouraged to think deeply about the differences between their two pictures and to note the metacognitive processes that allowed them to make their second drawing more detailed and accurate.

Talking Drawings *(cont.)*

Grades 1–2 Example

Text: *Harry the Dirty Dog* by Gene Zion

Before Reading	**After Reading**
Close your eyes and think about the topic. Draw what you see. Talk about your drawing with your partner.	Read the selection and then draw a new picture of what you learned.

What's Different?

Explain what is different about your before and after pictures.

My first picture is a dog with dirt on it. I didn't know what Harry looked like before I read the book. My second drawing shows Harry when he was dirty and Harry after a bath.

Talking Drawings (cont.)

Grades 3–5 Example

Text: *The Keeping Quilt* by Patricia Polacco

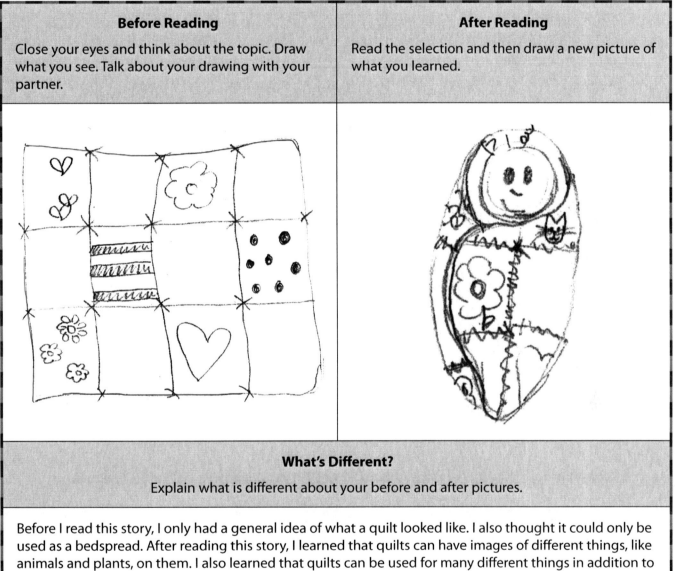

Before Reading	**After Reading**
Close your eyes and think about the topic. Draw what you see. Talk about your drawing with your partner.	Read the selection and then draw a new picture of what you learned.

What's Different?

Explain what is different about your before and after pictures.

Before I read this story, I only had a general idea of what a quilt looked like. I also thought it could only be used as a bedspread. After reading this story, I learned that quilts can have images of different things, like animals and plants, on them. I also learned that quilts can be used for many different things in addition to a bedspread.

Talking Drawings

Text: _____

Before Reading	After Reading
Close your eyes and think about the topic. Draw what you see. Talk about your drawing with your partner.	Read the selection and then draw a new picture of what you learned.

What's Different?

Explain what is different about your before and after pictures.

_____

_____

_____

_____

_____

Imagine, Elaborate, Predict, and Confirm

Background Information

Imagine, Elaborate, Predict, and Confirm is a mental imagery strategy combined with prediction skills that helps students comprehend text better. It requires students to use their imaginations as they predict and confirm what they will be reading. This strategy has been field tested and proven to increase student motivation and interest in addition to improving comprehension and writing skills (Wood 2002).

In the imagine phase, the teacher asks students to close their eyes and use their imaginations to create pictures about the reading selection prior to reading the text. The teacher can direct students to formulate their pictures based on the book cover, title, pictures, etc. Students are encouraged to use all of their senses during this phase. The teacher then shares everything students report with the class using a document camera.

In the elaboration phase, students use their visual images to add details and prior knowledge to expand their original images. By sharing their pictures with the whole class, students may stimulate one another to describe more details. Students make simple predictions based on their images during the prediction phase. They are then instructed to keep their predictions in mind as they complete the reading task.

During the confirmation stage, students return to their predictions and determine whether or not they were correct. The teacher and students modify the original predictions and integrate the new information learned to improve their comprehension of the text.

Grade Levels/Standards Addressed

See page 220 for the standards this strategy addresses, or refer to the Digital Resource CD (standards.pdf) to read the correlating standards in their entirety.

Activity

Instruct students to close their eyes and try to picture everything they can about a central topic from the text. Encourage them to use all of their senses to experience the images. Ask them to report on their mental images, and record them on an *Imagine, Elaborate, Predict, and Confirm* activity sheet (page 230, iepc.pdf) for the class to review, using a document camera to display their responses. Next, model how to use their visual images to add more details and information and record this on the activity sheet. Encourage students to follow your lead. Again, using the think-aloud technique, make at least one prediction about what you expect to find in the reading based on the visual images, and have students do the same. Ask students to complete the reading task. After reading, have students review their predictions to see if they were correct. Model how to revise the predictions and integrate them with the new information being learned. Make sure to explicitly model how to go back to the text and locate the key details in order to accurately check predictions.

Differentiation

English language learners will be able to comprehend the reading selection better if it is read aloud to them as they follow along with the printed material in front of them. Above-level students might prefer to read silently to themselves, while below-level students may prefer to conduct the reading in pairs and summarize or retell sections to partners.

Imagine, Elaborate, Predict, and Confirm

Imagine	Elaborate

Predict

_____

_____

_____

_____

Confirm

_____

_____

_____

_____

Adapted from Karen Wood (2002, 164–165)

Examining Visuals

Background Information

Another way teachers can work to improve their students' comprehension abilities is to teach them how to analyze the visuals included in the text. Taking a closer look at the pictures and illustrations in fictional narratives helps students focus on the main ideas, highlight the important details, learn additional information that is not included in the text, and expand their understanding of the content. This strategy also teaches students to make connections between the text of a story and the visual representations in the text. By comparing the visual representations to the text itself, students learn to analyze how visuals contribute to a story's overall tone, meaning, and plot sequence. It is best to introduce this strategy with a picture book containing colorful illustrations. Model for students in a think-aloud what elements to consider as they examine the pictures. Invite students to share their thoughts in a class discussion.

Grade Levels/Standards Addressed

See page 221 for the standards this strategy addresses, or refer to the Digital Resource CD (standards.pdf) to read the correlating standards in their entirety.

Activity

Select a portion of the text that includes colorful pictures or illustrations. Ask students to study the pictures closely to consider the following questions:

- What do the illustrations depict?
- What important information is contained in these pictures?
- Which details does the visual reveal?

Next, assign the reading task. As students read, they should consider how the visuals help them to understand the reading better. Depending on the grade level, ask students if the illustrations help to depict key concepts, identify the main idea, highlight important details, introduce new information, or expand their understanding of the information in the text. Have students report their findings during a whole-class discussion. Record their observations on the board or display them with a document camera. Using the explanations of the pictures, create a summary of the reading.

Differentiation

English language learners and below-level students will benefit from paired reading and small-group discussion prior to a whole-class discussion. This will provide them with adequate time to prepare and lower their anxiety. Above-level students should be encouraged to find any additional visuals that could accompany the reading selection.

Plot Sequencing

Background Information

When given the opportunity, young children actively participate in narrative play, oftentimes using graphics and drawings to depict stories. During this type of play, research shows that they naturally include many literary elements, such as character development, plot scheme, and action sequences (Wright 2007). The Plot Sequencing strategy takes students' natural inclination to visually depict plot schemes and teaches students to apply and further develop this skill with fictional texts. After reading a text selection, students create a series of drawings that show the main points of action in the story's plot. Through the process of developing these drawings, students gain a greater understanding of the story's plot and learn to selectively identify and summarize the most important events in the story's plot sequence. Students also gain familiarity with using important sequencing language such as *first*, *next*, *then*, and *finally*.

Grade Levels/Standards Addressed

See page 221 for the standards this strategy addresses, or refer to the Digital Resource CD (standards.pdf) to read the correlating standards in their entirety.

Activity

Before beginning the lesson, review the basic elements of a plot sequence with students: introduction/exposition, rising action/conflict, climax, and resolution. Explain each element, providing examples from recent class reading selections or well-known stories. Next, display the *Plot Sequencing* activity sheet (page 235, plotsequencing.pdf) for students with a document camera or re-create it on the board, and explain that students will be creating brief drawings to illustrate the plot elements of an upcoming reading selection. As a class, read the introduction to the story aloud and discuss what types of illustrations could capture the main point of the exposition. Distribute the *Plot Sequencing* activity sheet to students, and draw a scene in the first box on the *Plot Sequencing* activity sheet displayed for the class to model the process. Then, have students draw their own scenes on their own activity sheets. Next, have students read the rest of the text independently, and hold a class discussion about the remaining plot elements. Ask students to complete their drawings that illustrate these events. Allow time for students to discuss and share their drawings with a partner. Once they have shared their drawings, ask students to write a summary of the plot on the *Plot Sequencing* activity sheet. To support students as they write, distribute the *Sequencing Words Reference Sheet* in Appendix A (page 275, sequencingwords.pdf) to students to aid them during this process. Demonstrate how they can use these words to tie the events in the drawings together in a written summary. Allow students to work independently or with a partner to write an objective and succinct plot summary.

Plot Sequencing *(cont.)*

Differentiation

This is a great strategy for English language learners because it relies primarily on drawing rather than speaking or writing to demonstrate comprehension. Make sure to pre-teach new vocabulary from the text so that English language learners can understand the narrative, and provide them with written descriptions of the plot elements so they can refer back to these definitions as necessary. Below-level students will benefit from reading the text multiple times before illustrating the plot sequence. If possible, read the text aloud with these students before asking them to read it independently. While above-level students may easily grasp the concept of plot, they may become frustrated if drawing is not their strong suit. Remind them that they are not being assessed on their drawing abilities but rather on their understanding of plot. Above-level students may also benefit from using a more challenging text that utilizes more complex plot elements.

Grades 1–2

Text: *Lilly's Purple Plastic Purse* by Kevin Henkes

| **Exposition/Introduction** | **Rising Action/Conflict** | **Climax** | **Resolution/Conclusion** |

Summary
At first, Lilly was happy because she got a new purse. It was purple and plastic. She took the purse to school. But her teacher took it away. He said it was too distracting. Next, Lilly got very angry at her teacher. Lilly drew a mean picture of him. In the end, Lilly apologized to her teacher. He gave the purse back to her.

Plot Sequencing *(cont.)*

Grades 3–5 Example

Text: *The Secret Garden* by Frances Hodgson Burnett

Exposition/Introduction   **Rising Action/Conflict**   **Climax**   **Resolution/Conclusion**

Summary

In the beginning, Mary lives with her miserable Uncle Craven after her own parents die. Mary discovers the key to a secret garden and begins to tend to the garden. Next, she befriends Uncle Craven's sickly son, Colin. She persuades him to come out of isolation and into the garden with her. When a gardener discovers Colin out of bed, he assumes he is a cripple and, to prove Ben wrong, Colin stands up by himself for the first time in his life. Ultimately, Uncle Craven returns home and is happily surprised to find that his son is healthy and that Mary, Colin, and their friends have restored the secret garden.

Grades 6–8 Example

Text: *Where the Red Fern Grows* by Wilson Rawls

Exposition/Introduction   **Rising Action/Conflict**   **Climax**   **Resolution/Conclusion**

Summary

To start, Billy gets two coonhound puppies, Old Dan and Little Ann, and teaches them to hunt raccoons. They become very good hunters and Billy hunts with them every night. Eventually, the dogs tree a mountain lion and, although the dogs ultimately kill the mountain lion, Old Dan dies of his wounds and Little Ann dies of a broken heart shortly after. At the conclusion of the story, Billy is very distraught over their deaths and only finds peace when he sees that a red fern, which legend says are planted by angels, has grown on the dogs' graves.

Plot Sequencing

Directions: Choose the most important event for each of the four designated plot elements and complete a drawing depicting the event in the appropriate box. At the end, write a summary of the story with one or two sentences that describe each element of the plot. Be sure to use sequencing words to connect your sentences.

Text: _____

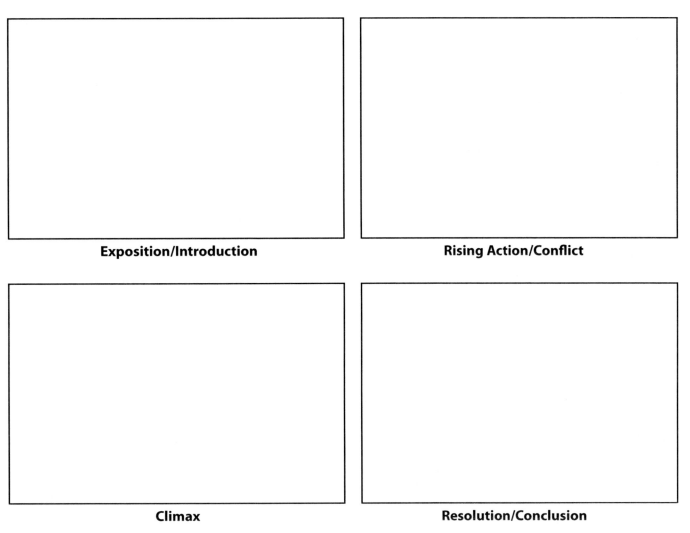

Exposition/Introduction

Rising Action/Conflict

Climax

Resolution/Conclusion

Summary

_____
_____
_____
_____

Character Portrait

Background Information

An understanding of fictional character development not only enhances reading comprehension but also has a positive effect on a student's own character (Block and Parris 2008). Through the study of literary characters, students have the opportunity to examine characters' goals and motivations, consider characters' differing perspectives, and explore characters' feelings and emotions. This type of character analysis increases reading comprehension and also improves students' ability to empathize with other people (Block and Parris 2008). The Character Portrait strategy provides students with a tool to examine a fictional character from multiple angles in order to learn from this character's thoughts, actions, and emotions. The central component of this strategy is the visual imagery used to take on the character's perspective and the visual depiction of the character created by students. Before reading the text, the teacher guides students through the visualization process to help students adopt the character's perspective. Then, students read the text and create a drawing of the character based on their visualizations. To complete the portrait, they add other character information such as personal attributes, history, temperament, etc.

Grade Levels/Standards Addressed

See page 221 for the standards this strategy addresses, or refer to the Digital Resource CD (standards.pdf) to read the correlating standards in their entirety.

Preparation

Prepare a Guided Imagery script (see pages 223–224 for implementing the Guided Imagery strategy) for one of the main characters in the story students are or will be reading. The script should include a brief description of the character and the situation he or she is facing in the story. Include enough detail to allow students to take on the character's perspective, but not so much detail that you give away crucial elements of the plot.

Activity

Read the Guided Imagery script for the selected character. Encourage students to close their eyes and visualize the situation from the character's perspective as you read the script aloud. After you are done reading, ask students to open their eyes and comment on the thoughts and feelings elicited from the visualization experience. Keeping the character's perspective in mind, have students read the text selection (or read it to them aloud), and then ask students to create a drawing of the character on the *Character Portrait* activity sheet (page 240, characterportrait.pdf). Once they have finished drawing, ask them to provide other information about the character in the designated boxes.

Character Portrait (cont.)

Variation

Adapt the activity sheet to include the setting and plot of the story. Variations of the Character Portrait strategy have students creating Wanted Posters, obituaries, yearbook pages, or website profile pages for the character. Any of these variations should include a student-generated drawing of the character and additional relevant character details.

Differentiation

When reading the prepared Guided Imagery script to English language learners, make sure to read slowly and enunciate your words clearly. Give these students ample opportunities to ask clarifying questions about both the visualization process and the text before beginning to illustrate on the activity sheet. Below-level students should be allowed to preview the text with the help of the teacher. Above-level students should be encouraged to draw on specific details in the text to describe the character in depth. If they finish the activity with time to spare, encourage them to compare and contrast the chosen character with another character from the same story.

Grades 1–2 Example

Text: *Tacky the Penguin* by Helen Lester

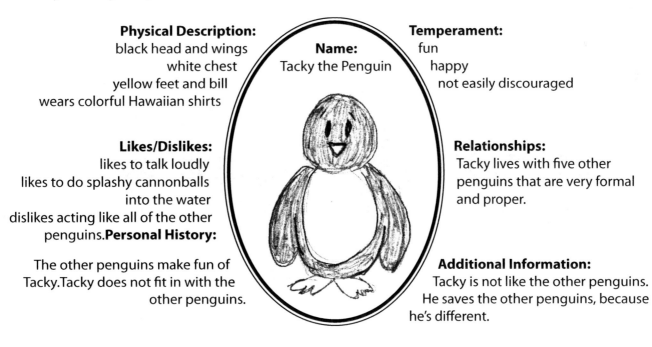

Physical Description:
black head and wings
white chest
yellow feet and bill
wears colorful Hawaiian shirts

Name:
Tacky the Penguin

Temperament:
fun
happy
not easily discouraged

Likes/Dislikes:
likes to talk loudly
likes to do splashy cannonballs
into the water
dislikes acting like all of the other
penguins.**Personal History:**

The other penguins make fun of
Tacky.Tacky does not fit in with the
other penguins.

Relationships:
Tacky lives with five other
penguins that are very formal
and proper.

Additional Information:
Tacky is not like the other penguins.
He saves the other penguins, because
he's different.

Character Portrait *(cont.)*

Grades 3–5 Example

Text: *Guinea Dog* by Patrick Jennings

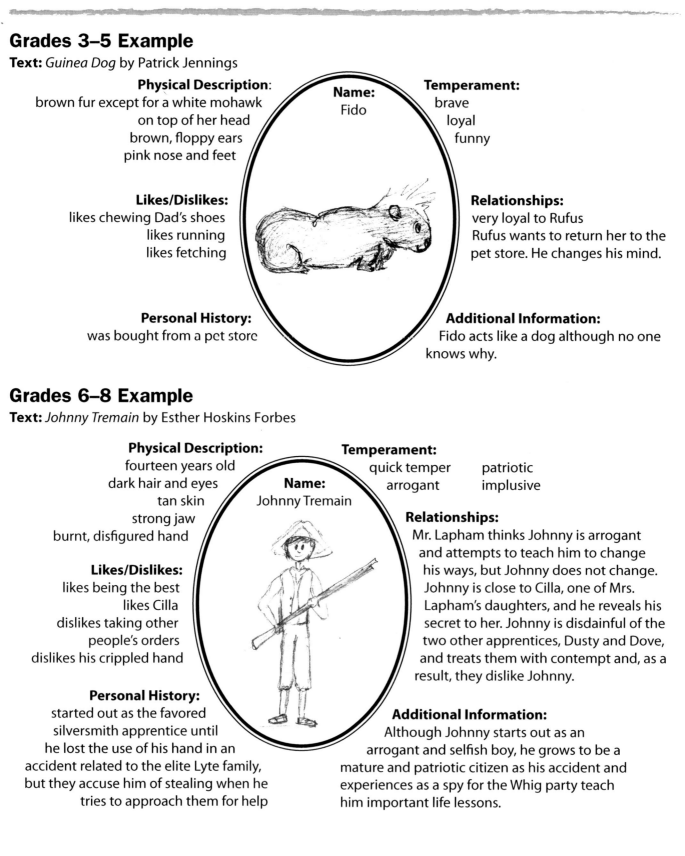

Physical Description:
brown fur except for a white mohawk
on top of her head
brown, floppy ears
pink nose and feet

Name:
Fido

Temperament:
brave
loyal
funny

Likes/Dislikes:
likes chewing Dad's shoes
likes running
likes fetching

Relationships:
very loyal to Rufus
Rufus wants to return her to the
pet store. He changes his mind.

Personal History:
was bought from a pet store

Additional Information:
Fido acts like a dog although no one
knows why.

Grades 6–8 Example

Text: *Johnny Tremain* by Esther Hoskins Forbes

Physical Description:
fourteen years old
dark hair and eyes
tan skin
strong jaw
burnt, disfigured hand

Name:
Johnny Tremain

Temperament:
quick temper   patriotic
arrogant   implusive

Likes/Dislikes:
likes being the best
likes Cilla
dislikes taking other
people's orders
dislikes his crippled hand

Relationships:
Mr. Lapham thinks Johnny is arrogant
and attempts to teach him to change
his ways, but Johnny does not change.
Johnny is close to Cilla, one of Mrs.
Lapham's daughters, and he reveals his
secret to her. Johnny is disdainful of the
two other apprentices, Dusty and Dove,
and treats them with contempt and, as a
result, they dislike Johnny.

Personal History:
started out as the favored
silversmith apprentice until
he lost the use of his hand in an
accident related to the elite Lyte family,
but they accuse him of stealing when he
tries to approach them for help

Additional Information:
Although Johnny starts out as an
arrogant and selfish boy, he grows to be a
mature and patriotic citizen as his accident and
experiences as a spy for the Whig party teach
him important life lessons.

Character Portrait (cont.)

Grades 9–12 Example

Text: *To Kill a Mockingbird* by Harper Lee

Physical Description:
six-year-old girl
Caucasian
dark, short hair
wears overalls

Name:
Jean Louise
"Scout" Finch

Temperament:
intelligent
good-natured
confident
always has good intentions

Likes/Dislikes:
likes climbing trees
likes playing with Jem and Dill
dislikes school
dislikes her teacher, Miss Caroline

Relationships:
Scout is close with her father and he teaches her to be open-minded and fair.
Jem also serves as a mentor and role model for Scout.
Calpurnia plays an important role in Scout's life, too, and teaches her how to interact with people.

Personal History:
Scout lives with her father, Atticus, and her brother, Jem.
Scout's mother died when she was two and their cook, Calpurnia, helps take care of Scout and Jem.
They live in the fictional town of Maycomb, AL.
Atticus makes a decent living as a lawyer even though most of the town lives in poverty during the Great Depression.
Scout's father does not force Scout to conform to the fussy social expectations held for most young girls in the South.

Additional Information:
At the beginning of the story, Scout is an innocent young girl, oblivious to the racial prejudice that surrounds her. As the story progresses, she becomes more exposed to the evil around her, but her belief in the good of humankind and her intelligence allows her to remain conscientious and optimistic.

Name: _____ **Date:** _____

Character Portrait

Directions: As your teacher reads the script, close your eyes and visualize the scene from the character's perspective. Then, read the text selection and draw a portrait of the character. Provide additional information about your character in the space around the portrait.

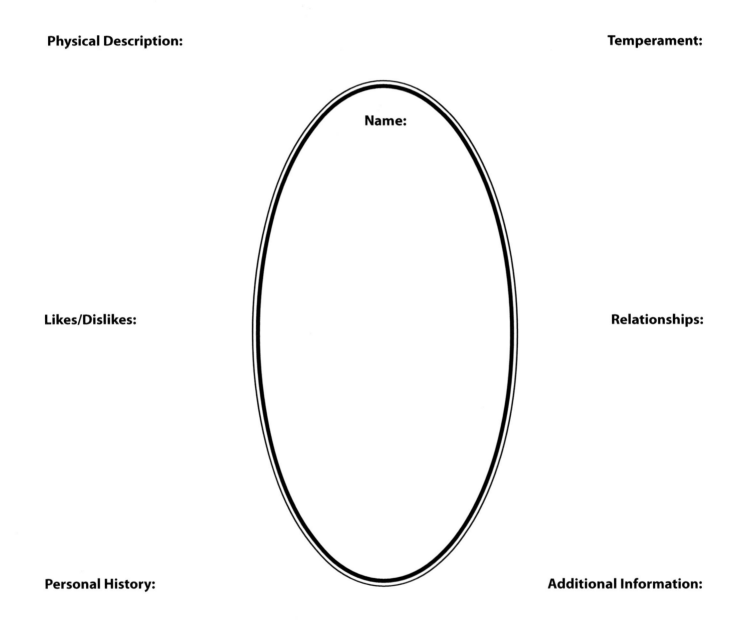

Physical Description:

Temperament:

Name:

Likes/Dislikes:

Relationships:

Personal History:

Additional Information:

Using Text Structure and Text Features Overview

Strategic Planning

Teaching students to read fiction strategically involves instructing them to examine how important information and ideas are organized in the literature. Skilled readers automatically search for the underlying structure of a text to identify how the relationships of the ideas are hierarchically arranged and can readily differentiate important ideas from less important ideas in the selection (Vacca and Vacca 2005).

Text Structure

There are different elements to text structure worthy of examination in the language arts classroom. These approaches range from highlighting external text features (e.g., illustrations, chapter headings, and captions) to identifying sentence and paragraph organizational patterns (e.g., plot sequence and description) to visually representing the organization of the ideas in the text through graphic organizers. In general, reading research suggests that almost any approach to teaching the structure of texts improves the comprehension and recall of key information in readers (Duke and Pearson 2002).

The direct instruction of text structure is intended to assist students to anticipate, monitor, and comprehend what they are reading. Looking for and using text structures helps students to study texts in order to make connections and think more deeply about the ideas they encounter while reading. If students know what to expect in a text selection, they spend more time thinking about the content and less time thinking about how it is put together. In addition, students who are familiar and comfortable with a wide variety of text structures can read with greater fluency and can choose to write in the structure that best suits their needs.

Text Frames

The more students understand the traditional formats of fictional books, the better equipped they are to remember what they have read, construct meaning about the information, develop new understandings, and apply the ideas they have encountered to different situations.

Teachers should attend to text structures the first time they introduce new books in their classrooms. Teachers can focus students' attention on the text features as they preview and skim through their books. Furthermore, teachers should periodically point out how text features affect understanding and highlight various organizational patterns throughout the school term in order to reinforce strategy instruction.

Using Text Structure and Text Features Overview (cont.)

External and Internal Text Structure

All types of literature include both external and internal text structures. Reading comprehension strategy instruction should assist students in identifying and utilizing both external and internal structures.

External Text Structure

Books contain format features, or external text structures, that serve as organizational aids to help the reader find information. While fictional texts do not include as many of these structures as traditional textbooks or informational texts, they often include several important features such as a title page, a dedication page, an acknowledgments page, or a story synopsis on the book jacket or the back cover. Depending on the type of book, fictional narratives may also include a table of contents, preface, glossary, chapters, illustrations, captions, headings, etc. Examining external structures is a valuable strategy if it is acknowledged and utilized. For example, students who look at the chapter titles carefully will notice that they often guide the reader by highlighting key concepts and ideas.

See the *External Text Structure Reference Sheet* in Appendix A: Additional Resources (page 276, externaltextstructure.pdf) for a list of text features frequently found in literary works. Students should know to discuss and work with external text features. When teachers discuss text features with students, it is important to be precise and consistent in the use of text terms.

Internal Text Structure

The internal text structure refers to how the words and paragraphs are logically put together. For the reader to comprehend new information easily, the information must be presented through the logical connections that exist between ideas. In fiction, stories often follow a general plot sequence that includes an introduction/exposition, rising action, conflict, climax, falling action, and resolution. The exposition, or introduction to the story, usually introduces the story's main characters, provides a setting for the story, and describes any background information relevant to the plot and characters. During the rising action, a series of events and conflicts occur that lead to the main problem, or climax, of the story. A story's resolution explains what happens to the characters after they overcome the main crisis presented in the climax. During the resolution, the author provides a conclusion to the story and wraps up the plot for the reader.

As students mature and begin to read more advanced material, they gain exposure to a wider variety of plot sequences and story structures. More complex books often contain a number of different plots, themes, conflicts, and resolutions that are interwoven into one another and do not follow the obvious plot sequence present in more basic picture books. However, a strong understanding of traditional plot sequence allows students to organize, differentiate, and comprehend these more complex structures as they gradually gain exposure to more challenging texts.

Using Text Structure and Text Features Overview (cont.)

Literary Devices

Authors of fictional texts also use a wide variety of literary devices to embellish plot schemes, enhance character development, create the tone for the story, and add depth to the literature. An understanding of these devices enables the reader to comprehend the text at a deeper level and gain more from the reading experience. The following chart is not an exhaustive list of literary devices but includes some of the most common ones and their definitions.

Common Literary Devices in Fictional Literature

Literary Device	Definition
foreshadowing	the use of indicative words and phrases to suggest the upcoming events or outcomes in a story
personification	the attribution of human traits and characteristics to non-human objects, animals, and phenomena
point of view	the perspective from which a story is being told
symbolism	the use of an object or action to represent something else
theme	the central message the author wants to communicate to the reader
tone	the attitude implied in the text

Using Text Structure and Text Features Overview (cont.)

Standards Addressed

The following chart shows the correlating standards for each strategy in this section. Refer to the Digital Resource CD (standards.pdf) to read the correlating standards in their entirety.

Strategy	McREL Standards	Common Core State Standards
Text Feature Scavenger Hunt	Grades 1–2 (5.2) Grades 3–5 (6.2) Grades 6–8 (6.2) Grades 9–12 (6.2)	Grade 1 (RL.1.5, RL.1.5) Grade 2 (RL.2.5, RL.2.5) Grade 3 (RL.3.5, RL.3.5) Grade 4 (RL.4.5, RL.4.5) Grade 5 (RL.5.5, RL.5.5) Grade 6 (RL.6.5, RL.6.5) Grade 7 (RL.7.5, RL.7.5) Grade 8 (RL.8.5, RL.8.5) Grades 9–10 (RL.9-10.5) Grades 11–12 (RL.11-12.5)
Read, Note, Sort	Grades 1–2 (6.2) Grades 3–5 (6.2, 6.3) Grades 6–8 (6.2, 6.3) Grades 9–12 (6.2, 6.3)	Grade 1 (RL.1.3, RL.1.5) Grade 2 (RL.2.3, RL.2.5) Grade 3 (RL.3.3, RL.3.5) Grade 4 (RL.4.3, RL.4.5) Grade 5 (RL.5.3, RL.5.5) Grade 6 (RL.6.3, RL.6.5) Grade 7 (RL.7.3, RL.7.5) Grade 8 (RL.8.3, RL.8.5) Grades 9–10 (RL.9-10.3, RL.9-10.5) Grades 11–12 (RL.11-12.3, RL.11-12.5)
Point of View	Grades 1–2 (6.2) Grades 3–5 (6.5) Grades 6–8 (6.4) Grades 9–12 (6.2)	Grade 1 (RL.1.6, RL.1.10) Grade 2 (RL.2.6, RL.2.10) Grade 3 (RL.3.6, RL.3.10) Grade 4 (RL.4.6, RL.4.10) Grade 5 (RL.5.6, RL.5.10) Grade 6 (RL.6.6, RL.6.10) Grade 7 (RL.7.6, RL.7.10) Grade 8 (RL.8.6, RL.8.10) Grades 9–10 (RL.9-10.6, RL.9-10.10) Grades 11–12 (RL.11-12.6, RL.11-12.10)
Graphic Organizers	Grades 1–2 (6.2, 6.3) Grades 3–5 (6.2, 6.3) Grades 6–8 (6.2, 6.3) Grades 9–12 (6.2, 6.3)	Grade 1 (RL.1.5, RL.1.10) Grade 2 (RL.2.5, RL.2.10) Grade 3 (RL.3.5, RL.3.10) Grade 4 (RL.4.5, RL.4.10) Grade 5 (RL.5.5, RL.5.10) Grade 6 (RL.6.5, RL.6.10) Grade 7 (RL.7.5, RL.7.10) Grade 8 (RL.8.5, RL.8.10) Grades 9–10 (RL.9-10.5, RL.9-10.10) Grades 11–12 (RL.11-12.5, RL.11-12.10)

Text Feature Scavenger Hunt

Background Information

A fun way for students to familiarize themselves with the features of the text is to have them complete a scavenger hunt (Robb 2003). Students can complete the activity all at once or it can be organized for students to complete over a number of days. Students can complete the activity with partners or in small groups.

Grade Levels/Standards Addressed

See page 244 for the standards this strategy addresses, or refer to the Digital Resource CD (standards.pdf) to read the correlating standards in their entirety.

Activity

Activate students' prior knowledge about text features through whole-class questioning. Review the purpose of different text features with the class while skimming through a fictional text. Divide the class into groups of four students. Distribute the *Text Feature Scavenger Hunt* activity sheet (page 246, textscavenger.pdf) to students, and instruct them to work together to complete the activity. As students work, circle the room to provide assistance, as necessary. When they have completed the activity sheet, call on the different teams to share their findings. Write their findings on the board or display them with a document camera, and discuss them further.

Differentiation

English language learners should have a vocabulary list of text terms with definitions available to them during the activity. Provide them with extra time to complete the task or have some of the questions answered for them. Below-level students should approach the questions in the order which they find most comfortable and should not be rushed to complete the task. Above-level students should compete to see who finishes the task first and has all of the answers correct.

Text Feature Scavenger Hunt

Directions: Work with your team member(s) and use the book to complete the following questions.

1. **Title Page**   **present?** yes____ no ____ page number _____

   Describe how the page differs from the front cover.

   _____

2. **Table of Contents**   **present?** yes____ no ____ page number _____

   List three interesting chapters.

   _____

3. **Dedication Page**   **present?** yes____ no ____ page number _____

   To whom is this book dedicated? List the dedication below.

   _____

4. **Glossary**   **present?** yes____ no ____ page number _____

   What kind of information does it contain? How can a glossary help you?

   _____

5. **Chapters**   **present?** yes____ no ____ page number _____

   How many pages are in the first chapter? How many in the last chapter?

   _____

6. **Photographs**   **present?** yes____ no ____ page number _____

   Study one of the pictures and its caption (if present) and write down what you learned.

   _____

7. **Illustrations**   **present?** yes____ no ____ page number _____

   Locate an interesting illustration. Examine it closely and explain what this visual aid can teach you.

   _____

8. **Acknowledgments Page**   **present?** yes____ no ____ page number _____

   What kind of people does the author acknowledge. Why?

   _____

9. **Other features**   **present?** yes____ no ____ page number _____

   What other features are in your book? How do these help you learn new information?

   _____

   _____

Read, Note, Sort

Background Information

One of the most prominent features in fictional literature is the narrative text structure. From a young age, students begin to notice elements such as characters, setting, conflict, and resolution when reading or listening to stories (McNamara 2007). Despite their propensity to notice these literary elements on a basic level, it is only through explicit instruction that students gain a deeper sensitivity to text structure that they can use to improve their reading comprehension. The Read, Note, Sort strategy teaches students how to explicitly examine the elements of plot sequence by noting the plot components and categorizing them according to their purpose. The kinesthetic action of physically sorting the plot elements helps students visualize the text structure and explicitly teaches them how text structure can enhance reading comprehension.

Grade Levels/Standards Addressed

See page 244 for the standards this strategy addresses, or refer to the Digital Resource CD (standards.pdf) to read the correlating standards in their entirety.

Activity

To begin this lesson, review the structural elements of a traditional plot sequence with the class: introduction/exposition, rising action/conflict, climax, falling action, and resolution. Discuss the purpose of each component of plot sequence, and give examples from well-known stories or fairy tales to demonstrate your points. Distribute blank notecards or sticky strips (sticky notes cut into strips) to each student, and explain that they are going to use these to take notes on the events in the story as they read the text selection. Have students read the text selection and record notes for each separate event that occurs in the plot. As a class, discuss the events, and have students sort their notes according to where they fall in the plot sequence. Next, distribute the *Read, Note, Sort* activity sheet (page 253, readnotesort.pdf) to each student, and ask them to attach the events to the diagram according to the plot element. When they have completed the diagram, ask students to write an objective summary of the story using their notes.

Differentiation

For English language learners, ensure that they understand the story before they begin the activity. It may be helpful to read the text aloud to them in order to clarify difficult vocabulary. Above-level students should be encouraged to analyze the plot sequence on a deeper level using the extension ideas listed in this lesson. Below-level students will benefit from extra scaffolding on this activity. Provide these students with some or all of the notecards already completed with the events from the story so they can focus on determining where these events fit on the plot diagram.

Read, Note, Sort (cont.)

Extension

For older students, this activity can be extended to encompass more complex plot schemes and teach more challenging literary-analysis skills.

- For books with parallel plots, have students sort the events for each of the plots separately. Use two different colored markers or notecards to differentiate between the plot lines, and have students attach the events for one plot above the line on the plot diagram and the other series of events below the line. Ask students to compare how these two plot lines interact and how the author's choice of text structure creates effects such as suspense, tension, or surprise.

- After reading two different text selections, divide the class in half and ask each group to complete the *Read, Note, Sort* activity sheet for one of the two texts. Use a document camera to display the plot diagrams for each book, and compare and contrast the text structures for the books. Have students analyze how the similarities and differences affect the two texts' meanings and styles.

- For longer chapter books, divide students into small groups and assign each group of students a chapter. Have them complete the *Read, Note, Sort* activity sheet for their assigned chapters, noting that each chapter will not necessarily contain all of the elements of the plot diagram. Once the groups have completed the activity for their designated chapters, use a document camera to display the Read, Note, Sort plot diagram for the class, and allow students to work together to sort their chapters onto the diagram. Use the completed diagram to analyze how each particular chapter fits into the overall structure of the text and contributes to the development of the plot.

Read, Note, Sort *(cont.)*

Grades 1–2 Example

Text: *Caps for Sale* by Esphyr Slobodkina

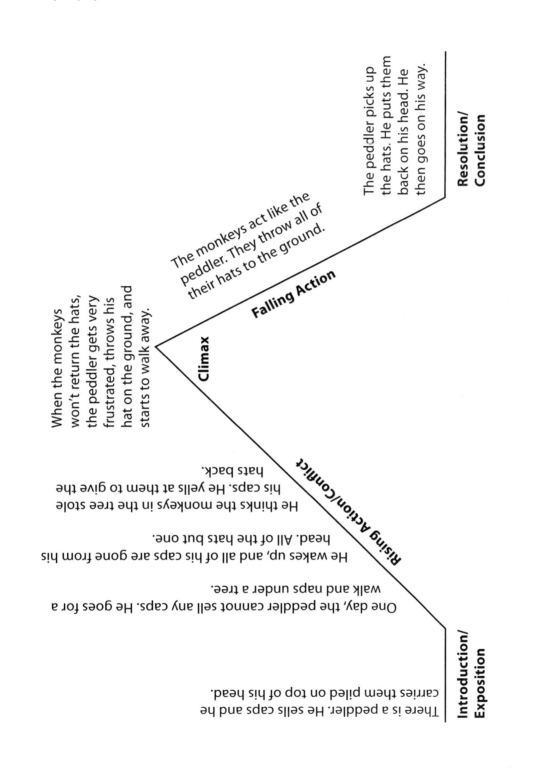

Resolution/Conclusion

The peddler picks up the hats. He puts them back on his head. He then goes on his way.

The monkeys act like the peddler. They throw all of their hats to the ground.

Falling Action

When the monkeys won't return the hats, the peddler gets very frustrated, throws his hat on the ground, and starts to walk away.

Climax

He thinks the monkeys in the tree stole his caps. He yells at them to give the hats back.

He wakes up, and all of his caps are gone from his head. All of the hats but one.

Rising Action/Conflict

One day, the peddler cannot sell any caps. He goes for a walk and naps under a tree.

Introduction/Exposition

There is a peddler. He sells caps and he carries them piled on top of his head.

Read, Note, Sort *(cont.)*

Grades 3–5 Example

Text: *Freckle Juice* by Judy Blume

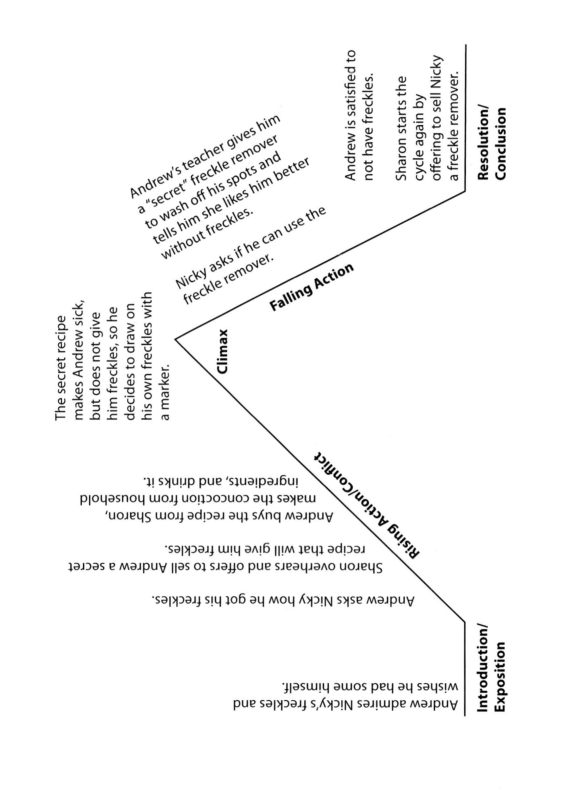

Andrew's teacher gives him a "secret" freckle remover to wash off his spots and tells him she likes him better without freckles.

Nicky asks if he can use the freckle remover.

Andrew is satisfied to not have freckles.

Sharon starts the cycle again by offering to sell Nicky a freckle remover.

Resolution/Conclusion

Falling Action

The secret recipe makes Andrew sick, but does not give him freckles, so he decides to draw on his own freckles with a marker.

Climax

Andrew buys the recipe from Sharon, makes the concoction from household ingredients, and drinks it.

Sharon overhears and offers to sell Andrew a secret recipe that will give him freckles.

Andrew asks Nicky how he got his freckles.

Rising Action/Conflict

Andrew admires Nicky's freckles and wishes he had some himself.

Introduction/Exposition

Read, Note, Sort *(cont.)*

Grades 6–8 Example

Text: Chapters 1–2, *The Lion, the Witch and the Wardrobe* by C.S. Lewis

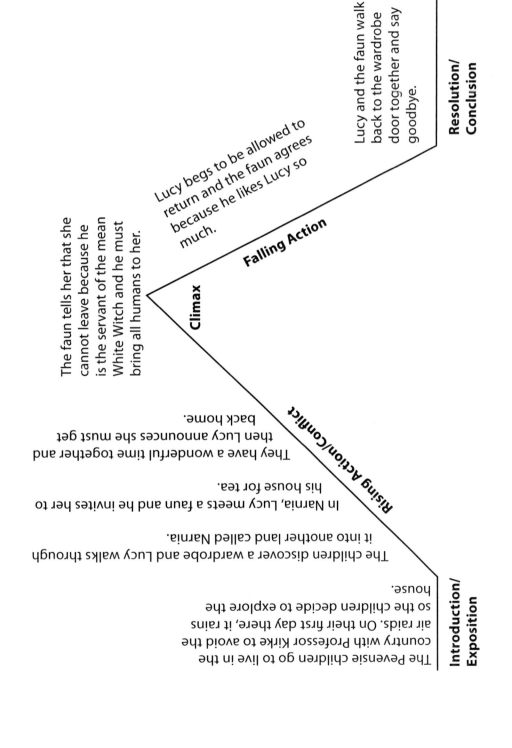

Resolution/Conclusion

Lucy and the faun walk back to the wardrobe door together and say goodbye.

Lucy begs to be allowed to return and the faun agrees because he likes Lucy so much.

Falling Action

Climax

The faun tells her that she cannot leave because he is the servant of the mean White Witch and he must bring all humans to her.

Rising Action/Conflict

They have a wonderful time together and then Lucy announces she must get back home.

In Narnia, Lucy meets a faun and he invites her to his house for tea.

The children discover a wardrobe and Lucy walks through it into another land called Narnia.

Introduction/Exposition

The Pevensie children go to live in the country with Professor Kirke to avoid the air raids. On their first day there, it rains so the children decide to explore the house.

Read, Note, Sort (cont.)

Grades 9–12 Example

Text: *To Kill a Mockingbird* by Harper Lee

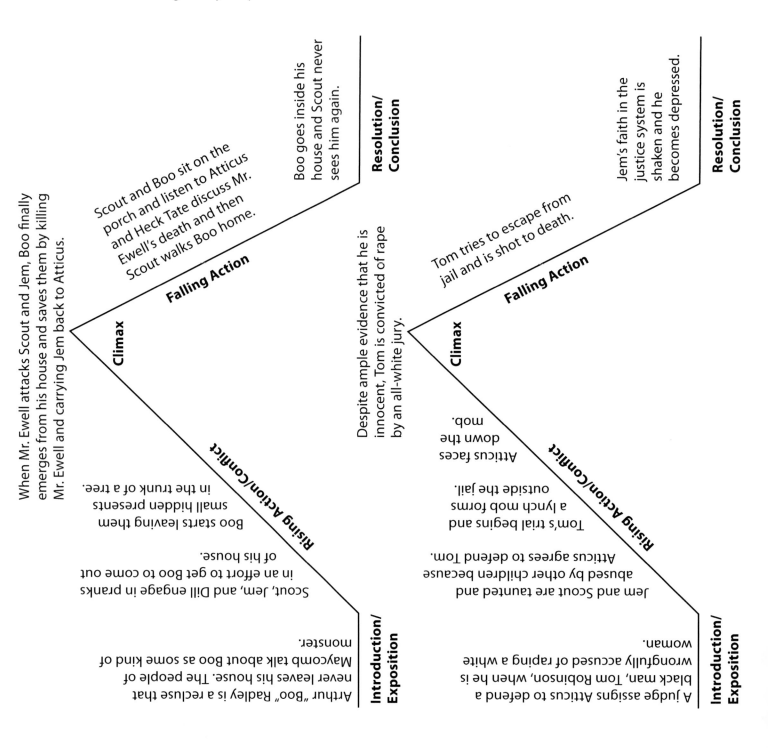

Left diagram:

Climax: When Mr. Ewell attacks Scout and Jem, Boo finally emerges from his house and saves them by killing Mr. Ewell and carrying Jem back to Atticus.

Falling Action: Scout and Boo sit on the porch and listen to Atticus and Heck Tate discuss Mr. Ewell's death and then Scout walks Boo home.

Resolution/Conclusion: Boo goes inside his house and Scout never sees him again.

Rising Action/Conflict: Boo starts leaving them small hidden presents in the trunk of a tree.

Scout, Jem, and Dill engage in pranks in an effort to get Boo to come out of his house.

Introduction/Exposition: Arthur "Boo" Radley is a recluse that never leaves his house. The people of Maycomb talk about Boo as some kind of monster.

Right diagram:

Climax: Despite ample evidence that he is innocent, Tom is convicted of rape by an all-white jury.

Falling Action: Tom tries to escape from jail and is shot to death.

Resolution/Conclusion: Jem's faith in the justice system is shaken and he becomes depressed.

Rising Action/Conflict: Atticus faces down the mob.

Tom's trial begins and a lynch mob forms outside the jail.

Atticus agrees to defend Tom.

Introduction/Exposition: Jem and Scout are taunted and abused by other children because Atticus agrees to defend Tom.

A judge assigns Atticus to defend a black man, Tom Robinson, when he is wrongfully accused of raping a white woman.

Name: _____ **Date:** _____

Read, Note, Sort

Directions: As you read the text, take notes on the different events that occur in the story. Write each event on a separate notecard or sticky strip. When you have completed the reading, sort and attach your notes according to where they belong on the plot diagram.

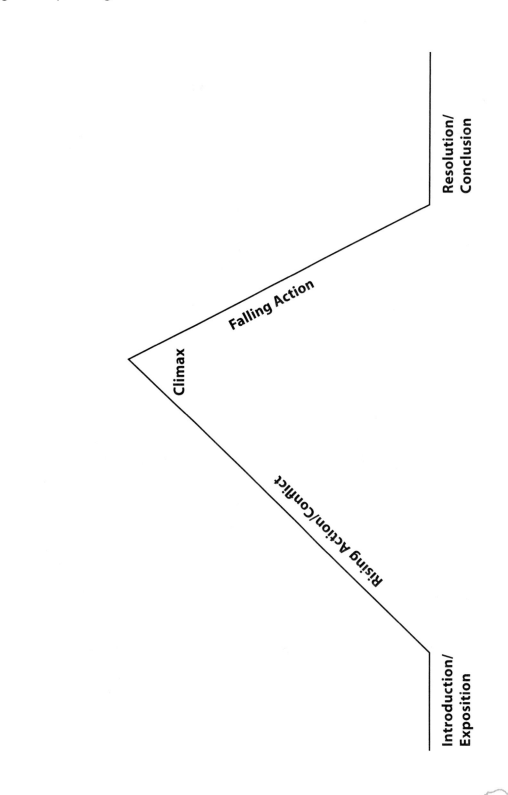

Text:

Point of View

Background Information

The point of view from which a story is told plays an important role in the development of a story's plot, characters, theme, and tone. Different types of narrators offer different perspectives so an author's choice of narrator immediately provides the reader with a sense of focus and direction for the story. The ability to assume different perspectives is a difficult task for many students, so it is important that teachers provide explicit instruction in the determination and examination of point of view. Students need to learn about the different types of point of view: first person central, first person peripheral, second person, third person objective, third person limited, and third person omniscient. They should also learn how the narrator's qualities, such as reliability, age, and attitude, affect the story. The Point of View strategy guides students in identifying the narrator's point of view, recording the evidence they used to make this determination, and analyzing the ways in which this particular point of view impacts the story.

Grade Levels/Standards Addressed

See page 244 for the standards this strategy addresses, or refer to the Digital Resource CD (standards.pdf) to read the correlating standards in their entirety.

Activity

Begin this activity by introducing or reviewing the different types of point of view that an author can give a narrator. With younger students, start with the difference between first person and third person narration. Older students can learn to differentiate between types of first and third person narrators. As appropriate for your students' ages, share the different types of point of view:

- first person central—The main character of the story is the narrator. The narrator refers to himself or herself as I.

- first person peripheral—The narrator of the story is not the main character but rather one of the secondary characters. The narrator refers to himself or herself as I and the reader experiences the story through his or her eyes.

- second person—The story is told from the perspective of you. This point of view is rarely used in fiction.

- third person objective—The narrator only knows what can be seen or observed from outside the characters. This point of view uses he, she, and it pronouns.

- third person limited—The narrator is not a character is the story but has access to the thoughts and feelings of one of the characters.

- third person omniscient—The narrator is not a character in the story but knows the thoughts and feelings of all of the characters.

As a class, practice identifying different types of point of view by reading the opening paragraphs of various stories to determine the point of view, and have students cite the textual evidence that led to that conclusion. Once students comprehend how to identify the point of view, introduce the following activity with students to encourage them to think about the effects of the narrator's perspective.

Point of View *(cont.)*

Place a medium-sized object, such as a basketball, in a central location in the classroom where all students can see it. Have students verbally describe the object. Students should describe the object from a variety of different perspectives. How would the object appear from an ant's perspective? How would the object appear if you were viewing it from an airplane? How do your emotions or attitudes change as your shift between various perspectives?

Hold a class discussion about how the narrator's point of view affects the meaning, tone, style, and theme of the story. Use examples from well-known stories to illustrate the effects of various points of view. Once you feel that students have a comprehensive understanding of point of view, distribute the *Point of View* activity sheet (page 258, pointofview.pdf) to students, and ask them to read a text selection to complete the chart with information from the story. To encourage deeper understanding, repeat the activity with different fictional text selections written from various points of view.

Differentiation

For below-level students and English language learners, make sure to highlight how the use of particular pronouns can be used to determine the narrator's point of view. Provide these students with a written description of the different types of point of view and the pronouns associated with each type. Encourage above-level students to complete an in-depth exploration and analysis of how the narrator's personal qualities and point of view affect the story.

Point of View *(cont.)*

Grades 1–2 Example

Text: *Little Bear* by Else Holmelund Minarik

Point of View	Evidence	Impact
Third Person Objective	The narrator uses the characters' names or uses *he and she*. The narrator does not know the characters' thoughts or feelings.	I think the author chose to use the third person perspective. The narrator only talks about the character's actions and words. It doesn't talk about thoughts or feelings.

Grades 3–5 Example

Text: *Pippi Longstocking* by Astrid Lindgren

Point of View	Evidence	Impact
Third Person Omniscient	The narrator uses everyone's names and the pronouns *he and she*. The narrator is omniscient because the thoughts and feelings of the characters are told. For example, the text says, "Her father had bought the old house in the garden many years ago. He thought he would live there with Pippi." (2)"	I think the author chose to use the third person omniscient point of view so she could provide different perspectives on Pippi. Pippi is such an unusual girl and it helps me understand the story better when the narrator provides information about Pippi's thoughts and also the views and perspectives of the people around her.

Point of View *(cont.)*

Grades 6–8 Example

Text: *Bridge to Terabithia* by Katherine Paterson

Point of View	Evidence	Impact
Third Person Limited	The narrator uses Jess's name and the pronoun *he* to refer to him, making it a third person narration. The narrator also knows Jess's thoughts and feelings but not the other characters', making it third person limited. For example, it says, "His body was begging him to quit, but Jess pushed it on." (5)	By using the third person point of view, the author is able to give the reader a more objective perspective on the conditions surrounding Jess, such as the poverty in which he lives. The limited omniscience also allows the reader to gain a better understanding of Jess's emotions and mental state, drawing the reader into the story and emphasizing the important theme of friendship throughout the book.

Grades 9–12 Example

Text: *Heart of Darkness* by Joseph Conrad

Point of View	Evidence	Impact
This book has two narrators: an anonymous passenger that listens to Marlow's story and Marlow himself. The anonymous passenger narrates from the first person plural (peripheral), representing four other passengers. Marlow speaks in first person (central) about his experiences and thoughts.	"The Director of Companies was our captain and our host. We four affectionately watched his back as he stood in the bows looking seaward." (37)—Anonymous passenger "I believe I dozed off leaning over the rail, till an abrupt burst of yells, an overwhelming outbreak of a pent-up and mysterious frenzy, woke me up in a bewildered wonder." (109)—Marlow	I think the author chose to use two narrators and points of view to provide multiple perspectives on Marlow's tale. By using the first person point of view, the narrators are able to give insight into the psychological effects of the journey, both on the Thames and the Congo rivers. The two narrators also allow the author to build on the parallels between Africa and Europe, white Europeans and black Africans, etc. Furthermore, the multiple narrators and points of view add a quality of unreliability to the narration and force the reader to question whose view is more trustworthy.

Point of View

Directions: Fill in the chart with correct information from your story.

- first person central—The main character of the story is the narrator. The narrator refers to himself or herself as *I*.

- first person peripheral—The narrator of the story is not the main character but rather one of the secondary characters. The narrator refers to himself or herself as *I* and the reader experiences the story through his or her eyes.

- second person—The story is told from the perspective of *you*. This point of view is rarely used in fiction.

- third person objective—The narrator only knows what can be seen or observed from outside the characters. This point of view uses *he, she*, and *it* pronouns.

- third person limited—The narrator is not a character in the story but has access to the thoughts and feelings of one of the characters.

- third person omniscient—The narrator is not a character in the story but knows the thoughts and feelings of all of the characters.

Text: _____

Point of View	Evidence	Impact

Graphic Organizers

Background Information

The term graphic organizer is a visual depiction of how ideas in a text are interrelated, connected, and organized. Graphic organizers are a visual form of traditional outlining that can highlight, summarize, or represent various literary elements. Because of their visual nature, students often find graphic organizers more effective and stimulating than traditional outlines. Graphic organizers require students to process information that they have read and have seen, thereby enhancing their retention and recall. Using graphic organizers helps readers remember what they read and improves reading comprehension and achievement (Trabasso and Bouchard 2002). There are hundreds of graphic organizers available to teachers. The examples for this activity are specific to teaching students the components of different text structures and literary features. Enlarged versions of the graphic organizers are provided on the Digital Resource CD (graphicorganizers.pdf).

Grade Levels/Standards Addressed

See page 244 for the standards this strategy addresses, or refer to the Digital Resource CD (standards.pdf) to read the correlating standards in their entirety.

Activity

Begin by explaining that when readers understand the structural features of a book, they are better able to understand and organize new information. Explain that graphic organizers help students organize and remember what they have read.

Select a passage from a piece of fictional literature for students to read. Prepare students for the activity by explaining that you will model how to use a graphic organizer to help them understand how the information is organized to improve comprehension and memory. Instruct students in the internal text patterns and literary devices found in the selected text. Model how to use the graphic organizer by displaying it with a document camera or re-creating it on the board. Then, distribute to the students the graphic organizer most appropriate for the activity. Explain how to read the text and identify the important information to include in the graphic organizer. As you read the passage aloud, pause and do a think-aloud to show students exactly how to identify the important information from the text. Ask them to read the rest of the passage and add more information to their graphic organizers. Invite students to discuss their graphic organizers to clarify and expand on their information.

Differentiation

Teachers scaffold the information to be placed in the graphic organizers for English language learners and below-level students to lower their anxiety (e.g., provide strategic answers or a word bank). Both groups of students may benefit from working in pairs or small groups to complete the graphic organizer. Above-level students may require little or no instruction and may be given an alternative assignment, if warranted.

Graphic Organizers (cont.)

Plot Sequence

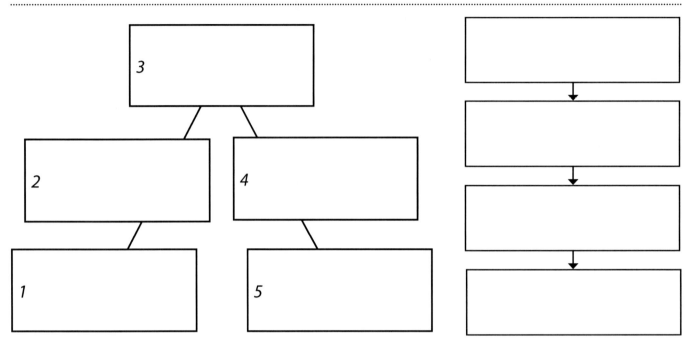

Character Analysis

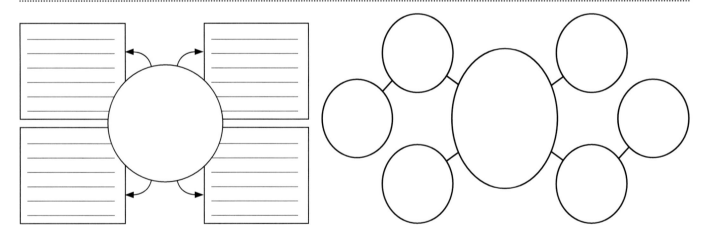

Graphic Organizers (cont.)

Character Comparison

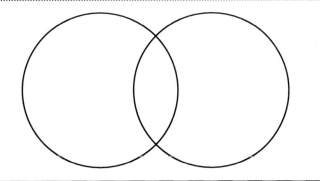

	Name 1	Name 2
Attribute 1		
Attribute 2		
Attribute 3		

Story Map

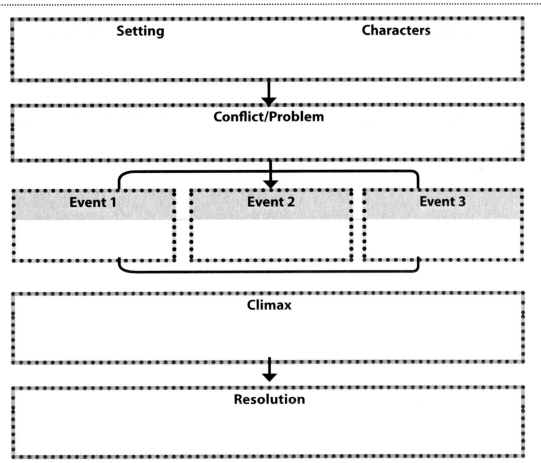

Graphic Organizers *(cont.)*

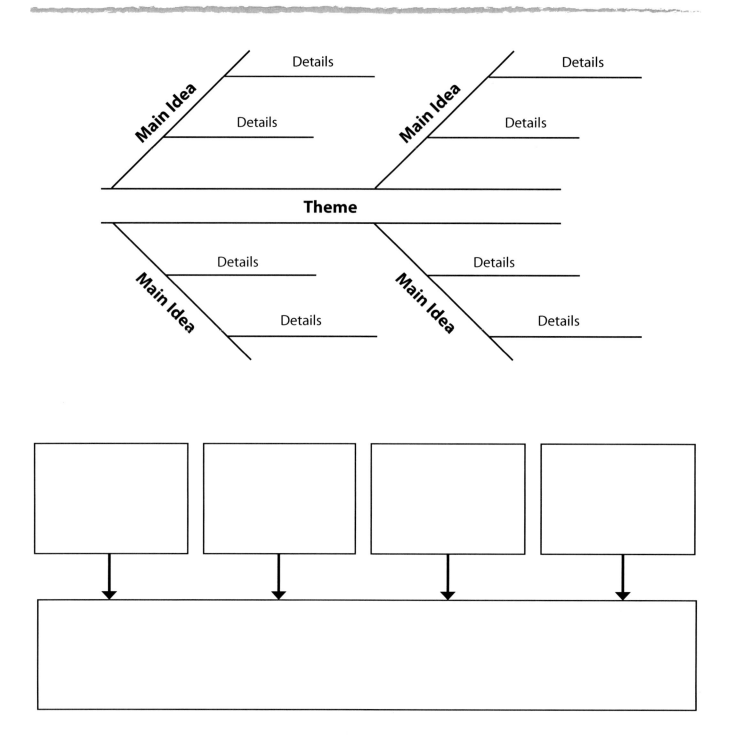

Using Multiple Reading Comprehension Strategies Instruction Overview

What Is Multiple Strategies Instruction?

While many researchers have focused on how the explicit instruction of individual reading strategies enhances students' ability to comprehend textual materials, combining reading strategies in a multiple strategy approach has proven to be very effective. The National Reading Panel (2000) makes it clear that the multiple strategies approach to reading comprehension is highly effective in assisting students in becoming more efficient and effective readers.

The multiple strategies approach in reading comprehension has been given a number of names by researchers: comprehension routines (Duke and Pearson 2002); process-based comprehension instruction (Block et al. 2002); multiple strategy intervention (Baker 2002); and comprehensive approach to comprehension instruction (Pearson and Duke 2002). A rose is a rose, no matter what the name. The National Reading Panel (2000) reviewed 38 multiple strategy studies—more significant studies were conducted in the area of the multiple strategy approach to improving reading comprehension in the classroom than any other topic. As the National Reading Panel (2000) states, "The multiple strategy instruction model represents an evolution in the field from the study of individual strategies to their flexible and multiple use" (4). The research reviewed provides considerable scientific support for the use of multiple strategies when instructing in reading comprehension (2000).

Why Does Combining Strategies Work?

Reading is a cognitive task that requires readers to coordinate multiple skills simultaneously. Skilled reading involves an ongoing adaptation of multiple cognitive processes (National Reading Panel 2000). When students are instructed to use reading comprehension strategies in combination, they learn how to think in terms of the two strategies simultaneously. As a result, they develop greater flexibility and coordination to better understand what they are reading. If one strategy does not work effectively, students will still comprehend the text because another strategy has been utilized. This approach to reading comprehension teaches students how to relate multiple strategies at specific points in the text when needed (Block et al. 2002). Because students are made aware that the reading strategies do not have to work in isolation, they indirectly learn to select which strategies will work best for different reading situations. As a result, considerable success has been achieved in improving text comprehension by instructing students how to use more than one strategy during the course of reading (National Reading Panel 2000).

Using Multiple Reading Comprehension Strategies Instruction Overview *(cont.)*

Teaching How to Interrelate Comprehension Strategies

The multiple strategies approach described later in this chapter explains teaching approaches that have been tested and proven effective in the classroom. Teachers, however, can combine reading comprehension strategies in their instruction on their own. The National Reading Panel (2000) suggests that this technique best serves students in grades 3–8. In this approach, teachers can choose to teach the following (Block et al. 2002):

- How to add depth and breadth to knowledge through intertextuality, summarizing, inferring, imaging, interpreting the author's intentions, reflecting, paraphrasing, identifying the gist, organizing, predicting, and making connections among words, facts, and concepts, and the historical and political context in which they are written and read

- How to simultaneously comprehend literally, inferentially, and applicably by establishing different purposes for reading

- How to think metacognitively and to clarify by using fix-up strategies and continuous self-monitoring

- How to fill in the gaps in both narrative and expository texts by processing the text continuously while reading

Reciprocal Teaching

Four comprehension strategies—predicting, questioning, clarifying, and summarizing—are combined in Reciprocal Teaching. Reciprocal Teaching (Palinscar 1982, as cited by Duke and Pearson 2002) utilizes the gradual release of responsibility from the teacher to students in each part of the process. In the first stage of the process, the teacher models different reading strategies, explains exactly what the strategies are, and explains exactly how they are used. The teacher selects two or more combinations of four strategies: questioning, summarizing, clarifying, and predicting, and uses direct instruction with students. Initially, the teacher guides the readers as they apply and practice the strategies together while reading a selection of the text. The teacher models how to use the strategies by providing examples and conducting think-alouds during the reading to demonstrate how to use the strategies in conjunction with one another. After much practice, students can work in small groups. When students demonstrate proficiency in using the strategies within small groups, the teacher gradually releases the responsibility of utilizing the reading strategies to the individual students to use independently.

Duke and Pearson (2002) describe a typical Reciprocal Teaching session as such:

The session usually begins with a review of the main points from the previous day's reading, or students may make predictions about the upcoming reading based on the title and pictures. Next, all students read the first paragraph of the text silently to themselves.

A student assigned to act as teacher asks a question about the paragraph, summarizes the paragraph, asks for clarification if needed, and predicts what might be in the next paragraph. During the process, the teacher prompts the student-teacher as needed and in the end provides feedback about the student-teacher's work.

Reciprocal Teaching sessions usually last 20–40 minutes, and more than one student can take on the role of the teacher during the session. The teacher's role is to guide students through modeling and scaffolding. Throughout the session, the teacher regularly reminds students of why learning the reading comprehension strategies is important and how it will improve their skills.

Reading researchers have reviewed a number of studies of Reciprocal Teaching and have concluded that it is effective at improving comprehension of text (Duke and Pearson 2002). Dramatic improvements in reading comprehension skills are evident after about 20 sessions of properly conducted Reciprocal Teaching (Snowball 2006).

Students Achieving Independent Learning

The reading comprehension strategies emphasized in Students Achieving Independent Learning (SAIL) are predicting, visualizing, questioning, clarifying, making associations (connecting prior knowledge to text), and summarizing. As in Reciprocal Teaching, this strategy asks the teacher to instruct students in using these strategies through explicit instruction and think-alouds. However, the focus is to help students learn how to choose the most effective strategy to use for any given text. Therefore, students focus on interpreting the text as they practice the reading comprehension strategies with a variety of texts. When using the SAIL routine, students are encouraged to articulate what the strategies are and how to use them, so they are working on developing their metacognitive skills. Furthermore, the routine enables students to discuss with each other the advantages and disadvantages of each strategy in different situations, so students learn to determine when it is most appropriate to use a particular strategy and why.

When using the SAIL routine in the classroom, there is no particular order in which to teach the strategies. Because strategy use really depends on the given situation, students should learn when it is best to use a particular strategy. The teacher provides a wide variety of texts to work with and models which thinking processes work best for different texts. Students learn how to apply multiple strategies as needed. Also, there is a greater focus on students' interpretation of the text rather than "the right answers" (Duke and Pearson 2002). SAIL requires many small-group and whole-class discussions so that students can talk to one another about the reading. They should also practice their own think-aloud skills as they read independently and share their thinking with each other.

Duke and Pearson (2002) summarize the qualitative research on SAIL by stating that it provides students with rich, motivating interactions with reading materials. Furthermore, with SAIL, students become more sophisticated at using reading comprehension strategies over time. In addition, students in classrooms that use SAIL outperform students in non-SAIL classrooms in standardized reading comprehension and vocabulary tests, and they also have better recall of the content in the reading.

Collaborative Strategic Reading

Collaborative Strategic Reading (CSR) (Klingner and Vaughn 2002) combines both reading comprehension strategy instruction and cooperative learning strategies that many teachers already comfortably employ in their classrooms. Due to peer interaction, CSR has been successful in improving comprehension in learning for disabled students and students learning English.

In CSR, teachers place students in small, mixed-ability, cooperative groups to work together as they apply four reading strategies to their text. The framework utilizes prior knowledge, prediction, monitoring comprehension, summarizing, and generating questions in the four stages of reading called preview, click and clunk, get the gist, and wrap-up.

The teacher begins by introducing CSR to the whole class and models the entire CSR framework to help students understand the plan. The teacher provides explicit instruction for using each of the reading strategies in the subsequent days. Using think-alouds, the teacher models how to verbalize thinking as he or she applies each of the strategies while reading a section of text. The teacher increases student involvement as they become more proficient at using the strategies and gradually releases responsibility to them.

Preview

Prior to reading a selection, the teacher models how to activate prior knowledge before reading so that students can make accurate predictions about the content of the reading. In doing so, the teacher helps generate interest in the topic. Teachers instruct students to spend approximately eight minutes to determine what the passage is about, who is described in the text, when the passage takes place, and where the text describes information that they already know about the topic. Students are encouraged to use titles, headings, pictures, and illustrations to help them preview the text.

Click and Clunk

This strategy teaches students to monitor comprehension during reading by identifying difficult words and concepts in the passage and using fix-up strategies when the text does not make sense. Students "click" it when they recognize information in the reading and know it well, and they "clunk" it when they encounter information they do not understand or need to know more about. Teachers instruct students in how to monitor their reading comprehension by recording clunks in their learning logs or on a separate sheet of paper to discuss with their peers and the teacher. They "declunk" words by applying the fix-up strategies they learn from cue cards that instruct them to reread the sentence with the clunk, reread the sentences before and after the clunk, look for prefixes or suffixes in the word, and break the word down to find smaller, recognizable words.

Collaborative Strategic Reading (cont.)

Get the Gist

By "getting the gist," students learn how to restate the main ideas or the most critical information in the text during reading. They are taught how to identify the most important points and retell what they have read in their own words. To teach students how to summarize effectively, they are instructed to get the gist in as few words as possible (10 words) and exclude unnecessary details while conveying the most meaning. Students should interact to review what aspects of their gist should be kept or dropped.

Wrap-up

When students "wrap-up" the reading, they summarize what has been learned from the reading and generate possible questions. They also answer the questions they have formulated as this helps them review the important information. In doing so, students improve their comprehension of the content and their recall of the information. Teachers can instruct students to use question stems on index cards to help them formulate literal and higher-order thinking questions.

CSR Materials

Cue cards—The teacher can generate cue cards for each of the members of the cooperative groups with instructions for the different roles that students can take. These cards help students stay focused on the task. For example, during the preview, a cue card might read, "Let's brainstorm and write everything we know about the topic in our learning logs."

Learning logs—Learning logs can take many forms but all help students record their ideas and facilitate cooperative learning. The learning log should ask students to identify what they already know about the topic, what they predict they will learn, questions they have about the important ideas in the passage, and the gist of the reading. Students should write down the clunks they encounter, as well.

Question Answer Relationships

Question Answer Relationships (QAR) (Raphael and Au 2005) is a multiple-strategy approach that gives students and teachers a common language about prior knowledge and questioning strategies. The creators argue that students and teachers need to use a common language about reading so that they can more easily discuss the processes involved in listening and reading comprehension during think-alouds and modeling. The QAR strategy allows students to categorize types of questions easily, which enables them to more readily answer them.

The first step in beginning QAR with students is to introduce them to the common language. Students learn that they use either prior knowledge (In My Head) or information gained from the book (In the Text) to generate and answer questions. Teachers use explicit instruction to teach students In the Text strategies, such as how to skim or scan the text for information, to reread, or to use clues from the title of the reading or from chapter headings, to locate or recall relevant information. The teacher can begin by introducing a text and asking students to generate questions based on the title, pictures, and other text features prior to reading and to record the information on sticky notes. The teacher then asks them to consider whether the information is located In My Head or In the Text and records the information on a large wall chart to make the distinction clear to students.

As students gain greater skill at using QAR, the teacher can build on their understanding of the strategies involved in the framework. Once students are confident in using In the Text, the teacher can introduce Right There questions and Think and Search questions. And once students show proficiency at using In My Head, the teacher can introduce Author and Me questions and On My Own questions.

Right There Questions

The answers to Right There questions are located directly in the reading materials. They are the literal level of questions that ask *who, what, where, when, how,* and *why*. These questions sometimes begin with *according to the passage,* or *include the aforementioned journalistic words*.

Think and Search Questions

Think and Search questions require students to think about what they have read and make connections in order to relate the information and ideas in a passage to each other. Students must look back at the reading selection, try to find the information needed to answer the question, and then think about how the information or ideas fit together. These questions sometimes include the phrases *compare and contrast, the main idea of the passage*, and *what caused*.

Question Answer Relationships *(cont.)*

Author and Me Questions

These questions require students to use ideas and information that are not directly stated in the reading selection to find the answers. Students must think about what they have read to formulate their own opinions. These questions are inferential and sometimes begin with what the author implies, what the passage suggests, and the speaker's attitude.

On My Own Questions

Students can answer On My Own questions using their prior knowledge and experiences. These questions usually do not appear on tests because they do not refer to the reading passage. On My Own questions usually include the phrases *In your opinion* or *Based on your experience*.

When teaching students how to correctly identify the four different types of questions, teachers should begin with whole-class instruction. The teacher can use a read aloud and ask students to pose questions about the reading after they have completed the passage. The teacher can write their questions on sticky notes and then place them in the appropriate categories on chart paper. To further students' understanding of the different types of questions, the teacher can prepare a number of questions about the reading passage and ask them to place the questions in the correct category. Gradually, the teacher releases the responsibility to students as they work in small groups to label the different question-answer relationships. Eventually, the teacher can give students a reading selection to complete in pairs and require the pairs to generate a given number of questions for each question-answer relationship.

QAR is an effective approach to teaching reading comprehension strategies because it emphasizes the value of scanning, skimming, and rereading to locate information as well as differentiating new knowledge from prior experiences.

Metacognitive Instruction for Multiple Strategy Use

Metacognitive awareness is the tool that allows students to assess and choose which reading comprehension strategies to use when reading written text. Through this strategic process, students evaluate their own knowledge and skills, make decisions about which skills to employ, and monitor their own comprehension in order to determine the effectiveness of their choices. While this type of metacognitive awareness may occur naturally for some students, the majority of students benefit from explicit instruction in how to use metacognitive awareness to improve reading comprehension. In this strategy, students learn how to use their metacognitive awareness and a combination of strategies, including activating prior knowledge, questioning, semantic word mapping, word analysis, think-alouds, and summarizing to improve their reading comprehension (Boulware-Gooden et al. 2007).

Activation of Prior Knowledge

To begin, the teacher introduces a main idea or central theme of the text and asks students several related questions. Students quickly jot down their thoughts about the questions. Then, as a class, students brainstorm words related to the main topic or theme and add them to a semantic word map that the teacher creates at the front of the class. The class works together to connect words and ideas in the map, while also adding semantic information to clarify the definitions or the meanings of challenging words. Students discuss how each new addition to the map helps them activate their prior knowledge or gain new knowledge about the meanings of related words. In addition, students talk about the purpose of asking and answering questions at the beginning of the activity and how these questions also helped to activate prior knowledge.

Questioning and Think-Alouds

Before they start to read the text selection, students revisit the questions asked by the teacher at the beginning of the activity. The teacher prompts students to think aloud while reading and to quietly vocalize answers to the comprehension questions. This part of the activity reinforces the value of thinking aloud and questioning to monitor reading comprehension.

Summarizing

When they have completed the reading, the teacher displays a graphic organizer appropriate to the task at hand and asks students to help identify the important elements in the text to include in the organizer. As students discuss, the teacher records the theme, the main ideas, the supporting ideas, and the details on the graphic organizer. The teacher reviews the purpose of a summary with the class and demonstrates how they can use the information from the graphic organizer to write a summary of the reading. When they have completed their summaries, students share them with a partner. Next, they review and answer the comprehension questions asked at the beginning of the lesson. To conclude the activity, the class reviews the numerous comprehension strategies they used to understand the text and examines the reasoning behind why each specific strategy was chosen to facilitate different types of comprehension.

Greek and Latin Roots

Root	Meaning	Examples
act (L)	do	action, active, actor
agon (G)	struggle, contest	protagonist, antagonist, agony
anthrop (G)	man	anthropological, philanthropist, misanthrope
arch (G)	rule	archetype, matriarch, monarch
aud (L)	hear	audition, audible, auditorium
aug (L)	increase	augment, augmentative, August
auto (G)	self	automatic, automobile, autograph
belli (L)	war	bellicose, belligerent, rebellion
biblio (G)	book	bibliophile, bibliography
bio (G)	life	biography, biopsy, autobiography
cad, cas (L)	to fall	cadence, cascade, cadaver
cand (L)	glowing	incandescent, candle, candid
carn (L)	meat	carnivore, carnal, incarnate
centr (L)	center	central, eccentric, egocentric
cide, cise (L)	cut, kill	homicide, incisor, genocide
cred (L)	believe	credulous, incredible, credence
culpa (L)	fault, blame	culpable, culprit
cur (L)	care	cure, curable, curator
dem (G)	people	demogogue, democracy, epidemic
dict (L)	speak	predict, dictionary, dictate
duc (L)	lead	conduct, abduct, deduct
fac (L)	make	factory, faction, benefactor
fer (L)	bring	transfer, confer, ferry
flect, flex (L)	bend	inflection, reflex, flexible
fract, frag (L)	break	fracture, fragment, fragile
fug (L)	flee	refugee, fugitive, refuge
gen (L)	kind, class	genre, gender, generation
grad, gress (L)	step, go	gradual, graduate, progress
gram (G)	letter	telegram, diagram, grammar
graph (G)	write	autograph, biography, lithography
grat (L)	pleasing	gratify, grateful, gratuity
homo (L)	like	homogenous, homonym, homogenize
idio (G)	peculiar	idiosyncrasy, idiom, idiot
jud (L)	law	judicial, judge, judgment
laps (L)	slip	elapse, collapse, prolapse
liber (L)	free	liberate, liberty, liberal
liter (L)	letter	literature, alliteration, literacy
luc, lum (L)	light	translucent, illuminate, luminous

Greek and Latin Roots (cont.)

Root	Meaning	Examples
lud (L)	play, game	allusion, allude, ludicrous
luna (L)	moon	lunar, lunacy, lunatic
mal (L)	bad	malcontent, malaria, malicious
melan/o (G)	black	melanoma, melancholy, melodrama
meta (G)	change, alter	metaphor, metastasis, metamorphosis
miss, mit (L)	send	dismiss, emit, admittance
mono (G)	one	monologue, monochromatic, monotheism
mort (L)	death	mortician, mortuary, mortal
mut (L)	change	mutate, immutable, mutant
mytho (G)	traditional story	myth, mythology, mythological
narr (L)	tell	narrator, narrate, narrative
nat (L)	born	natal, innate, natural
neg (L)	no	renege, negative, negligent
not (L)	mark	annotate, notabe, connotation
noun (L)	declare	announce, denounce, pronounce
nov (L)	new	novel, novelty, novelist
omni (L)	all	omnipotent, omniscient, omnivore
orig (L)	beginning	origin, original, originate
path (G)	feeling	antipathy, apathy, empathy
per (L)	throughout	permeate, permanent, perennial
phil (G)	love	philanthropist, bibliophile, philosophy
phobe (G)	fear	phobia, claustrophobic, arachnophobia
port (L)	carry	porter, transportation, portable
post (L)	after, behind	postscript, posthumous, postpone
purg (L)	clean	purge, purgatory, expurgate
rid (L)	laugh	deride, ridiculous, ridicule
rupt (L)	break	rupture, erupt, interrupt
san (L)	health	sanitary, sane, sanitation
scrib (L)	write	scribe, describe, inscribe
sens, sent (L)	feel	sensation, sensory, dissent
sery (L)	watch over	conserve, preserve, reservation
spec (L)	see	inspect, spectrum, spectacles
strict (L)	draw tight	restrict, constrict, restrictive
syn (G)	together	synonym, synthesis, syntax
topo (G)	place	utopia, topology, dystopia
vern (L)	word	verbose, verbal, verbatim
vir (L)	worth, manliness	virile, virtue, virtuoso

Adapted from Edward B. Fry and Jacqueline E. Kress's *The Reading Teacher's Book of Lists*, 5th edition.

5 Types of Context Clues Reference Sheet

Type	Description	Example
Definition	Author provides the definition of the unknown word directly within the text.	An anthology is a collection of poems, short stories, or plays.
Synonym	Author implies word meaning by using another word with a similar meaning in the text surrounding the unknown word.	My indolent dog refused to get up to go for a walk. He is the laziest dog I've ever met!
Antonym	Author conveys meaning by contrasting the unknown word with a word of opposite meaning.	I expected to find an abundance of blueberries still on the bush, but instead the berries were scarce and hard to find.
Example	Author suggests meaning by giving examples of the unknown word.	She had to choose a nocturnal animal, such as an owl, skunk, badger, or hamster, to study for her science project.
General	Author provides non-specific clues about the meaning of an unknown word through various words and phrases in the text surrounding the target word.	Her answer was very ambiguous. It did not reveal her thoughts or opinions on the matter. We had no idea which way she would vote.

Sequencing Words Reference Sheet

Beginning Terms

At the beginning

Initially

To start

First

To begin

Middle Terms

Additionally

Next

Then

Following

Subsequently

Ending Terms

At the end

Lastly

Ultimately

Finally

To conclude

External Text Structure Reference Sheet

appendix	introduction
caption	italicized type
chapter	map
citation	margin
column	page
conclusion	paragraph
drawing	passage
excerpt	photograph
font size	picture
glossary	publisher
heading	quotation
illustration	references
indenting	section
index	sketch

References Cited

Anderson, Lorin W., David R. Krathwohl, and Benjamin S. Bloom. 2001. *A Taxonomy for Learning, Teaching, and Assessing: A Revision of Bloom's Taxonomy of Educational Objectives.* New York: Longman.

Aronson, E., N. Blaney, C. Stephan, K. Sikes, and M. Snapp. 1978. *The Jigsaw Classroom.* Beverly Hills, CA: Sage.

Baker, Linda. 2002. "Metacognition in Comprehension Instruction." In *Comprehension Instruction: Research-Based Best Practices*, edited by Cathy Collins Block and Michael Pressley, 77–95. New York: The Guilford Press.

Baker, L., and A. L. Brown. 1984. "Metacognitive Skills and Reading." In *Handbook of Reading Research*, edited by P. D. Pearson, R. Barr, M. L. Kamil, and P. Mosenthal. Mahwah, NJ: Lawrence Erlbaum Associates.

Beck, Isabel L., Margaret G. McKeown, Rebecca L. Hamilton, and Linda Kucan. 1997. *Questioning the Author: An Approach for Enhancing Student Engagement with Text.* Newark, DE: International Reading Association.

Blachowicz, Camille L. Z., and Peter Fisher. 2000. "Vocabulary Instruction." In *Handbook of Reading Research, Volume III*, edited by Michael L. Kamil, Peter B. Mosenthal, P. David Pearson, and Rebecca Barr, 503–24. Mahwah, NJ: Lawrence Erlbaum Associates.

Block, Cathy Collins, and Susan E. Israel. 2004. The ABCs of performing highly effective think-alouds. *The Reading Teacher* 58 (2): 154–67.

Block, Cathy Collins, and Sheri R. Parris. 2008. *Comprehension Instruction: Research-Based Best Practices.* 2nd ed. New York: The Guilford Press.

Block, Cathy Collins, and Michael Pressley. 2003. "Best Practices in Comprehension Instruction." In *Best Practices in Literacy Instruction.* 2nd ed., edited by Lesley Mandel Morrow, Linda B. Grambell, and Michael Pressley, 111–26. New York: The Guilford Press.

Block, Cathy Collins, Joni L. Schaller, Joseph A. Joy, and Paola Gaine. 2002. "Process-Based Comprehension Instruction: Perspectives of Four Reading Educators." In *Comprehension Instruction: Research-Based Best Practices*, edited by Cathy Collins Block and Michael Pressley, 42–61. New York: The Guilford Press.

Boulware-Gooden, R., S. Carreker, A. Thronhill, R.M. Joshi. 2007. "Instruction of Metacognitive Strategies Enhances Reading Comprehension and Vocabulary Achievement of Third-Grade Students." *The Reader Teacher* 61 (1): 70–77.

Buehl, Doug. 2009. *Self-Questioning Taxonomy. Classroom Strategies for Interactive Learning.* 3rd ed. Newark, DE: International Reading Association.

Calkins, Lucy, Mary Ehrenworth, and Christopher Lehman. 2012. *Pathways to the Common Core: Accelerating Achievement.* Portsmouth, NH: Heinemann.

Casteel, C. A. 1990. "Effects of Chunked Text Material on Reading Comprehension of High and Low Ability Readers." *Reading Improvement* 27: 269–275.

Christen, William L., and Thomas J. Murphy. 1991. *Increasing Comprehension by Activating Prior Knowledge.* ERIC Digest. Bloomington, IN: ERIC Clearinghouse on Reading, English, and Communication. ERIC Identifier: ED328885.

Clark, Kathleen F., and Michael F. Graves. 2005. "Scaffolding Students' Comprehension of Text." *The Reading Teacher* 58 (6): 570–80.

References Cited (cont.)

Clinton, V., and P. Van Den Broek. 2012. "Interest, Inferences, and Learning from Texts." *Learning and Individual Differences* 22: 650–63.

Cotton, Kathleen. 1988. "Classroom Questioning." *School Improvement Research Series: Research You Can Use*. Portland, OR: Northwest Regional Educational Laboratory. http://educationnorthwest.org/webfm_send/569/. October 14, 2013.

Dechant, Emerald. 1991. *Understanding and Teaching Reading: An Interactive Model*. Hillsdale, NJ: Lawrence Erlbaum Associates.

Duke, Nell K., and P. David Pearson. 2002. "Effective Practices for Developing Reading Comprehension." In *What Research Has to Say About Reading Instruction*, 3rd ed., edited by Alan Farstup and S. Jay Samuels, 205–42. Newark, DE: International Reading Association.

Dunlap, Carmen Zuñiga, and Evelyn Marino Weisman. 2006. *Helping English Language Learners Succeed*. Huntington Beach, CA: Shell Educational Publishing.

Durkin, D. 1978–1979. "What Classroom Observations Reveal About Reading Comprehension Instruction." *Reading Research Quarterly* 14 (4): 481–533.

Edwards, Elizabeth C., George Font, James F. Baumann, and Eileen Boland. 2012. "Unlocking Word Meanings: Strategies and Guidelines for Teaching Morphemic and Contextual Analysis." In *Vocabulary Instruction: Research to Practice*, edited by James F. Baumann and Edward J. Kame'enui. New York: The Guilford Press.

Fink, Rosalie. 2006. *Why Jane and John Couldn't Read—And How They Learned*. Newark, DE: International Reading Association.

Frayer, Dorothy A., Wayne C. Frederick, and Herbert J. Klausmeier. 1969. "A Schema for Testing the Level of Concept Mastery." *Working Paper No. 16*. Madison, WI: Wisconsin Research and Development Center for Cognitive Learning.

Fry, Edward B., Jacqueline E. Kress, and Dona L. Fountoukidis. 2006. *The Reading Teacher's Book of Lists, Grades K–12*. 5th ed. San Francisco, CA: Jossey-Bass.

Gambrell, Linda B., and Paula B. Jawitz. 1993. "Mental Imagery, Text Illustrations, and Children's Story Comprehension and Recall." *Reading Research Quarterly* 28: 264–76.

Gambrell, Linda B., and Patricia S. Koskinen. 2002. "Imagery: A Strategy for Enhancing Comprehension." In *Comprehension Instruction: Research-Based Best Practices*, edited by Cathy Collins Block and Michael Pressley, 205–18. New York: The Guilford Press.

Gambrell, L., J. Malloy, and S. Mazzoni. 2007. "Evidence-Based Best Practices for Comprehensive Literacy Instruction." In *Best Practices in Literacy Instruction*, edited by L. B. Gambrell, L. M. Morrow, and M. Pressley, 11-29. New York: The Guilford Press.

Garner, R. 1987. *Metacognition and Reading Comprehension*. Norwood, NJ: Ablex.

Goldman, Susan R., L. G. Jason, Jennifer W. Brach, Arthur C. Graesser, and Kamila Brodowinska. 2012. "Comprehending and Learning From Internet Sources: Processing Patterns of Better and Poorer Learners." *Reading Research Quarterly* 47 (4): 356–81.

References Cited *(cont.)*

Gourgey, A.F. 1998. "Metacognition in Basic Skills Instruction." *Instructional Science* 26: 81–96.

Hacker, Douglas J., John Dunlosky, and Arthur C. Graesser. 1998. *Metacognition in Educational Theory and Practice*. Hoboken, NJ: Taylor & Francis.

Hammond, W. Dorsey, and Denise D. Nessel. 2011. "The Power of Inquiry: Supporting Students' Reading of Informational Texts." In *The Comprehension Experience: Engaging Readers Through Effective Inquiry and Discussion*. Portsmouth, NH: Heinemann.

Hansen, Jane. 1981. "The Effects of Inference Training and Practice on Young Children's Reading Comprehension." *Reading Research Quarterly* 16 (3): 391–417.

Hansen, Jane, and P. David Pearson. 1983. "An Instructional Study: Improving the Inferential Comprehension of Fourth Grade Good and Poor Readers." *Journal of Educational Psychology* 75 (6): 821–29.

Hayes, David A. 1989. "Helping Students GRASP the Knack of Writing Summaries." *Journal of Reading* 32: 96–101.

Hedgcock, John, and Dana R. Ferris. 2009. *Teaching Readers of English: Students, Texts, and Contexts*. New York: Routledge.

Hoyt, Linda. 2002. *Make It Real: Strategies for Success with Informational Texts*. Portsmouth, NH: Heinemann.

Keene, Ellin Oliver. 2002. "From Good to Memorable: Characteristics of Highly Effective Comprehension Teaching." In *Improving Comprehension Instruction*, edited by Cathy Collins Block, Linda B. Gambrell, and Michael Pressley 80–105. San Francisco, CA: Jossey-Bass.

Keene, Ellin Oliver, and Susan Zimmerman. 1997. *Mosaic of Thought: Teaching Comprehension in a Reader's Workshop*. Portsmouth, NH: Heinemann.

Klingner, Janette K., and Sharon Vaughn. 2002. "Promoting Reading Comprehension, Content Learning, and English Acquisition Through Collaborative Strategic Reading." *The Reading Teacher* 52 (7): 738–47.

Kragler, Sherry, Carolyn A. Walker, and Linda E. Martin. 2005. "Strategy Instruction in Primary Content Textbooks." *The Reading Teacher* 59 (3): 254–261.

Krashen, Stephen. 2009. "81 Generalizations About Free Voluntary Reading." *International Association of Teachers of English as a Foreign Language*. 9: 1-6. http://successfulenglish.com/wp-content/uploads/2010/01/81-Generalizations-about-FVR-2009.pdf. October 14, 2013.

Kujawa, Sandra, and Lynne Huske. 1995. *The Strategic Teaching and Reading Project Guidebook*. Rev. ed. Oak Brook, IL: North Central Regional Educational Laboratory.

Lapp, Diane, James Flood, and Nancy Farnan, eds. 1996. *Content Area Reading and Learning Instructional Strategies*. 2nd ed. Boston: Allyn & Bacon.

Law, Y.K. 2011. "The Effects of Cooperative Learning on Enhancing Hong-Kong Fifth Graders' Achievement Goals, Autonomous Motivation and Reading Proficiency." *Journal of Research in Reading* 34 (4): 402–425. http://dx.doi.org/10.1111%Fj.1467-9817.2010.01445.x.

Lenski, Susan Davis, Mary Ann Wham, and Jerry L. Johns. 1999. *Reading & Learning Strategies for Middle & High School Students*. Dubuque, IA: Kendall/Hunt.

References Cited (cont.)

Lesesne, Teri S. 2006. *Naked Reading: Uncovering What Tweens Need to Become Lifelong Readers.* Portland, ME: Stenhouse Publishers.

Long, S. A., P. A. Winograd, and C. A. Bridge. 1989. "The Effects of the Reader and Text Characteristics on Reports of Imagery During and After Reading." *Reading Research Quarterly* 24, 353–72.

Manzo, Anthony V. 1969. "The ReQuest Procedure." *Journal of Reading* 13 (2): 123–26.

Maria, Katherine. 1990. *Reading Comprehension Instruction: Issues & Strategies.* Parkton, MD: York Press.

Mastropieri, M. A., and T. E. Scruggs. 1997. "Best Practices in Promoting Reading Comprehension in Students with Learning Disabilities." *Remedial and Special Education* 18 (4): 197–214.

Mayer, R. 1998. "Cognitive, Metacognitive, and Motivational Aspects of Problem Solving." *Instructional Science* 26, 49–63.

McNamara, Danielle S., ed. 2007. *Reading Comprehension Strategies: Theories, Interventions, and Technologies.* Mahwah, NJ: Lawrence Erlbaum Associates.

Moreillon, Judi. 2009. "Coteaching Reading Comprehension Strategies in Elementary School Libraries: Maximizing Your Impact." In *Matrix: Relationship Between Reading Comprehension Strategies and AASL's Standards for the 21st–Century Learner.* http://storytrail.com/Impact/matrix.htm. October 14, 2013.

Morrow, Lesley Mandel. 2003. "Motivating Lifelong Voluntary Readers." In *Handbook of Research on Teaching the English Language Arts*, edited by James Flood, Diane Lapp, James R. Squire, and Julie M. Jenson, 857–67. Mahwah, NJ: Lawrence Erlbaum Associates.

Nagy, William E., and Judith A. Scott. 2000. "Vocabulary Processes." In *Handbook of Reading Research, Volume III*, edited by Michael L. Kamil and Rebecca Barr, 269–84. Mahwah, MJ: Lawrence Erlbaum Associates.

National Center for Education Statistics. 2013. *120 Years of Literacy: National Assessment of Adult Literacy.* http://nces.ed.gov/naal/lit_history.asp. October 14, 2013.

National Governors Association Center for Best Practices, Council of Chief State School Officers. 2010. *Common Core State Standards: English Language Arts Standards.* Washington, DC: National Governors Association Center for Best Practices, Council of Chief State School Officers.

National Reading Panel. 2000. "Teaching Children to Read: An Evidence-Based Assessment of the Scientific Research Literature on Reading and Its Implications for Reading Instruction." In *Report of the National Reading Panel: Teaching Children to Read.* Bethesda, MD: National Institutes of Health. https://www.nichd.nih.gov/publications/pubs/nrp/Documents/report.pdf. October 14, 2013.

Neufeld, Paul. 2005. "Comprehension Instruction in Content Area Classes." *The Reading Teacher* 59 (4): 302–12.

Neuman, Susan B. 1988. "Enhancing Children's Comprehension through Previewing." In *Dialogues in Literacy Research. Thirty-Seventh Yearbook of the National Reading Conference.* Edited by John E. Readence and R. Scott Baldwi, 219-24. Chicago, IL: National Reading Conference.

Ogle, Donna M. 1986. "K-W-L: A Teaching Model that Develops Reading of Expository Text." *The Reading Teacher* 39 (6): 564–70.

References Cited (cont.)

Paris, S. G., B. A. Wasik, and J. C. Turner. 1991. "The Development of Strategic Readers." In *Handbook of Reading Research, Volume II*, edited by R. Barr, M. L. Kamil, P. B. Mosenthal, and P. D. Pearson, 545–62. Mahwah, NJ: Lawrence Erlbaum Associates.

Pearson, P. David, and Nell K. Duke. 2002. "Comprehension Instruction in the Primary Grades." In *Comprehension Instruction: Research-Based Best Practices*, edited by Cathy Collins Block and Michael Pressley, 247–58. New York: The Guilford Press.

Perez, Lisa. 2013. "Re-Imagine Your Library with iPads." In *Learning & Leading with Technology* 40 (6): 22–25.

Pressley, Michael. 2000. "What Should Comprehension Instruction Be the Instruction Of?" In *Handbook of Reading Research, Volume III*, edited by Michael L. Kamil, Peter B. Mosenthal, P. David Pearson, and Rebecca Barr, 291-309. Mahwah, NJ: Lawrence Erlbaum Associates.

Pressley, Michael. 2002a. "Comprehension Stategies Instruction: A Turn-of-the-Century Status Report." In *Comprehension Instruction: Research–Based Best Practices*, edited by Cathy Collins Block and Michael Pressley, 11–17. New York: The Guilford Press.

Pressley, Michael. 2002b. "Metacognition and Self-Regulated Comprehension." In *What Research Has to Say About Reading Instruction*, 3rd ed., edited by Alan E. Farstup, and S. Jay Samuels, 11–27. Newark, DE: International Reading Association.

Raphael, Taffy E., and Kathryn H. Au. 2005. "QAR: Enhancing Comprehension and Test Taking Across Grades and Content Areas." *The Reading Teacher* 59 (3): 206–21.

Rasinski, Timothy, Nancy Padak, Rick M. Newton, and Evangeline Newton. 2008. *Greek & Latin Roots: Keys to Building Vocabulary*. Huntington Beach, CA: Shell Education.

Rasinski, Timothy, Nancy Padak, Rick M. Newton, and Evangeline Newton. 2012. *Practice with Prefixes*. Huntington Beach, CA: Shell Education.

Rasinski, Timothy, Nancy Padak, Rick M. Newton, and Evangeline Newton. 2013. *Starting with Prefixes and Suffixes*. Huntington Beach, CA: Shell Education.

Readence, John E., Thomas W. Bean, and R. Scott Baldwin. 2000. *Content Area Literacy: An Integrated Approach*. Dubuque, IA: Kendall/Hunt.

Robb, Laura. 2003. *Teaching Reading in Social Studies, Science, and Math*. New York: Scholastic.

Rupley, William H., John W. Logan, and William D. Nichols. 1999. "Vocabulary Instruction in a Balanced Reading Program." *The Reading Teacher* 52 (4): 336–46.

Ryder, Randall J., and Michael F. Graves. 2003. *Reading and Learning in Content Areas*. 3rd ed. New York: Wiley & Sons.

Schwartz, Robert M., and Taffy E. Raphael. 1985. "Concept of Definition: A Key to Improving Students' Vocabulary." *The Reading Teacher* 39 (2): 198–205.

Shefelbine, J. 2002. *Reading Voluminously and Voluntarily*. New York: The Scholastic Center for Literacy & Learning.

Smith, Frank. 2004. *Understanding Reading: A Psycholinguistic Analysis of Reading and Learning to Read*. Mahwah, NJ: Lawrence Erlbaum Associates.

References Cited *(cont.)*

Snowball, Diane. 2006. "Comprehension For All." *In Teaching Pre K–8* 36 (8): 62–63.

Sullo, Bob. 2007. *Activating the Desire to Learn.* Alexandria, VA: Association for Supervision and Curriculum Development.

Trabasso, Tom, and Edward Bouchard. 2002. "Teaching Readers How to Comprehend Text Strategically." In *Comprehension Instruction: Research-Based Best Practices*, edited by Cathy Collins Block and Michael Pressley, 176–200. New York: The Guilford Press.

Vacca, Richard T., and Jo Anne L. Vacca. 2005. *Content Area Reading: Literacy and Learning Across the Curriculum.* 8th ed. Boston: Pearson Education.

Wagner, Tony. 2008. *The Global Achievement Gap.* New York: Basic Books.

West, Charles K., James A. Farmer, and Phillip M. Wolff. 1991. *Instructional Design: Implications from Cognitive Science.* Upper Saddle River, NJ: Prentice Hall.

Wolk, Ronald A. 2011. *Wasting Minds: Why Our Education System Is Failing and What We Can Do About It.* Alexandria, VA: Association for Supervision and Curriculum Development.

Wood, Karen D. 2002. "Differentiating Reading and Writing Lessons to Promote Content Learning." In *Improving Comprehensions Instruction: Rethinking Research, Theory, and Classroom Practice*, edited by Cathy Collins Block, Linda B. Gambrell, and Michael Pressley, 155–180. Hoboken, NJ: Wiley & Sons.

Wright, Jim. 2007. *Response to Intervention Toolkit: A Practical Guide for Schools.* Port Chester, New York: National Professional Resource.

Literature Cited

Grades 1–2

Andreae, Giles. 2001. *Giraffes Can't Dance.* New York: Orchard Books.

Breen, Steve. 2008. *Violet the Pilot.* New York: Dial Books for Young Readers.

Cannon, Janell. 1993. *Stellaluna.* New York: Harcourt.

Carle, Eric. 1987. *The Very Hungry Caterpillar.* New York: Philomel Books.

Carle, Eric. 1999. *Rooster's Off to See the World.* New York: Aladdin Paperbacks.

Cole, Joanna. 1986–2010. *The Magic School Bus.* New York: Scholastic.

Dr. Seuss [pseud.]. 1989. *The Sneetches.* New York: Random House.

French, Jackie. 2003. *A Diary of a Wombat.* New York: Clarion Books.

Henkes, Kevin. 1993. *Owen.* New York: Greenwillow Books.

Henkes, Kevin. 1996. *Lilly's Purple Plastic Purse.* New York: Greenwillow Books.

Lester, Helen. 1988. *Tacky the Penguin.* New York: Houghton Mifflin Harcourt.

McCloskey, Robert. 1976. *Blueberries for Sal.* New York: The Viking Press.

Minarik, Else Holmelund. 1985. *Little Bear.* New York: HarperCollins.

Muldrow, Diane. 2001. *The Little Red Hen.* New York: Golden Books.

Piper, Watty. 1990. *The Little Engine That Could.* New York: Platt & Munk.

Slobodkina, Esphyr. 2008. *Caps for Sale: A Tale of a Peddler, Some Monkeys and Their Monkey Business.* New York: HarperCollins

Williams, Brenda, and Benjamin Lacombe. 2009. *Lin Yi's Lantern: A Moon Festival Tale.* Cambridge, MA: Barefoot Books.

Williams, Vera B. 1982. *A Chair for My Mother.* New York: Greenwillow Books.

Zion, Gene. 1984. *Harry the Dirty Dog.* New York: HarperTrophy.

Zion, Gene. 1986. *No Roses for Harry!* New York: HarperCollins.

Grades 3–5

Aesop. 1994. "The Boy Who Cried Wolf." In *Aesop's Fables.* Mineola, New York: Dover Publications.

Aesop. 1994. "The Hare and the Tortoise." In *Aesop's Fables.* Mineola, New York: Dover Publications.

Aesop. 1994. "The Town Mouse and the Country Mouse." In *Aesop's Fables.* Mineola, New York: Dover Publications.

Andersen, Hans Christian. 2010. "The Princess and the Pea." In *Hans Andersen's Fairy Tales,* translated by Naomi Lewis. London: Puffin Books.

Blume, Judy. 1971. *Freckle Juice.* New York: Bantam Doubleday Dell Books for Young Readers.

Blume, Judy. 1980. *Superfudge.* New York: Dutton Children's Books.

Burnett, Frances Hodgson. 1951. *The Secret Garden.* New York: Puffin Books.

Catling, Patrick Skene. 1952. *The Chocolate Touch.* New York: William Morrow and Company.

Cleary, Beverly. 1968. *Ramona the Pest.* New York: HarperCollins.

Literature Cited (cont.)

Dahl, Roald. 2007. *Charlie and the Chocolate Factory*. New York: Puffin Books.

Dahl, Roald. 2013. *Fantastic Mr. Fox*. New York: Puffin Books.

DiCamillo, Kate. 2000. *Because of Winn-Dixie*. Somerville, MA: Candlewick Press.

Fitzhugh, Louise. 1992. *Harriet the Spy*. New York: Yearling.

Freeman, Martha. 2010. *The Case of the Rock 'N Roll Dog*. New York: Holiday House.

Grimm, Jacob, and Wilhelm Grimm. 2003. "Snow White." In *Selected Folktales: A Dual-Language Book*, edited and translated by Stanley Appelbaum, 147–159. New York: Dover Publications.

Jennings, Patrick. 2010. *Guinea Dog*. New York: Egmont.

Kline, Suzy. 1989. *Horrible Harry and the Ant Invasion*. New York: The Viking Press.

Leaf, Munro. 2011. *The Story of Ferdinand*. New York: The Viking Press.

Lindgren, Astrid. 1950. *Pippi Longstocking*. New York: The Viking Press.

Lobel, Arnold. 1970. "The Letter." In *Frog and Toad Are Friends*. New York: HarperCollins.

Lowry, Lois. 1989. *Number the Stars*. New York: Houghton Mifflin Harcourt.

MacLachlan, Patricia. 1996. *Sarah, Plain and Tall*. New York: Scholastic

Polacco, Patricia. 1988. *The Keeping Quilt*. New York: Simon & Schuster.

White, E. B. 1945. *Stuart Little*. New York: HarperTrophy.

Wilder, Laura Ingalls. 1963. *Little House on the Prairie*. New York: HarperCollins.

Yelchin, Eugene. 2011. *Breaking Stalin's Nose*. New York: Henry Holt.

Grades 6–8

Alcott, Louisa May. 1983. *Little Women*. New York: Bantam Doubleday Dell Books for Young Readers.

Andersen, Hans Christian. 2010. "The Emperor's New Clothes." In *Hans Andersen's Fairy Tales*, translated by Naomi Lewis. London: Puffin Books.

Avi [pseud.]. 1990. *The True Confessions of Charlotte Doyle*. New York: Scholastic.

Ayres, Katherine. 1998. *North By Night: A Story of the Underground Railroad*. NewYork: Yearling.

Balliet, Blue. 2012. *Chasing Vermeer*. New York: Scholastic.

Carroll, Lewis. 1993. *Alice's Adventures in Wonderland*. Mineola, NY: Dover Publications.

Cushman, Karen. 2012. *The Midwife's Apprentice*. New York: Houghton Mifflin Harcourt.

Forbes, Esther Hoskins. 1943. *Johnny Tremain*. New York: Houghton Mifflin Harcourt .

Golding, William. 1954. *Lord of the Flies*. New York: Penguin Putnam.

Knowles, John. 1987. *A Separate Peace*. New York: Scribner.

L'Engle, Madeleine. 1962. *A Wrinkle in Time*. New York: Square Fish.

Levine, Gail Carson. 1998. *Ella Enchanted*. New York: Scholastic.

Lewis, C. S. 1978. *The Lion, the Witch and the Wardrobe*. New York: HarperTrophy.

Literature Cited *(cont.)*

Lowry, Lois. 1993. *The Giver.* New York: Houghton Mifflin Harcourt.

Mass, Wendy. 2009. *11 Birthdays.* New York: Scholastic Press.

O'Dell, Scott. 1988. *Island of the Blue Dolphins.* New York: Houghton Mifflin Harcourt.

Palacio, R. J. 2012. *Wonder.* New York: Alfred A. Knopf.

Paterson, Katherine. 1977. *Bridge to Terabithia.* New York: HarperCollins.

Paulsen, Gary. 1996. *Hatchet.* New York: First Aladdin Paperbacks.

Potok, Chaim. 1967. *The Chosen.* New York: Ballantine Books.

Raskin, Ellen. 2004. *The Westing Game.* New York: Puffin Modern Classics.

Rawls, Wilson. 1997. *Where the Red Fern Grows.* New York: Scholastic.

Riordan, Rick. 2012. *Rick Riordan's Heroes of Olympus Series Three Book Set.* New York: Hyperion.

Taylor, Mildred D. 1991. *Roll of Thunder, Hear My Cry.* New York: Puffin Books.

Grades 9–12

Alvarez, Julia. 1991. *How the Garcia Girls Lost Their Accents.* Chapel Hill, North Carolina: Algonquin Books.

Austen, Jane. 1995. *Pride and Prejudice.* Mineola, NY: Dover Publications.

Bradbury, Ray. 1995. *Fahrenheit 451.* New York: Simon & Schuster.

Brontë, Emily. 1996. *Wuthering Heights.* Mineola, NY: Dover Publications.

Buck, Pearl S. 1958. *The Good Earth.* New York: Washington Square Press.

Cisneros, Sandra. 1991. *The House on Mango Street.* New York: Vintage Books.

Collins, Suzanne. 2010. *The Hunger Games.* New York: Scholastic.

Conrad, Joseph. 2005. *Heart of Darkness and Selected Short Fiction.* New York: Barnes & Noble Classics.

Fitzgerald, F. Scott. 2004. *The Great Gatsby.* New York: Scribner.

Hawthorne, Nathaniel. 1994. *The Scarlet Letter.* Mineola, New York: Dover Publications.

Hemingway, Ernest. 1952. *Old Man and the Sea.* New York: Scribner.

Hemingway, Ernest. 2012. *A Farewell to Arms.* New York: Scribner.

Hurston, Zora Neale. 1990. *Their Eyes Were Watching God.* New York: Perennial Library.

Kesey, Ken. 2002. *One Flew Over the Cuckoo's Nest.* New York: Penguin Books.

Lee, Harper. 1960. *To Kill a Mockingbird.* New York: Grand Central.

O'Brien, Tim. 1990. *The Things They Carried.* New York: Houghton Mifflin Harcourt.

Remarque, Erich Maria. 1982. *All Quiet on the Western Front.* New York: Ballantine Books.

Rowling, J. K. 2009. *Harry Potter Paperback Boxed Set, Books 1–7.* New York: Scholastic.

Steinbeck, John. 1939. *The Grapes of Wrath.* New York: The Viking Press.

Zusak, Markus. 2006. *The Book Thief.* New York: Alfred A. Knopf.

Contents of the Digital Resource CD

Page	Resource	Filename
27–28	Correlation to Standards	standards.pdf
43	Rating Vocabulary	ratingvocabulary.pdf ratingvocabuary.doc
47	Word Knowledge Analysis	wordanalysis.pdf wordanalysis.doc
50	Root Word Tree	rootwordtree.pdf rootwordtree.doc
53	Roots/Prefixes/Suffixes Chart	rootschart.pdf rootschart.doc
57	Context Clue Analysis Chart	contextcluechart.pdf contextcluechart.doc
61	Concept of Definition Map	conceptdefinition.pdf conceptdefinition.doc
65	Frayer Model	frayermodel.pdf frayermodel.doc
70	Vocabulary Diagram	vocabularydiagram.pdf vocabularydiagram.doc
73	Keyword Association	keywordassociation.pdf keywordassociation.doc
84	KWL Chart	kwlchart.pdf kwlchart.doc
91	Think Sheet	thinksheet.pdf thinksheet.doc
97	Alphaboxes	alphaboxes.pdf alphaboxes.doc
101	Points of Confusion	pointsconfusion.pdf pointsconfusion.doc
109	Picture Prediction	pictureprediction.pdf pictureprediction.doc
112	Text and Subtext	textsubtext.pdf textsubtext.doc
116	Wordsplash	wordsplash.pdf wordsplash.doc
122	Inference Investigation	inferinvestigation.pdf inferinvestigation.doc
126	Character Inferences	characterinfer.pdf characterinfer.doc
160	Previewing the Text through Questioning	previewingquestioning.pdf previewingquestioning.doc
166	Scaffolding Reader Questions	scaffoldingreader.pdf scaffoldingreader.doc

Contents of the Digital Resource CD (cont.)

Page	Resource	Filename
176	Character Interview	characterinterview.pdf characterinterview.doc
182	Question Hierarchy	questionhierarchy.pdf questionhierarchy.doc
192	Rank-Ordering Retell	rankordering.pdf rankordering.doc
194	Key Words	keywords.pdf keywords.doc
200	Guided Reading and Summarizing Procedure	guidedreadingsummarizing.pdf guidedreadingsummarizing.doc
202	Jigsaw	jigsaw.pdf jigsaw.doc
206	Chunking Text	chunkingtext.pdf chunkingtext.doc
210	Determining the Theme	determiningtheme.pdf determiningtheme.doc
214	SWBST	swbst.pdf swbst.doc
228	Talking Drawings	talkingdrawings.pdf talkingdrawings.doc
230	Imagine, Elaborate, Predict, and Confirm	iepc.pdf iepc.doc
235	Plot Sequencing	plotsequencing.pdf plotsequencing.doc
240	Character Portrait	characterportrait.pdf characterportrait.doc
246	Text Feature Scavenger Hunt	textscavenger.pdf textscavenger.doc
253	Read, Note, Sort	readnotesort.pdf readnotesort.doc
258	Point of View	pointofview.pdf pointofview.doc
260–262	Graphic Organizers	graphicorganizers.pdf
272–273	Greek and Latin Roots	greeklatinroots.pdf
274	5 Types of Context Clues Reference Sheet	contextclues.pdf
275	Sequencing Words Reference Sheet	sequencingwords.pdf
276	External Text Structure Reference Sheet	externaltextstructure.pdf

Notes